Beyond Boundaries

Helen Parry Jones

To Dear Prisca
With Healing love
Helen xxx

First Published in Australia by Aurora House
www.aurorahouse.com.au

This edition published 2017
Copyright © Helen Parry Jones 2017
Typesetting: PrePress Plus
Cover design: Simon Critchell

ISBN: 9780648185123 (Paperback)

NATIONAL LIBRARY OF AUSTRALIA

A catalogue record for this book is available from the National Library of Australia

Dedication

Emancipation

Acknowledgements

Every book starts with a concept, but it also needs help from people to assist in its journey to completion. Those who have helped me reach publication, either with their professional contribution or by contributing their personal stories, carry equal importance and the order of my thanks has no bearing on my gratitude.

My thanks firstly goes to three very respected and professional ladies. To Gillian Holmes, my editor, for her never-ending patience; Josie Dietrich, my proofreader, for her painstaking scrutiny; and Linda Lycett, my publisher at Aurora House Australia, for enabling this book to reach out to a global audience. Thereafter comes a big hug for Ruth Johnston for allowing me to use her poem 'Spirit', in dedication to all fathers in spirit. A sentiment I hold most dear, as sadly I lost my own father in his fiftieth year.

Sincere love and gratitude for all the many personal contributions that have enabled me to share some of the most extraordinary experiences I have been a part of. In particular, I would like to thank the following for their story contributions: Margaret and Maurice Grey, Nigel Williams, Margaret Orams-Hampton, Gill and Pat Joseph, Tom O'Connor, Rachel Bull, Johnny and Angie Marr, Ruth Johnston, Audrey Parry-Jones, Heidi Price Zerivitz, Lee Zerivitz, Betty Price, Professor Keith and Linda Garfield, Anne Bates, Jenny Williams, David and Simone Lewis, John Eccles and Ceidiog Hughes. And, in some circumstances, my association with you has been life-changing for me in ways you might not have even considered.

My thanks to Jean Palmer for spontaneously inviting me, a total stranger, into her beautiful home to share her skills to start developing a screenplay.

A special thank you to Aunty Joan, whose devotion in looking after my mother in her final stages of terminal cancer was admirable.

For those people who I have been unable to contact, or where it might be appropriate, I have changed their names, but the stories are painstakingly accurate. Where the experiences have happened in a public arena, I have endeavoured to use the real identities to complement the accuracy of the story.

Also, a special mention of Joanne Jones who sadly lost her fight with cancer before I could publish, and to my mother-in-law Elsie Bull who recently, at the age of eighty-seven, passed over. You were both genuine advocates of my work.

To Yvonne for taking the time to write to Gay Byrne about me, an act that changed my life beyond recognition at a most critical point.

To the iconic presenter Gay Byrne, for giving me the opportunity to embrace the Irish nation and set off a chain of events that has been ongoing for twenty-two years to date.

These acknowledgements wouldn't be complete without mentioning the encouragement from many of my clients, but the list is too long to identify everyone. Please know that your support is greatly appreciated.

To all my children, whose love makes everything worthwhile. Last but not least, I want to thank with all my heart, my soulmate and husband Richard, who has supported me unconditionally in everything I do from the moment we met. There are always highs and lows involved with any creative project, so without his help I doubt I would've ever had the stamina to complete this book. I know your criticisms are made with love – and your attention to historical detail has been meticulous, if not a little infuriating at times.

SPIRIT

I am that shadow
deep
within the recess
of your mind
familiar
kind
I am as light
filtering through leaves
caressing your skin
soft
like a warm summers breeze
soothing
calm
shielding from harm
cradling whilst you heal
stroking your tears
letting them flow
my love
wraps around you
enveloping
in unconditional embrace
my mission to care
I will always be there
I am spirit
I am you
we are one.

Ruth Johnston

Contents

Author's Note

The ultimate aim of my books are to take away the fear about the process of dying and death, and address some of the questions about our continued existence in the next dimension. Without doubt, the answers to these questions are of paramount importance to everyone, as physical death is inevitable for every living being.

By writing about my spiritual lessons and experiences with Sam – my childhood spirit friend, guide and mentor who was once a slave and shipped to Liverpool before he tragically died – in the context of my own life narrative, I hope to enlighten you in an inspirational way about an unseen dimension, to which we are all naturally connected and where our life force will continue. Science's understanding of the universe is constantly changing, even more so in the last twenty years. It is discovering more and more about the vibrations and energy that surround and connect us to our physical form, and how that energy relates and interacts with our universe. Many scientists are now embracing the notion of other dimensions, which leads to endless possibilities for our very existence. History has taught us that our minds should not be limited by what we think we know or understand, and what our eyes can see.

Please rest assured, when describing what I perceive as a spiritual dimension and relating how I can naturally interact with it at a conscious level, I am not trying to challenge people's religious beliefs. Historically, religion has endeavoured to establish a social, spiritual and environmental consciousness within a framework of fundamental morals, and this is a very positive objective. However, we have witnessed how, when the establishment aligns itself with religious leaders and their dogma, religion can also become a vehicle for controlling the masses. Such abuse has contributed towards creating a fractionalized world and the appalling destruction of countless lives.

As science uncovers the truth and eventually proves the existence of another dimension of continued existence – and one day it will – society will be given the opportunity to enter a new era. My only concern is that our leaders, who have demonstrated a desire for control and personal gain, do not hijack this potential revolution for the benefit of the few.

Time will tell, it always does!

Following the release of my first book, *Hands of an Angel*, many people asked me to write about my continuing journey with Sam, and the spiritual lessons he has taught me, but for untold reasons, it has taken me five years to get this manuscript published.

But now, here it is!

Beyond Boundaries begins with me meeting my soulmate, Richard, after a repressive and failed marriage. Richard's presence was the catalyst for breaking the inner shackles that had restrained me from speaking out confidently about who and what I am. With his earthly love and Sam's metaphysical presence, I have changed from a naïve young woman into one of a strong character who understands her own self-worth and her life purpose.

My personal contribution to this journey is that I have devoted my life to learning as much as possible from Sam. And what I have learned, I have tried to impart by means of individual consultations, seminars, media opportunities and, more recently, through writing.

I hope this book will make fascinating reading and that – as a longstanding professional therapist – I have imparted the emotional tools you might need, not only to deal with death and grief, but for you to embrace all the energies around you; to bring spiritual growth, fulfilment and true happiness into your own lives.

From my earliest recollection, the underlying message in everything I have been taught is love. Love is an essence that can soften a single heart, united it can move mountains to change a world.

Preface

As a professional therapist, people often ask me: "Helen, what is it that you do?"

In answer to this, I say, "I connect with a reality beyond the boundaries of our understanding and communicate with a greater consciousness existing outside the physical laws that are the materiality of our dimension."

Irrespective of what name your culture chooses to label this greater consciousness and where it exists, I embrace the opportunity to share my insight and understanding of it with you without the bias of theology.

My life has been devoted to honing my ability to link with this consciousness and channel an energy that seems essential to our very wellbeing. I believe that this energy can fill a person with a renewed positivity, which naturally transforms into a healing energy.

Whether I am administering the healing energy to alleviate a physical illness in person or from a distance in the form of absent healing, delivering a communication from your family in this reality, or sharing the infinite wisdom of the greater consciousness, it all comes under the auspices of a therapeutic healing experience.

I have noticed when communication is involved, I become the equivalent of a telephone line between the two dimensions; when physical healing is performed I become a transformer, enabling the spiritual energy to pass quickly into the earthly body.

My insight allows me to locate illness and discover malfunctions within the human body and that of animals, with astounding detail and accuracy.

And what I have learned is that LOVE is the key. We can only feel love, we cannot see it. It's through this invisible force that everything flourishes, and it provides the nourishment necessary for our spiritual growth.

So many people glibly state that there is no such thing as a reality in an unseen dimension, often labelled as the spirit world.

Well, I say to those people – prove that it doesn't exist!

The Flicker of Love

"A flicker of love, ignites the heart, fires the soul,
and lights a path of hope."
~Helen Parry Jones~

My spirit guide Sam walked in silence beside me. He was as clear and physical to me as the crowd of Chester shoppers that passed by. Sam had been a loyal companion since childhood, and together we had shared a lifelong journey of spiritual growth.

His formal introduction to me still makes me smile. When I was four years old Mum and I went to Mum's sister Aunty Joan's house in Queensferry, Wales – a town near the English border. Like so many tenement houses of that era, the toilet was in the backyard next to the coal shed. On this occasion, after I had spent my penny and started to make my way back indoors, sitting on the back doorstep just a couple of yards in front of me was this large black-skinned man, unusually dressed in a loosely fitted robe.

I believe I'd had previous sightings of him, but up until that moment he seemed more like a shadowy figure following me around in the background, especially at night while I tried to sleep. At times, I remember being a little frightened as I thought he was the bogeyman my friends often talked about. However, no matter how many times I ran into my parents' bedroom and told my mother what I could see, she would tell me not to be so silly, I was imagining things.

I knew these glimpses weren't a figment of my imagination and it frustrated me that I was disbelieved so adamantly, especially by the person I loved most in all the world. However, the incident at Aunty Joan's house was the first time I was aware of coming face-to-face so clearly with him, his unusually dark-black skin and really sensing his physical presence.

At the time, he looked a very young man, probably in his late teens. His demeanour was not threatening and his face was soft and full of compassion. One could even say he was very handsome. His gaze penetrated mine. Even as a child I felt his youthful presence held a greater depth of wisdom than that of my parents.

Even though every bit of me was riveted by his unique appearance, strangely I didn't fear this peculiar looking man. Nevertheless, I realised if I was to go back inside the house, I would have to ask him to move so I could climb the steps. Obviously, I now know I could have walked straight through him, but at the time he seemed as solid to me as my own flesh and blood.

Although I was anchored to the spot, I felt no tension, no threat, no fear; in fact a wave of overwhelming love flooded through me, the like of which I had never felt before. I remember witnessing his smile for the first time, it hasn't changed to this day, and always shows a remarkable array of perfectly formed white teeth.

"Hello, Helen – I am here as your friend." He spoke softly. His voice was deep and full of warmth, but he had an accent I had never heard before. I had never seen a black person so it was particularly odd for me to actually talk to one ... especially in my aunty's backyard! You have to remember British life in the early 1960s was not as multicultural as it is today, especially on the Welsh borders.

It was then he explained he was not the bogeyman as I had thought, and he told me I could call him Sam. He said that I shouldn't fear him and he was there to protect me. Although I had been warned many times by Mum not to talk to strangers, meeting this man was like reuniting with an old friend.

I fondly remember it was the first time he referred to me as *my child*, which in his accent sounded like *my chile*. Even to this day it is an endearment he uses when talking to me.

Sam went on to explain he was my Guardian Guide and I was to think of him like a school teacher, helping me learn new subjects. He said at first I wouldn't follow everything he might try to teach me, but as I grew up I would understand more. It was on this occasion he first spoke to me about spirit people and the spirit world.

I remember asking why my parents couldn't see him. He explained how I was very different and that most people couldn't see spirit people nor their spirit guides, even though they were always there, standing near them. I remember it was in this moment of revelation that I became aware I was able to see and communicate with dead people, which strangely didn't frighten me ... it made me very inquisitive.

However, there was one thing on my mind that troubled me considerably. I asked, "Why do my mummy and daddy say I do not see you?"

He answered, "It is because they do not understand your gift ... and fear what they do not understand."

I now realise my parents must have been terrified when their only child talked about seeing the invisible. The implications of experiencing such phenomena must have seemed out of this world to them. It was no wonder my parents scolded me throughout my childhood each time I mentioned seeing, amongst other things, my black man called Sam.

I longed for my parents to believe me and recognise my special ability, not only to give their approval but show parental pride in it. Their disapproval forced me into an intolerable position. I wanted them to know I didn't tell lies, that my visitors were not a figment of my imagination. I needed and craved their validation, not rejection. My parents doubt in me was isolating, as if I had been banished to a desert island.

Nan Ada, my mum's mother, was the only person to accept I could see what to others was invisible. I loved her so very much. Although she didn't have any pets, I would often tell her there was a big fat ginger cat and a black and white moggy sleeping on her sofa.

Whenever I spoke about them to Nan she would laugh lovingly and tell me not to worry about them. She always referred to them as Tigger and Arthur, and explained they were her cats, but they had died long ago. She told me she felt happier knowing they were still around the house and was pleased I could see them. It gave me such a sense of peace having someone I loved believing I spoke the truth.

My mother, on the other hand at one point in my childhood, took me down to our local GP, Dr Cornforth, to be assessed in case I was suffering from a form of mental illness. Thankfully he gave me a clear bill of health. At the time, I could sense my mother's disappointment at not finding an explainable medical reason for my conversations with a multitude of invisible visitors.

No matter how many times I closed my eyes, the spirit world was always there when I opened them. Essentially, growing up with this reality was as natural as breathing to me. As I got older, and throughout our many chats together, I realised Sam seemed to know how lonely a world it was for me to be so 'different' from the other kids.

As I was recalling these childhood memories, I hadn't noticed how quickly I had made my way through the city centre streets and arrived at my car, an old Austin Mini – my pride and joy, my independence. When I got in, I couldn't help thinking how bizarre it was for this thin, black man, unusually tall at about six foot six inches, nobly dressed in a floor-length robe, to stoop to half his body height and awkwardly climb into the small passenger seat beside me as if his spiritual presence had to adhere to the physical laws of my world.

It was incredible to believe we sat a little more than fifteen miles from where he was brutally murdered in 1797 on the cobbles of a dank Liverpool dock after months of confinement in the hull of a slave ship. Considering he had lived only nineteen years of earthly life, many would consider that he had little to share with me, a mother and housewife, who had recently celebrated her twenty-eighth birthday.

During his time here he was considered by my forefathers to be a slave of little worth or intelligence, comparable to a working beast to use or trade. In his own country, he was a proud, young warrior with a full and exciting life in front of him, surrounded by a loving family and positively driven by a strong cultural identity. The last months of his earthly life were an agonising experience for him, filled with heartache and extreme suffering. He had been so violently abused, it was hard to imagine how any society could rationalise inflicting such pain on another human being.

I had learned these things about him eleven years earlier when I was seventeen after he reluctantly succumbed to my constant requests to know about his earthly life. I remember him telling me he would only ever talk about this the once, and out of respect I have never pressed him again to relive his earthly memories. It is only with his consent I am now sharing with you, my reader, the details of his life.

Sam's birth name was Se-Se Samba (pronounced Seh-seh, meaning God has heard or God hears), but his mother would often call him by his second name Samba. Once enslaved, his captors issued him and his brother with the last name Bartholemy, and specifically for him with the prefix of Sam.

He was abducted from his African homeland along with many more young men and women after his village was ravaged and burnt to the ground by a gang of slave traders. All the village elders, including his own parents, were slaughtered in front of his eyes and even the pregnant women were not spared abduction or death.

The surviving captives were beaten and bound together with wooden slats around their necks and their limbs chained with irons. Every part of their village was destroyed so they would have no identity or anything to return to if they escaped. All the young men, women and children were gathered and separated into different groups. Women were separated from their husbands - with child or not. The screams of those he loved are to this day still etched into his consciousness. Within the spirit world it took much spiritual growth to understand and forgive man's inhumanity and the crimes that were committed against his family and tribesmen.

His three sisters and two brothers were also taken. All his siblings, except one younger brother, were separated from him when they were divided among the various ships carrying the human cargo. His youngest brother was chained to him as they embarked upon their allocated ship. Many around them were forcibly dragged screaming and whimpering like animals.

His sea journey lasted several months before arriving in America. On arrival, Sam was stripped naked, examined by the Master Captain and placed into a specific group classified by age, gender, or strength. The pretty young women were singled out by the Masters into yet another section, to be sold on as concubines or housemaids. Sturdy men and strong young boys were chosen to fetch the highest price for their muscle power. Sam and his brother were among a group sold at auction to travel on board another ship bound for Liverpool, England.

The travel conditions aboard this ship were even worse. They were packed together below deck, lined side by side, and treated savagely. Bodies were bound together in heavy metal chains that constantly flayed their flesh causing pain and infection.

Sam told me that such tight confinement caused his muscles to cramp uncontrollably and every part of his body was racked in pain. During his journey, sickness overcame him as it did many of his companions. Their bodies were constantly drenched in urine, vomit and faeces – a wretched cocktail that saturated the timbers they were bound upon. He remembered how at times he thought he would suffocate from the oven-hot air and stench. When the weather was good and the putrid smell became too insufferable for the ship's captain to bear, they were taken onto the top deck in small groups to be doused with buckets of salt water. It became entertainment for the crew to watch the slaves writhe as the sea water bit into their open cuts. On one occasion, Sam was picked out to be hauled into the air by a noose around his feet and dunked over the side for the crew's amusement. This was a regular spectacle the crew seemed to enjoy. Beatings and rape were commonplace, not only to manage the slaves' behaviour, but for general amusement. Those that died or were close to death were hauled overboard for the sea to consume.

Sam told me how, during their long journey, they were given only the foulest gruel to sustain them. Those who wouldn't eat had metal funnels pushed into their mouths to force-feed the concoction into their stomachs. Out of desperation, some managed to commit suicide. The voyage not only destroyed their bodies, but also their minds and their will to live. Sam had no shame in telling me that he was so utterly and completely distraught, there were many times he would have welcomed death to rescue him from this hell. He only fought this inclination as he knew somewhere in the ship was his brother, and in their father's absence he felt that it was his duty to try and protect his sibling.

Although they were bound together while walking up the ramp to the ship, he and his brother had been separated on boarding. Sam was so much taller than his brother, and the tiers of bodies were arranged according to height to maximise cargo-to-volume in the ship's hold. He tried calling out many times to find his brother, even passing on messages from man to man. Unfortunately, it never worked, as so many had the same name or were too distraught to even speak. The guilt of not being able to find and protect his brother during the journey was a huge burden for him. A combination of disease and inadequate food took a heavy toll on the captives and even some of the crew. One in every five Africans died on board. Some of the living considered those were the lucky ones!

When they finally arrived in Liverpool, Sam was thin from starvation and stricken with tuberculosis. He coughed uncontrollably and blood oozed from his mouth. As he disembarked the ship, he could barely support his own bodyweight. He had hardly taken twenty steps along the dockside when he collapsed.

After a swift beating it became evident to his captors he was too sick for the auction block. To hide his sickness from the potential buyers, Sam was taken by one of the crew and chained to a wall in a quiet area of the dock well away from view. There were several others chained to the same wall. At first Sam thought this was an act of kindness and they had been singled out to receive urgent medical treatment. It gave him time to think about his brother, and he prayed he had survived the long journey and might be sold to someone who was kind enough to let him sleep on dry straw. However, the respite was short-lived. The captain from the ship appeared and without any hesitation or emotion pulled a gun from inside his coat and placed it against Sam's head. In that instant he was murdered in cold blood and his earthly journey was over.

Enough melancholy, I thought.

I turned and looked at Sam's kind features. It was impossible not to be moved by him when remembering the horrific experiences he had endured. Through spiritual enlightenment, he had progressed far beyond revenge or retribution.

Sam looked ahead into the distance, his face devoid of any expression. I began to focus on the large round dials in the Mini's dashboard. Without thinking, I slid the key into its slot and turned it. The engine started straight away, breaking the silence.

Despite his detachment, I knew from a lifetime of experience he could hear my every thought. I didn't feel he was angry or even displeased with me, but rather that he was contemplating what to say. Having Sam constantly at my side, I had experienced many of these silent waits and I knew there was no rushing him.

Normally, when in his presence, he would engage me in spiritual discussion or some sort of meaningful tutorial. However, such silent periods were often Sam's way of considering the many outcomes of my actions so he could advise me, if and when it was appropriate for him to do so.

I had experienced a life-changing day and I was in turmoil. I needed him to reassure me everything was going to be all right. I was in a dilemma. One minute I believed my life was empty of marital happiness and the next I had met this wonderful man, called Richard. He had been catapulted into my life less than three weeks before, predominantly as a client wanting spiritual guidance. His purpose was to discuss the consequences of his own failing marriage and concerns about how any marital break-up might affect his position within the growing family business.

The very first time he walked through the door to meet me for his consultation, I knew in my heart of hearts he was different, even special in some way. Despite it being the third time I had met this man, we had never been alone together socially.

Three days prior we'd arranged a casual meeting-up in Richard's Chester shop, to go for a quick coffee. When I walked in, I saw him emptying a box of clothes pegs into a display basket. I was shocked to see such a large array of toys and home accessories stacked high on the shelves. Little did I know he had positioned himself so that he could see me the moment I walked in. Our eyes met, and then we gave each other a quick hug. The ice was broken.

Richard linked my arm in his and in one sweeping motion ushered me towards to door. "Come on! We can't stay in here. Let's go down the road and have that coffee you promised me."

Afterwards, I spent the most perfect romantic afternoon in the August sunshine, walking and talking alongside the River Dee and meandering through the rose beds in the park. Just holding hands and looking into this man's eyes had sent my heart racing.

Even after just a matter of minutes of being together, my life seemed full of endless possibilities for a new future. The tenderness and care he showed me was a revelation. I had not felt this special in a long time. It proved to me that my life had to change if I was ever to be fulfilled and find true happiness.

But ... like so many of us, I feared change.

My husband, John, and I had recently reconciled for the children's sake after a six-month trial separation. So my failing marriage, which had been in steady decline over the past three years, was no secret. Despite this, never in a month of Sundays did I expect I would meet someone else who could potentially be a new relationship in my life.

I knew by the way we talked, Richard had an instinctive understanding of my work. He had witnessed first-hand during both of his consultations with me the accuracy of my spiritual communications. Playfully, he had told me that I was either telling the truth, telling lies or I was completely mad! But he believed without any doubt I spoke the truth, and had a healthy appetite to learn more. What I treasured most in this man was that he had genuine belief in me.

Yet, despite this belief, if Richard was going to have a meaningful relationship with me, was he prepared to accept the colossal importance of Sam in my life – a relationship between three people, no less? I believed he would!

Sam had an earthly life in certain aspects very similar to our own, full of hope and expectation. I vowed to myself that one day I would take Richard to Liverpool Docks to make Sam's life here in the physical world more tangible. Together we could try and find where the slave boats docked and maybe discover where Sam had been murdered.

In that moment, sitting in my car, I questioned myself with a hundred questions. What was happening to me? What had this man Richard done to my life? How do I deal with this? What about my children? Where does my life go from here? *Sam, help me. Why don't you speak to me?* I screamed out in my head, trying to provoke some answers from him. In my heart, I knew it was not his role to take away my freedom of choice. Making personal life choices was my own responsibility.

Despite this confusion, all my senses were heightened. I was consumed with a passion for Richard I had never felt before. Instinctively, I tried in vain to shield these alluring thoughts from Sam, as though it was my father who was sitting next to me. I could sense he was listening as there is no hiding the truth from your spirit guide, but there was no judgement in his manner.

I gathered my concentration and engaged the gears. It was time to pick up my two young children, Fiona, aged seven years, and Anthony, aged four years, from my parents' home in Kinmel Bay, about forty-five miles away. My children had long become the only source of happiness in my loveless marriage. Of course, it hadn't always been this way, but they filled a void in my life that was not their role to fill. Was I now prepared to irrevocably change their lives forever?

Why is life governed by so many difficult choices?

About an hour later, I arrived at my parents' bungalow. Despite being about six p.m., the summer day was still in its full glory. Under my mother's watchful eye, the children were happily playing in the garden, oblivious to my emotional turmoil. Their presence was a welcome distraction for my mother, as my father was in hospital again recuperating from one of his recurrent breathing attacks.

Dad was only forty nine years of age and had been suffering from emphysema for nearly twenty years. He had been a smoker all his life and the result was ravaging his body. More recently, his time was spent having attacks, being admitted to hospital, and once stabilised, enjoying brief respites until his next incident. Unfortunately, the episodes had become progressively worse during the last twelve months. My father had been brought back from the brink of death on far too many occasions.

I knew Dad didn't have long with us, as Sam had told me when I was a child that he would pass over into the spirit world during his fiftieth year. This was a huge responsibility for anyone to bear, let alone a child. For me, it was yet another consequence of having spiritual sight that I had had to accept, whether I liked it or not.

On reflection, I am glad I knew, as it ensured I treasured every living moment with him. When I originally found out, I had tried to warn my mother about his premature death. Once was enough! A huge row ensued between us and I knew I was forbidden to mention my conversations with Sam ever again.

Even after a lifetime of spiritual tutorials from my guide, I accepted that my perception of the spiritual dimension is not only beyond my understanding, but also most people's basic acceptance. Even the most advanced scientists struggle with the concept of another dimension. Without doubt, there is so much in this universe of ours that remains unexplainable. As science constantly uncovers many mysteries about the world around us, logical explanations about who we are and where we originate are continually evolving and pushing the boundaries of what we consider to be the basis of our reality. One day, society will look back and ridicule our ignorance of the spiritual essence within us that is fundamental to our existence.

From what I understand, we are not human beings on a spiritual quest but spiritual beings on a human journey.

Geographical culture also places boundaries on the way we perceive our own world, specifically how we should eat, drink, dress, be educated and observe religion. Without thought, we assume the intellectual mindset of the society we are born into. Understanding my own cultural background, it is no wonder people often consider my conversations with an invisible spiritual world absolutely unbelievable.

My father was no different. He saw his life so deeply rooted to the material world that his belief system made it impossible for him to even imagine a progression into another dimension. 'Once you are dead you are dead', was his belief. A sentiment he voiced often.

In my role as a medium, it is my duty to reassure you that death is not the end. I have no reservations about that; there *is* life after death and a continuance of our existence for all of us, irrespective of our colour, creed or sexual orientation.

It was unfortunate I was not able to instil that reassurance into my parents. I failed with the two people I loved most in all the world. To make it worse, I had to watch their constant suffering. My mother in her silence worrying about my father's terminal condition and my father locked into his degenerative sickness. Knowing by accessing the spiritual dimension I could ease his suffering exasperated me and it was a huge emotional barrier between us when he denied me the chance to try to help him. However, it must be said that throughout my rocky marriage my parents had been a constant source of emotional support.

My marital stress was something they really didn't need right then. Knowing Dad's time with us was short provoked guilt when I brought any type of problem to his door.

Since meeting Richard, I had spoken to my mother about him several times, and although she was not happy I was meeting him socially, I knew deep down she had accepted that my future was not with my husband.

Mum called the children inside to watch television and insisted on having a chat with me over a pot of tea in the kitchen before we dashed off to see my father in hospital. The day's events were still fresh in my mind and I wanted to keep reliving every touch and every smile. It was as though Richard was no stranger to me, but rather that we had just rediscovered each other after waiting our lifetimes to reunite. Our conversation flowed effortlessly as we discussed everything about our lives, our dreams, our expectations and ultimately about a new life together as one. Then, as we said our goodbyes, that fateful first kiss, not a passionate embrace, but a nervous, clumsy, crash of teeth.

My mother looked worried as I told her about the afternoon's events and my feelings towards this man. Her concern was natural and she tried to balance my enthusiasm with scepticism and doubt. She focused on how hard it was for a man to take on the responsibility of someone else's children. But I was having none of that negativity! A depth of love had anchored itself so quickly in my heart. I knew if he cared about me enough, nothing else would matter to him. However, we agreed I would not tell my father so as not to worry him – and in Mum's mind, the possibility of a new relationship was all very premature. She insisted she would tell my dad when she felt the time was right, which had in recent years become the norm when telling him about my marital predicaments.

So that evening at my father's hospital bedside, the conversation centred on the children playing in the garden. I so much wanted to talk about this new man coming into my life. But seeing Dad lying there, fighting for every breath, thin and gaunt from his disease, I felt my mother was right, it could wait ... for now. I reached out and touched his hand; I wanted him to know how much I loved him.

He turned and smiled at me.

In that instant, I noticed a young spirit girl standing beside the metal bed-frame. She looked at my father and seemed oblivious to the fact I could see her. Within seconds she disappeared. I looked around for Sam to enquire of her purpose, but he was nowhere to be seen.

I so wished I could tell my father what I could see.

2

We've Only Just Begun

*"Hours, days, weeks, months or even years can
pass trying to fix something unfixable,
… or you can leave the fragments and move on."*
~Helen Parry Jones~

Fortunately, the children had had their tea at Mum's house, so later that evening when I arrived back at our new home in Upton, Chester, I was able to put them straight to bed. Actually, the house was in need of major renovation. Despite all my objections, John had just sold our lovely family home in St Asaph and moved us so we could be nearer to his workplace. Even though we were living like campers, I was trying to create as normal a family life as possible.

Already well past nine p.m., John still hadn't come home from work; he rarely did these days until very late. He was having to do overtime, apparently, but I had suspected otherwise for a while now.

Fortunately, there was plenty of hot water as the boiler had just been replaced. I drew myself a bath so I could relax for a while to reflect on the day. I climbed in gently, and soon acclimatised to the initial stinging on my skin. Once completely immersed up to my neck, the hot water became very comforting. I heard John arrive home. As much as I wanted to blank him from my mind and avoid him, this was my cue to get dried and change into my pyjamas so I could undertake my domestic responsibilities.

Downstairs, I put the kettle on to make tea. We exchanged some pleasantries and a brief conversation about my hospital visit to see my father. He declined food as he had grabbed something earlier. We rarely ate as a family these days. Fifteen minutes later I excused myself to go up to bed. I said I was tired, but in reality I just wanted to be alone to reflect on my day. He said he would use the spare room again, so as not to disturb me in the morning on his early start. For a while now, separate bedrooms had become our normality. This was no life for a young woman!

Once in bed, I found reassurance in snuggling up in my luxurious old quilt, as the linen still had the familiar scent of my last home. Eventually, summer darkness came. My eyes focused on the solitary light bulb limply hanging from old cable in the centre of the ceiling. As if in an altered state, I reminisced on the day and my mind filled with questions about my future.

I wondered why my deceased grandparents, Nan Ada and Granddad Joe, had showed themselves to me in the park earlier that day. My nan had died just before her fiftieth wedding anniversary, so to see them so happy together walking alongside Richard and me, I interpreted as a very good omen for our future together. I felt this was a spiritual sign giving me their blessing with this new relationship.

My thoughts ran wild as I created scenarios in my mind and tried to imagine the many different futures each choice would bring. I now realised my life could be changed, that my struggle in this loveless marriage might possibly end. Then I called myself stupid to even think the outcome of my leaving would lead to anything good. Yet deep inside, I knew meeting this new man was to forever change my life in some way, even if all I had was this one day with him.

My experience of men was limited – I had married when I was only nineteen. Maybe it was my naïvety that allowed me to believe a stranger could now romantically sweep into my world and bring happiness to my life after just one kiss. Yet here I was, about to plan my future with him. Some would say this choice was complete and utter madness!

Then there were the children – the innocents in every marital breakdown. All they wanted from life was two loving parents. How could I possibly impose such change upon them? Contrary to the modern lifestyle, I believed whole heartedly in marriage, yet I was confused as to why, when my husband and I loved the children so very much, this wasn't enough to sustain our union? But as much as I tried – it wasn't.

My head pounded! The consequences of all my different choices played out in front of my mind's eye as if I were watching actors on a stage.

John often told me he loved me, but I felt the words were said through obligation, not from the heart. I wanted to be loved by someone who wanted to love me in a way I wanted to be loved. Was that so wrong? It felt selfish to even think of my own happiness above that of my children's. But the longing to be free of the indescribable loneliness and the anxiety of feeling unloved, overwhelmed me.

In my professional role as a spiritual medium, I give voice to the guidance offered by the collective consciousness of my spirit guides. Part of that process is to identify problems and explore the likely outcomes of addressing them. It is then up to the recipient to make their own choices based on that guidance.

This is a shock for some people when they come to see me, as they often have the misconception they are going to be told what to do for the best or have important decisions made for them. In life, a good parent doesn't dictate how a child should lead their life, they offer advice from wisdom, and trust the child will make good choices based on that advice. Accordingly, when I have a problem, Sam will often try to explain the possible outcomes of my actions, however he will never tell me what to do with my life.

Right here, right now, needing to make life-changing decisions for myself, that spiritual law felt extremely lacking! Although still silent, Sam was there in the darkness of the bedroom. I couldn't see him; I could only sense his presence.

In all honesty, I had only had an afternoon walk in the park with this man, so really there was no way of knowing whether a relationship would grow between us. However, deep inside I sensed we were twin flames on the same path. Nevertheless, I knew the only way to have a committed and meaningful relationship was if I was unhindered by marriage. If I had learned anything from imparting the wisdom from my guides to others in similar circumstances, it was that if you truly want an open and honest partnership, it cannot be through clandestine meetings and grabbed affection. A relationship built upon lies and deceit would be doomed to disappointment from the start.

After a while, my mind slowly emptied as it tried to find sleep.

Just as I was about to close my eyes Sam appeared before me. He smiled compassionately and spoke quietly in his usual endearing manner, "Hello, my chile."

In my adult years, Sam referred less and less to me as his chile, but when he did, I knew there were some difficult times on the horizon for me. I was so happy he had at last broken the silence between us, but I was a little apprehensive as to what he was about say. However, I was ready to hear his wisdom.

He began, "Having listened to your inner conversations and emotional struggle, my chile, there are no right or wrong answers to this dilemma, only a choice of heart. You are consciously reacting to this situation seeking a positive outcome for the greater good. This is an honourable process. However, what you have to ask yourself is for whose greater good are you making this choice? Is it for selfish pursuit of your own happiness, or do you genuinely feel that staying in the present relationship will eventually damage your children by hearing constant arguments and seeing you continuously unhappy?"

I felt confused and asked, "How can I know whether my choice will be the right choice? How can I know whether my desire to be loved completely, both sexually and emotionally, is a selfish desire, especially when I genuinely believe this new love will ripple out and radiate to my children?"

"Only you can answer this," Sam answered. "Remember, whatever your choice, there is no judgement. It is you that has to live with the outcome of your decisions."

I knew there was wisdom in his words, but in reality all I wanted him to do was tell me what the right decision would be in the best interest of my children and for my own happiness. However, being told what was right to do was never going to be an option.

Sam carried on. "While women generally seek enduring love, men are primarily hunters – they are often looking to find prey. You need to discern if this man finds you prey or a soul mate. This doesn't make men the cause of failed relationships, as there are many women who don't look for lasting love or lasting relationships. Many women send out signals to attract the baser element of the male hunter and to have their lust satisfied, and yet these same women all too often wonder why there is no lasting relationship for them afterwards. Women often believe that this kind of lustful, sexual relationship will help them through their moments of crisis, which in some cases of course it will. However, when they believe this is the way to a lasting relationship, all too often they can be disappointed."

I listened attentively to Sam's every word.

"I can only advise you love is the only real, solid foundation that can sustain a positive and lasting relationship. Remember, true love requires trust and loyalty, and it is those qualities that successfully binds two people together. My advice, chile, is to understand this. I feel that in your heart you have chosen your path, and you are determined to leave your present relationship and move forward. This will have a direct effect not only upon you, but also on everyone close to you and most importantly on your children. So you need to understand what sort of relationship Richard may offer you ... if any. That is his choice and in a short time you will know. Due to your progressed spirituality, your life journey is always faster and more intense than most. Helen, my chile, draw on your spiritual essence from deep inside, and trust your inner self to guide you."

My eyes closed as exhaustion overwhelmed me, and Sam's words of wisdom faded into the background. The day had finally caught up with me, and my body forced me to sleep.

Around four a.m., or so, I was disturbed by the feeling of someone sitting at the end of my bed. It startled me, and as I opened my eyes I could see quite clearly a woman. She was of slight stature with her hair in curls hanging on her tiny shoulders, and her face was pale and thin. However, she had huge, piercing brown eyes that stared directly into mine. Although I was very familiar with seeing the spirit world when they visited unexpectedly, it could be very shocking. At first, I wanted to scream out, but somehow I managed to compose myself.

Despite the darkness giving way to the early morning light, I could see a glow around the outline of her petite body. She smiled at me tenderly, "Please don't be frightened. You are so lucky to have two such beautiful children. They are so precious. I would have loved to have had children of my own."

Immediately I became alert and listened to her intently. She spoke with an American accent, and I was puzzled as to her identity. There was something familiar about her face, but I couldn't place her. Intuitively, I posed the question in my mind of who she was and why she was with me. As if in answer to my thought, she smiled and replied, "I am the musician Karen Carpenter."

Her reply staggered me. *The* Karen Carpenter was sitting on *my* bed, whether she was a spirit or not! This was the first time I had ever been visited by a celebrity, so naturally I was a little awestruck.

Since that time, I have been visited by countless celebrities and people of substantial notoriety, but I have learned it is only our society that has differentiated them in that way. Earthly accolades have no importance in the spirit world, so when working professionally I have learned to address all my visitors from a position of respectful equality.

She continued speaking, "One day I would like you to talk to my family, especially my brother Richard."

Then, as if we were old friends, Karen started talking about how she too had experienced a loveless marriage with her husband, Tom, and although she filed for divorce, she died before it was finalised.

Karen wept as she explained that secretly she regularly took a cocktail of thyroid and laxative medication to deplete her body of the extra pounds she thought she needed to lose. I could sense her pain as she explained that although she wanted to be free from her condition, the thought of putting on weight was hideous to her. She talked of how her dieting consumed every part of her.

There was an essence of true sadness in her voice. Intuitively, I knew she had genuine remorse as she had accepted her actions contributed to her early death, four years prior.

She continued, "I felt bad about my illness. Inside I was sad and alone. There were things I couldn't speak of to those who were close to me, particularly to my parents. When you meet my brother, please tell him that I love him and that I never thought I would die this way."

Karen's tone changed and her manner became stronger, "You are suffering a little of what I went through, so I know you will understand."

I gasped in disbelief. Whatever gave her the impression I had an eating disorder?

However, where the spirit world is concerned, there is no hiding the truth. And the truth was, in recent years I had at times made myself sick after food to control my own weight in the belief that if I was thinner my husband would show me more affection and perhaps love me more. But now, with maturity, I have learned this is a misconception shared by many bulimics and is rarely the outcome.

Without any prompting, she smiled warmly and started to sing, 'We've only just begun' in her familiar mellow, melodic voice. How bizarre – I was being sung to by Karen Carpenter – now who would believe that?

I had learned over the years to be very selective about what I said to people about what I could see and hear from the spirit dimension. So my meeting with Karen was going to be my secret for a while. And then intuitively I felt *my* Richard would listen; in fact, I knew he would love to hear all about this extraordinary window of communication I had into the spirit dimension. At that moment, for the first time in my life, I felt totally liberated.

As the lyrics were ending, she gestured her hand as if blowing me a kiss goodbye and simply faded away. I lay there for a while wondering why she had chosen to speak with me when I was thousands of miles away from her family. My heart was still racing as a result of this bizarre encounter. Why did she sing that particular song to me? What was the purpose of her communication? How could I help her? Or maybe she had come to help me? It was all a mystery, as I doubted that I would ever have the opportunity to go to America, let alone ever meet any of her family.

If there is one thing for certain I have learned when talking with the spirit world – no matter how many questions you ask, in reality, whatever they say, whatever wisdom they try to share, it just evokes so many more questions. And this communication with Karen was no different.

However, I now believed that if I decided to leave my husband, it would free me to explore a new future. Then Karen's words returned to me and confirmed my thought, filling my heart with her rendition of 'We've only just begun'. I was now convinced this was a sign that starting a new life with Richard was my true destiny.

I looked at my bedside clock; it was eight a.m. John had already left for work, so I climbed out of bed, got dressed and packed a suitcase for the children and me.

After breakfast, I casually asked them to gather a few toys together and then ushered them into the car. Fortunately, they were always eager and excited to visit their grandparents.

As soon as we arrived, the children ran in to give their nan a kiss and then sat in the lounge to watch cartoons. At least they were distracted so I could have a serious talk with my mother. We sat next to each other at the small kitchen table and I poured my heart out over a pot of tea. As soon as I explained I had left John and wanted a divorce, Mum started to cry.

And then came my desperate plea, "Maybe I could stay with you for a couple of days while Dad is in hospital, until I have found somewhere to live?"

She reluctantly agreed, but there was a sense of anger and bitterness in her response. "How could you do this right now with your dad being in hospital? Isn't there enough for me to deal with?"

I replied, "I know, Mum, but I can't cope anymore. I just can't carry on being unhappy, day after day. Even if my life isn't with Richard, it's definitely not with John. I just can't stay with him a minute longer … even if Dad is in hospital."

My suitcase resting against the kitchen wall confirmed how serious I was.

Mum tried to reason, "You shouldn't make such rash decisions. Have you thought this through properly? What about your finances … especially for the children's sake?"

Her advice was sound. However, having already experienced a six-month separation, the decision was in no way rash as I had been visualising this day for a very long time. As far as the finances were concerned, yes, she made a very good point, but somehow we would have to manage. My marital unhappiness was beyond any financial consideration.

I now had to step into my own light.

Sam stood by the back door, seemingly leaning on the kitchen worktop. He hadn't spoken to me since last night. However, on this occasion, he didn't have to say any words. Just by looking into his eyes, I knew the time had come to do what was morally correct and honestly tell my husband of my intentions. The thought made me feel sick.

After taking a deep breath, I walked into my mother's lounge and sat in the armchair by the large bay window overlooking the front garden. Mum switched off the television and took the children outside for a play to allow me some privacy to call John. Nervously, I dialled him at work.

Sam followed me into the lounge and although he never spoke a word, he smiled at me reassuringly from across the room. The warmth and understanding behind that smile gave me the strength I needed.

John didn't like me calling him at the office, so when he answered the phone I could hear in his voice he was very annoyed with me. I explained I was sorry to have to break this news to him this way, but I wanted a divorce. After a long conversation talking about our irrevocable differences, John started to cry. At first I was very moved by his emotional outburst and cried with him. However, as our conversation progressed I began to feel these tears were as a result of his lost pride rather than losing me from his life. The mood changed as I told him I had just met someone. I explained it was a client who I had only met once socially, and that was for a walk in the park only. He started to shout at me and we were seconds away from slamming the phone down on each other.

Sam stepped forward and held his hand up. His body seemed to give off waves of energy, similar to a pebble disturbing calm water. As the energy engulfed me, it instilled an inner peace within me. John momentarily stopped ranting and I seized the opportunity that Sam's intervention had given me to speak calmly.

"I can assure you that no intimacy has taken place with this man. However, I want to be free of my marital commitments to you so I can have intimacy with him and explore the possibility of us having a new future together. I really don't know if a relationship will work out between us – but, if he is half the man I think he is, he is the right man for me. If it turns out he isn't, then I have lost nothing, as we are finished anyway."

These were harsh words, but honest.

Some people might wait weeks, months or even years for the right time to give such final news. Some might say that one day after a walk in the park and a single, short kiss was very premature. However, in my opinion, why put off what you intend to say, as there will never be a good time.

There was nothing more to be said. Everything was now in the open and I was free to pursue a new life unencumbered by the guilt of marital deceit – I had a brand-new future to live.

In retrospect, from the wisdom and emotional strength I have gained through maturity, I realise that I should have faced John and said what needed to be said at home in private when I decided to leave with the children. I shall always regret that mistake and I unreservedly apologise for not doing so. However, what is done cannot be changed, and so I have to live with that.

The next job was the solicitor. One phone call later, the receptionist had given me an appointment for that afternoon – job done!

Later that day, I arrived back from the family solicitor with the advice I should move back to the marital home with the children, and that, for the children's welfare, John had a responsibility to make the house habitable. However, the most shocking news was that some months earlier he had been to the solicitor to research a divorce strategy.

I could see the relief on my mother's face that I might still have a home to go back to. It made her a little more welcoming to our staying with her, as she knew I would most probably follow the solicitor's advice and move back.

I realised there was a difficult journey ahead. That being said, it seemed appropriate to meet up with John as soon as I felt emotionally strong enough and have a face-to-face chat with him to discuss what needed to be done and attempt to do so as amicably as possible.

For now, I was happy at the thought of a new future ahead of me.

3

What a Difference a Day Makes!

"Our life journey is made up of countless choices.
We are the result of them."
~Helen Parry Jones~

I had just spent my first night on my mother's sofa and although I'd had a restless night, I woke feeling confident that I'd made the right decision to divorce and pursue a new life. Sam had made an early appearance and was sitting silently in the armchair beside me.

After a short time, he turned his head and smiled warmly, "How are you, my chile?"

Despite the stressful events of the previous day, I felt a renewed sense of positivity. As soon as I rose, I put the kettle on and made Mum a mug of tea and took it into her bedroom to wake her. As I walked in, I nearly screamed out in shock as an overwhelming spiritual presence filled the room. Standing by my mother's bed was a spirit child, dressed in what could only be described as a jump suit made from the thinnest of white linen type material, tied at the waist with a white band. The sleeves were baggy, as were the leggings that clung tightly at her ankles where the apparition seemed to wane. She was adorned with bracelets of flowers around her wrists, a flowery chain worn as a necklace with a matching flowery headband in her hair. The flower buds were tiny and a mixture of vibrant colours, far brighter than any I had seen before. She appeared to be around nine or ten, but her eyes had the depth of much wisdom. I could discern from her spiritual essence she was a spirit guide.

In my mind, she spoke to me, not childish words, but with wisdom far greater than her outward appearance. The way she spoke was direct and precise, "Don't wake your mother. She sleeps so soundly. It is you I need to talk to. Take heed, my child, your father is very ill. Those in spirit are very near to him. Soon, he will hear us calling – time is of the essence for him."

A chill radiated throughout my body and made me shudder.

Dad had been hospitalised so many times in recent years with so many life-threatening attacks, and we'd had so many death-watch visits that I doubted his frail body could take much more living. My father was still only forty-nine, but his fiftieth birthday was just a few weeks away. Was this a spirit preparing my father to be taken from us like they had predicted so many years ago? I knew the end was near.

Sensing I needed to know who she was, she spoke to me again with the same resolute clarity, "I am your father's guide. Rest assured he will see me soon enough. Be prepared, dear child. You will know when the time has come for him to leave with us, as you will be called back from across water."

Although I felt sick my father's last day was imminent, I was reassured that just maybe it wasn't going to be today as I was not intending to cross any water. However, the words she spoke concerned me, so I kept repeating them in my mind to commit this prediction to memory. Then, as if to break the tension, I remember feeling vaguely amused by the way this child-like guide called me 'child'!

I stood in the doorway and looked at my mother. She was still asleep and her mug of tea was starting to burn my hand. I thought, when I wake her, should I tell her of this remarkable visitation? My mother had recently started to take a little more interest in my ability to see the spirit dimension, but still she gave me the impression that much of what I said was fanciful. It was a dilemma.

Then, like a fading candle, the spirit guide was gone. In the same instance the telephone rang, breaking the early morning silence. It was only seven thirty a.m., so this couldn't be good news. The adrenaline pumped around my body.

The sound startled Mum and without thinking she jumped out of bed. However, I had already run to answer it. It was the hospital – we were to go there immediately. My father had taken a turn for the worse and they doubted he would pull through.

Mum suggested I call John to take the children as their granddad's deathbed was not a place for them to be. She reasoned that he wouldn't want them upset. I reluctantly made the call. His reply was brief and curt: from now on, my father's illness and the children's daily routine were not his problem – he had work to do! Unfortunately, I had no option but to take the children with us to the hospital.

On arrival, the nurse made it clear they couldn't go onto the ward. I explained my circumstances and she volunteered to watch over them in the visitors lounge for a short while to settle them down. This was a specialist chest hospital and many of the patients shared my father's condition. In this place, death was always in the air.

Dad lay motionless, his head and shoulders resting on a stack of pillows. He looked old and haggard. His frail body was plumped up with drugs and steroids. I could hear the rasps of his weak breath. The nebuliser machine he relied upon was vibrating bedside him like a workman's drill.

My mother bent over him, holding one of his hands and soothing his brow with the other. I fetched her a chair and placed a second one for myself on the opposite side of the bed. Lovingly, I held his other hand. Dad was dying.

His breathing sounded strange, it was more of a gasp – noisy and laboured. It seemed to take every ounce of his strength to concentrate on breathing in, and then it was equally hard to breathe out. It was unbearable to watch.

Instantly, my hands began to burn and healing energy began to pass into him. When we were at home together, he would never let me administer any healing to him as he thought it all nonsense. But lying here waiting for death to take him, he didn't really have much choice.

I desperately wanted him to live.

After about five minutes or so, my hands were still burning. Weakly, he pulled his hand away from mine and grabbed at the mask tugging it off his face. He turned to me, and while trying to gulp a lungful of air, he whispered, "I'm glad you're here. I love you, Helen."

I took a deep breath and sobbed, I couldn't remember the last time he had said those tender words to me. With tears rolling down my cheeks, I wanted to cradle him in my arms but the pipes and cables were in the way. I took the mask out of his bony hand and put it back over his face so he could breathe more easily again.

The room was stunningly bright from the summer morning sun shining through the solitary window. A lifetime of spiritual sight had taught me such conditions were not the most ideal for seeing spirit. However, in a blink of an eye, I was aware of a spirit figure at the foot of my father's bed standing tall and silent.

Actually, the sight of him was quite intimidating. I looked into his eyes, they were deep blue and held a millennium's experience. I say he, but his soft features looked genderless, radiating youth and beauty, almost feminine, but not gentle like a woman's. I sensed this spirit was resolute and compassionate, but nevertheless unshakable in his opinion. I couldn't help but stare at him in absolute awe. He seemed to be immune to the grief of death and I instinctively knew he treated this situation as a task, it seemed it was his duty to be here. As he stood there, he stared intently at my father, watching his every breath as he struggled to remain alive.

The spirit wore a long gown made from a delicate golden material, and over it a swaying robe of deep purple that hung from his shoulders to the ground. His head was covered in the same piece of purple material, worn like a snood, draped and thrown back over his broad shoulders. Strangely, I could even see the faint outline of his perfectly proportioned body through the gown. All his garments seemed to have an iridescent vibrancy of their own; it was a remarkable sight.

Flowing from his back to the ground I saw what I can only describe as an energy of sorts, like the shimmer off a road on a hot day – but a thousand times more. I had seen something similar before but never to this degree or vivacity. It was shocking to observe.

His appearance was made more dramatic as he held a long staff in his left hand. I noticed that with each breath my father took, the long staff would pulsate in unison with him, almost like it had a life of its own. Naturally, I was transfixed by this spectacular visitation. Although I could not see Sam, I could hear him in my mind. He sensed my confusion and explained this visitor had come with a particular purpose. He said I would know him in my earthly world as the Angel of Hope. This angel apparently had two main duties, he was responsible for visions and also guiding souls into the spirit world when they passed.

This revelation confused me as to why he was here today. Sam explained that this presence was here to facilitate a spiritual change within my father. Mum started to speak to me and the sound of her voice disturbed my spiritual focus. I looked back to see the angel, but he bowed his head down as if to nod and just disappeared.

She looked at me from across the bed. "Your dad can't cope at the moment, Helen," she said. "Why don't you go and check up on the children and have a rest. Don't worry, I'll call you if I need you or when there's any change."

Perhaps Mum wanted a little alone time with my father. I was relieved at the respite as it was becoming increasingly difficult to keep my emotions under control watching my father suffer in this way.

The visitor's lounge had an overwhelming smell of stale cigarettes. Smoking had brought death closer to most of the patients in this hospital, yet many of them still sat in here for hours smoking with their families with the full consent of the hospital.

I explained to the children that their granddad was very poorly. Naturally they looked sad, but were oblivious to the severity of his illness and continued to play normally. I sat in a well-worn armchair and gazed through the old-fashioned metal-framed glass doors that opened onto the gardens. If it wasn't for our circumstance, I would have considered this to be a particularly beautiful morning.

While sitting there, my mind focused on giving Dad some strength through absent healing. Perhaps this might help him through this critical time and keep the Angel of Death at bay.

Absent healing is a term used for administering spiritual healing from a distance. By using a meditation technique, you can bring about physical and emotional change within the recipient that can be as dramatic as if the healer was with you in person. I wasn't going to let death take Dad without a fight. Actually, there wasn't a night that went by that I didn't send some absent healing to him, but his refusal to give up smoking resulted in limited success. It was like trying to fill a bucket with water that was peppered with holes. There was a part of me angry because he had spent a lifetime smoking that had aggravated his condition and contributed to these agonising hospital stays. I believed wholeheartedly that without my nightly absent healing, he would have died years before.

After about an hour, my meditation was disturbed by a smiling nurse bringing in a tray carrying a mug of tea and two small glasses of orange squash. "I can't believe it," she said. "Your father has stabilised and his breathing has improved. Why don't you pop down and see him and I will watch the children while they have something to drink."

I didn't need asking twice and almost ran down the corridor. Mum was still sitting in the same position holding Dad's hand. The oxygen mask had been temporarily removed and his breathing was a little less strained. I stroked his grey hair and gave him a light kiss on his clammy forehead. "Sorry to scare you, love," he whispered between short gasps of breath.

I smiled, and in my mind gave thanks that he had been given enough strength to live.

My mother said she was going to stay with Dad for the rest of the day and suggested I go back home so the children could have a play in the garden and then come back to collect her in the evening. If anything changed she would call me.

When I arrived back, it seemed a good idea to contact Richard and let him know that Dad was in hospital seriously ill. Also, I felt I should tell him I had left my husband and was now living at my parents' home for a while. To be honest, I was a little nervous about contacting him in case he wanted nothing more to do with me. This was a lot of heavy baggage for him to accept.

At the time, North Wales didn't have much mobile network coverage, so Richard was still dependent on telephone kiosks to keep in touch with everyone when he was driving between his shops. So it wasn't much of a surprise when I called his mobile phone to find it was out of range. It left me no alternative but to leave a message at his Chester shop for him to call me.

Hardly an hour passed before he phoned back. It was wonderful to hear his voice after such a stressful day. I shared all my news and Richard seemed genuinely concerned about my father and shocked I had left John.

I explained that my decision to divorce was made entirely on my own accord and as far as I was concerned, if our relationship was to progress, it would be honest, in the open and above board. I told Richard my husband mocked me saying that I was stupid to think somebody would be so committed to me after just one meeting.

On hearing all of this, there was an unusually long silence. My heart sank. Perhaps I had misjudged him and maybe he felt overcommitted to me too soon; pressurised even. Perhaps John was right after all!

Richard was unfazed and assured me that after three months of being separated, he realised his marriage was completely over. He added, as yet he had not filed for divorce, but under the circumstances that was now next on his agenda.

Inwardly, I glowed with happiness.

Later that evening I collected my mother from the hospital. Dad had sat up for a while, eaten something and had remained settled all day – so once again, fighting all the odds, he had cheated death.

Over the following days Dad had stabilised enough to enable me to ask Mum to babysit so Richard and I could go out on our 'first date' together. Reluctantly she agreed, on the understanding I would be home by eleven p.m., and it would be after the hospital visit. From my teenage years, I was used to strict curfews, so I readily accepted as it was a small price to pay to spend the evening alone with Richard.

We dined at the Bod Erw, in St Asaph, a very popular restaurant at the time. It was bliss being in Richard's company and I couldn't remember ever feeling so happy. Rather than silencing my opinions, he listened to me intently, embracing everything I told him about my life.

It felt wonderful! I was in love.

Naturally, I didn't want the evening to end, but my curfew approached. On the walk back to the car, Richard caught my arm and effortlessly turned me round so we were face to face. Pulling me close to him, we embraced. That's when we had our first passionate kiss. My heart melted and my pulse raced. It was so perfect.

Over the next week or so, Richard and I saw each other when we could.

My father recuperated sufficiently and came home from hospital, and after a family meeting it was decided the children and I could stay with them until the start of the September school term. After that, we would return to the Chester house.

Naturally, it was a little squashed with all of us in the bungalow now my father was back, but despite his illness, these were happy family days.

My relationship with Richard was evolving into something even deeper. It had reached a point where I wanted to have some intimacy with him. Discussing this openly with my mother, she agreed to a one night only 'sleep-away'. However, I was aware once this line was crossed there was no going back. It was make or break!

Our room at the locally famous Kinmel Manor Hotel turned out to be pretty ordinary. That night, though, we were determined to be in our little piece of paradise. With the lights turned off, the moon suffused the room with its silver light. I noticed how small our love nest truly was, as the double bed almost filled the space. I looked around and took in every little detail, this was one night I never ever wanted to forget.

That night, at twenty-eight years of age I felt truly fulfilled as a woman for the very first time in my life. This was beyond doubt a new and life-changing experience. With such energy and emotion spent, we were both intensely happy. We lay naked on the bed holding each other tenderly, our legs lovingly intertwined covered only with a loosely draped sheet and shared stories about ourselves. Nothing was taboo and no question was out of bounds. We discovered being together was the most natural thing in the world, and it was what we both wanted deep within our hearts. In reality, our love seemed inevitable and held no boundaries.

Richard began to tell me about his journey to find me. Like so many people, his experience of mediums, psychic clairvoyants or spiritual healers was minimal; in fact almost non-existent. He had a healthy scepticism of such things – out of ignorance rather than coming from a position of dogmatic disbelief. "Throughout my life I have always believed there had to be more to our existence than work, food and sleep, and then eventually dying into nothingness. Surely that would make life so pointless?"

His words spoke volumes to me.

However, I was still curious to know more about his opinions. I asked, "So before meeting me, what was your perception of the afterlife?"

Richard stroked my hair and replied, "I believed in the probability of life after death. It seems most religions tell us if we are good children or obedient servants of our deity, we will enjoy an afterlife of sorts."

He paused and reflected, "However, if this afterlife is available, it seems ridiculous it is open to some and not others based on which religion you are born into, or even how well you follow the rules. Actually, it seems more logical that whatever happens afterwards is the same for everyone, irrespective of their geographical birthplace or cultural or religious beliefs."

I smiled and felt good that the man of my dreams had a spiritually open mind and a desire to gain understanding.

Richard explained, "The trigger to learn more about spiritual communication happened when my wife was specifically warned by a psychic not to have a love affair with an old flame, five months before it happened. Despite the warning, events transpired as predicted. That's when I started to accept the spirit world could offer some guidance in making life-choices."

I lay gazing into Richard's eyes. I was fascinated by everything he said, even by the way he moved his lips.

He continued, "Soon after, I consulted two psychics before eventually meeting you. The first was an old lady who confidently told me I had been working abroad as an engineer, near a hot desert and long pipelines. Also, that I had two young children. She insisted my car looked as if it was painted like a patchwork quilt after having an accident. She told me I must get rid of it as it was nothing but trouble for me. Also, I was to have a promotion at work – with a new secretary."

Listening to this story, I was taken aback. What I had just heard was incredible.

Richard continued reminiscing, "I was convinced I was going to get some guidance, so I was really disappointed by this totally meaningless so-called psychic reading. However, it seemed rather heartless just to walk out on her, as she was a sweet enough old dear, really. So I politely told her I couldn't relate to anything she said – I had never worked abroad, I was a self-employed shopkeeper and a promotion with a secretary just didn't apply! Also, I was driving a brand-new silver sports car and had three children, not two.

"It was then I told her I wasn't sure whether I should continue with my marriage. The old lady seemed genuinely dumbfounded that her reading was absolutely meaningless to me. However, after some careful thought, she said, 'If you go back to your wife now, you will be able to make your life together work, but your marriage will only ever be what it is now. However, as an alternative, I see a second marriage for you. If you choose a new life, this second marriage is just around the corner and it will all happen very quickly. I believe her name will be Helen.'

"Well, to be honest, that confused me even more. What I wanted to hear was by returning home, my wife would love only me and we would all live happily ever after. So, I left my appointment feeling very disappointed and rather confused as it really wasn't what I wanted to hear."

He then smiled at me lovingly, "Well she guessed one thing right, didn't she? Your name is actually Helen!"

I remained silent, trying to fully digest everything he was saying to me.

He carried on, "Having been totally disillusioned by this woman, I had another psychic recommended to me. Although her reading shared many similarities that I could associate with, she offered more information. She told me, 'I believe you are at a crossroads in your marriage. If you choose to go back, you will make the marriage work, but it will only ever be what it is now, nothing more. If you are content to accept that, you will be fine, who is anyone to judge other than yourself? If you stay within this marriage, it will be you who will make the sacrifices to ensure it works. However, one day as you get older you might look back and question your choice and say, what if – what if I had made the break? If you do make the choice for a clean break now, I see a second marriage for you and it's just around the corner, it's very imminent. I am giving you the name Helen. She is younger than you and is twenty-seven years old with two children.'"

Richard paused and turned on his side to look directly at me, "Again, it wasn't what I wanted to hear, so I all but dismissed the information. After thinking about my situation, at least what she said made sound practical advice. At least she didn't make up stories about engineers, hot deserts and new secretaries!"

I couldn't contain myself any longer. I stopped Richard making any more derogatory remarks about the first old lady's reading. I recognised her interpretation and had to say something.

"Actually, she wasn't wrong at all. I know this might sound bizarre, but my husband recently worked in Saudi Arabia and his visa described him as a civil engineer. He was working on the designs of the Kings Terminal at Riyadh Airport where there was plenty of sun, hot desert and pipelines! While he was away, I had a very bad accident in our Dolomite Sprint. While I was waiting for it to be resprayed, it did look rather like a patchwork quilt, with big grey patches all over it. I was never happy with the car afterwards, as it always seemed to be going wrong, so we decided to get rid of it. On returning, he had a new job with a new secretary. And, I have two children!"

Tears started to slowly roll over Richard's cheeks, "Obviously, we were destined to be together before we'd even met. The old lady sensed we were to be married and was probably reading me as your husband. For me, this is confirmation that my destiny is with you. Truly, I am so very happy."

Richard's honesty and pure emotion touched my heart. I told him, "I have learned by experience that when in communication with the spirit world, it is not uncommon to offer information that might seem irrelevant at the time. However, it is human nature only to accept what we know to be true or believe is possible. When something is said that's not immediately recognisable, all too often it can be disregarded as irrelevant or nonsense, and then forgotten."

Richard asked if I had received any predictions about him. I shared my memories, even though over time they had drifted to the back of my mind. I said, "Several years ago, I had a sitting with a lady who told me of my own marriage failing and there was going to be a new man called Richard in my life. She said I would recognise him as he wore a tweed jacket, he came from a family of initial Rs and he'd have drawers full of socks."

Richard smiled. "Actually almost every member of my immediate family's first names begin with the initial R. Robert, my only brother who is ten years younger than me, Ralph, our father, Rachel, Rhian, Reece, my three children, Roy and Robina, my aunt and uncle. I always wear a jacket, several of which are tweed. As for the socks, the amount I have stored in my drawers is ridiculous, especially odd ones – I won't throw them away as you just don't know when the missing one will turn up!"

He was curious, "So how does it all work, how do you actually see the spirit dimension?"

I thought for a moment and tried to access all the years of Sam's tutorials about this very subject, and simplify a lifetime of learning into a few meaningful sentences. Of course it was impossible, so instead I asked Richard a question, "What is electricity? How does it work, and where does it come from?"

He looked puzzled, "I don't know, I haven't really thought about it."

I smiled. "Exactly! Electricity is probably one of the most important things in our lives. Almost everything we do depends on it and yet the majority of us just accept it is there for our benefit to make life easier. We don't really care how it works as long as things operate when we switch them on."

Richard nodded.

I continued, "In all aspects of life we rely on important facilities without having the need to understand them. Why then, when discussing the spirit dimension, do we need a full in-depth explanation and comprehensive understanding of the mechanics of it all? In the absence of an explanation, we tend to disregard its existence and then say its messengers are fraudulent liars."

"I take that onboard," Richard said. "But there are engineers who do understand electrical effects, so why can't you, as a professional, explain spiritual communication?"

I felt so invigorated as nobody had ever challenged me in this way before. I went on to say how our finest scientists had a limited understanding of the world we live in. How what was true for them at one time can so easily become a falsehood with new awareness.

I wanted Richard to remain mindful that what I had learned was subject to many limitations, especially my own level of understanding and limited vocabulary. I was not the fountain of all knowledge, and told him so.

My mind returned to Sam's tutorials. "However, I will attempt to explain your question as best I can. Firstly, we like to think of ourselves as solid, but we are not. All molecules are constantly vibrating, but seem solid only to our eyes."

Richard nodded. "Yes, I remember my O' Level physics lessons."

"Well, the spirit world is a dimension existing alongside our own, but at a different vibration. We can't see it, but within it, everything appears solid as does matter within our own existence."

Richard interrupted me, "Yes that seems feasible. But how can you access that dimension?"

"Perhaps this is better understood by accepting within our own dimension that waves at different frequencies occupy the same space all the time. For instance, there are hundreds of radio stations simultaneously broadcasting information that can only be heard if you have a receiver tuned into that particular frequency. Where the spirit dimension is concerned, I am a receiver tuned to receive that specific frequency."

Richard became a little anxious. "You make it sound so natural and easy to understand. I suppose because people can't access the spirit dimension for themselves, they don't believe it exists?"

"Actually, there are more people than you think who can access the spiritual, however perhaps not to the degree I do. So many people have the occasional sighting, sound and even smell of their family passed over. Nevertheless, you're right, people often regard what they can't see as nonexistent and yet there is so much around us in our normal daily lives that is undetectable to our senses, but it is definitely there.

"It was as recent as 1830 that Lister invented the achromatic microscope giving the proof there are things that actually exist in the invisible. Scientists know our eyes and ears sense only a small range of frequency of light and sound waves. Animals hear things we can't. Bees and other insects can see light in the ultraviolet range, which helps them feed. Birds rely on sex-dependent markings on their plumage, which are only visible in the ultraviolet range. All of this is invisible to us. But it's there and very real."

With some frustration in his voice, Richard asked, "At the end of the day what will it actually take for science to accept the spiritual dimension actually exists?"

I spoke with Richard about how the proof they want isn't a community of spiritual mediums telling them it's there. What they require is a mathematically based theory that backs up a consistent and repeatable experiment. A good example of this is proving the world is round and not flat, an absolute truth that would have had you tortured and executed as a heretic not so long ago.

Pythagoras was the first to document the world was round about two thousand six hundred years ago, but it was another three hundred years until Eratosthenes developed the mathematical theory. However, it still lacked proof, as the theory wasn't backed up by an experiment. This came much later when a man called Magellan sailed round the world in 1522. The experiment together with the mathematical theory completely smashed the beliefs of the mainstream medieval religious system.

I was in full flow by this stage and I knew Richard wanted more. "Then of course there was the debate about the orbit of the earth around the sun or vice versa," I said. "That dilemma was only resolved about three hundred years ago – how recent is that? All those learned people with their progressive minds were tortured and murdered for not conforming to the status quo."

Richard interrupted me, "So what does it take to prove you are not a charlatan?"

I smiled. "For the present-day science community proving surviving energy after death needs to follow the same procedure. But at the moment it's impossible, because we are dealing with phenomena beyond the range of our five physical senses, and as yet we haven't discovered a method that can measure the spirit world's wavelength frequency and its energies. Once it is scientifically proven, and one day it will be, there are going to be thousands of pompous self-proclaimed intellectuals having to eat humble pie ... as did their predecessors."

Richard seemed to absorb everything I was saying. Having someone listen in this way was such a joy. He demanded more, "How do you predict the future?"

"First of all, it's not me. Always remember, I am just the go-between, the message bearer, the link or whatever else you want to call being in the middle of a conversation. Actually, it's not that the future is being predicted, it is more like your spiritual guides use their collective wealth of experience to predict the likely outcome based on your current actions. Remember your basic schoolboy physics ... for every action there is a reaction – cause and effect.

"Years ago, Sam explained this same question to me with a very simple anecdote. Imagine you see a young boy about five years of age playing with razor blades. Based upon all the experience you have had with sharp objects you suggest to the child to stop what they're doing and put the razor blades down as unless they do so they are going to cut themselves. The child now has two choices, to trust your prediction and put the blades to one side, or ignore your suggestion and carry on playing. If the child chooses the latter and continues, there are two consequences, either the child will cut himself or he doesn't. If he does cut himself, in the child's eyes you have successfully predicted the future and your advice has credibility. Conversely, there might be a tiny chance that no harm comes to him, so he might surmise you cannot see into his future and your advice was worthless. Having failed, are you incompetent to give advice on other occasions? It was then he explained that predicting the future was not absolute, but it was the most likely event to happen based upon past experiences."

Richard nodded, and so I carried on explaining. "Those in spirit will suggest alternative life-choices, which bring about better outcomes to improve your life. However, the final call is up to you, as you are the one who is in charge of your own actions – that is your freedom of choice. Then the accuracy of all of this information is dependent on the medium's ability to accurately communicate that information. What adds to this complexity is your life is like a bowl of spaghetti! By that I mean it's hard to identify one specific problem from another as they are all intertwined in one mass. So it's not quite as easy as saying you have done *this* so *that* will happen."

I rolled my head to the side to make eye contact with Richard. "However, despite what you think, my guide Sam has explained to me that the future is not as straightforward as we might imagine."

Richard laughed a little. "How so? I thought it was quite clear-cut, the future is what is going to happen."

I shook my head, "You might think that! For my own understanding, I have asked Sam this question many times. The nearest I have been to getting to grips with the concept of time is in a very simple analogy he told me, 'Imagine you are travelling along in a railway carriage and you have a solitary window to see through. Whatever you see from that window is what your mind perceives to be the *now*, in a flash it has gone out of sight – into the *past*, so it becomes a memory. All the landscape that is ahead of the train you can't see – it is the unknown – it is in the *future*. Now imagine, if you could actually stand on top of the railway carriage. Standing there in the *now* you can see for miles in every direction, you can see a panoramic overview of the *future* as it approaches. You can also see every aspect of where you have been, what is *past* – all as one simultaneous panoramic experience.' That is how Sam tried to explain time to me."

Although he looked bewildered, I think Richard understood a little of what I was trying to say. Sympathetically I said, "It's hard for me to understand too. In the interest of not confusing ourselves anymore, let's just agree to be happy not fully understanding the concept of time and that there are truly many things far beyond our comprehension. Take solace in the fact that even the cleverest minds only understand a fraction of the truth our Universe holds."

Richard said, "Surely if spirit visitors are around you all the time, you mustn't get a minute's peace from them?"

I could understand what he was trying to say, so I offered my explanation, "Actually I can totally block out the spirit dimension in an instant. Imagine you are at a busy restaurant table having a conversation with friends. I guarantee the only people you can see and hear in that situation are your friends. You will blank out all the other sights and sounds, as if they were not there at all. Now imagine you stop talking and focus on your surroundings, you will immediately become aware of all the sights and sounds around you. We do this naturally all the time without even thinking. This is how I can control my exposure to the spirit world."

I could tell Richard understood my every word. Inwardly I felt so content. We stopped talking. Enough had been said for one night.

In the silence, our bodies intertwined, we basked in the moonlight, convinced fate had brought us together. Raw emotion was making my whole body tingle. I was overjoyed this man wanted me so much, with all his heart. I could sense the sincerity of his intentions. I knew he wanted to love me in the way I wanted to be loved.

We didn't want this night to end. A new life was ready to dawn for us – as one.

4

On the Move

"Every new beginning comes from some other beginning's end."
~Lucius Annaeus Seneca~

As the academic year started in early September, the children and I had to return to Chester so they could begin their new school. Only a few minor odd jobs had been addressed and little had been done to make the house properly habitable.

One dull morning, after a difficult month trying to live a normal life on my own with the children, Richard arrived unexpectedly and surprised me with a trip to Kinmel Bay. We stopped outside a new bungalow. Casually he showed me around the property, which apparently had been built by his family as an investment to sell. For no apparent reason, it had been on the market for about two years with absolutely no interest from prospective buyers.

While standing at the kitchen sink and looking at the fields outside, Richard came from behind, put his arms around me and whispered in my ear, "Do you think you and the children could live here and be happy with me?"

I was ecstatic, how could we not live happily here?

"You can decorate it however you like," he said.

I am rarely speechless, but this was one of those times. It was beautiful. It was a mystery to me how this property had been overlooked.

Richard cradled me in his arms, happy in the thought that he had secured a place for us all to live together.

Sam smiled and stretched his hand out. Strangely, he started rotating his arms causing waves of energy to pass through the air in a type of swirling motion, round and round, filling the whole room. It was like watching waves of heat rising from a hot road and then spiralling like a massive whirlpool. I had never experienced this phenomenon before. It was remarkable!

Sensing my curiosity, Sam explained, "The energy here exists on multiple levels, not because of where this place is, but because you are in this place."

Somehow, I knew there was a link between this mass of energy and that of my own chakras as I could sense one feeding off the other, creating a type of spiritual energy amplifier. It was evident this bungalow was going to be a place of much spiritual activity.

Sam walked into the centre of this whirling energy and it completely absorbed him. Then as if a switch was flicked, the room fell still. Sam had gone.

I knew with all my heart I was going to be happy and protected here, and without any doubt this was now my new home – our new home. We walked around the gardens and excitedly I planned out new borders and shrubberies. There was an ornamental bench in the back looking over the field, so we sat and chatted.

Out of interest, I asked Richard what his previous house looked like, as he often talked fondly of it having the most breathtaking sea views overlooking the Welsh Llyn Peninsular.

"I would love to go and visit so I could see where you once lived," I said.

In response, he just gave me a very long and dubious look, then frowned.

I laughed out loud and explained, "I don't mean actually visit in person, but to visit by 'astral travel'."

Astral travel is when you can take your spiritual body on a journey and leave your earthly body behind. Although I had never done any astral travelling, it was basically the same technique Sam had taught me many years before when I entered an altered consciousness for some of my tutorials with him.

Previously, when entering an altered state of consciousness, I didn't have a witness to confirm what I was visualising was actually true. However, on this occasion I had Richard to substantiate the accuracy of my visitation. This was a tough test I was giving myself, but how else can we push our own boundaries unless we choose to try to conquer the difficult.

I sat next to Richard on the bench and held his hand, so I would feel safe and relaxed. Instantly I became aware of Sam and he instructed me to close my eyes and listen to his voice in my mind.

Richard was rather sceptical and I wasn't sure if he actually believed I could do this.

In a more serious tone, he asked, "What if something goes wrong, will anything serious happen to you?"

I chuckled. "No, I will most probably just get a headache. The only way this can become a little tricky is if I travel too deep into an altered state. That's why I need you to hold my hand and keep me anchored by talking me through this."

With my eyes closed, I took three deep breaths. Barely ten seconds later, in my mind's eye I could see myself approaching a house, walking side by side with Sam. He told me quite clearly it was Richard's old home. Eager to discover the accuracy of my ability, I began to describe what I saw.

"I'm standing on the road facing the front of the house, but there's only one storey – it's actually a bungalow! You told me earlier it was a house. Also, it must be in a big dip, as the long grey roof seems to be low down at my eye level."

Richard confirmed my description and added that the house looked like a bungalow from the front road due to the slope in the land.

I walked forward leaving Sam standing alone in the road. "I seem to be going down a very steep slope – not steps. The front door is in the middle of the frontage. As I am getting nearer I can see there are some steps going down to the front door, but only a few."

Once again Richard confirmed my words. By the tone in his voice, I could tell he was very surprised at the detail of my description. In an attempt to challenge me further, he invited me to go inside. Actually, I was a little nervous just in case I saw any people walking about. However, Sam assured me the house was empty.

I continued, "As I walk inside, I find myself in a small hallway."

I heard Richard's voice encouraging me to look ahead, there was something there, quite specific and unique in appearance, he asked me to look and concentrate.

My focus was instant. "Oh yes, I can see what you mean. It's beautiful! I can only describe it as looking rather like a big square tapestry about four-foot by four-foot and it's really colourful."

Richard confirmed my description, however he explained it wasn't a tapestry, but a large piece of multi-coloured antique leaded glass, which he'd had built into the hall wall during its construction.

He asked me to walk through the rooms.

I followed his instructions and described each room in great detail, particularly the large panoramic windows in the lounge.

I even commented how the garden looked distinctly *au naturel* – but I was being kind, as it looked totally unkempt.

My final test was to walk outside onto the lounge balcony and look right down to the end of the garden. Excitedly I exclaimed, "Oh look at that! It's a little fairy house. It's so beautiful."

Richard explained it was a two-storey children's playhouse in brightly painted wood. Nevertheless, he agreed, it did look rather like a fairy house.

Still in my altered state, Sam came to meet me and held my hand again. Under his instruction, after three really deep breaths, I opened my eyes. In an instant, it was over.

Safely sitting on the garden bench, I cuddled in to the warmth of Richard's arms. As a newcomer to psychic phenomena, he was genuinely amazed at this experience. For me, I was amazed that at last I had someone by my side who loved me for what I truly was and wanted to share in my extraordinary life-journey.

During the following week, we made arrangements to choose all the necessary furnishings and planned to move in around December so that we could spend our first Christmas together.

Inexplicably, the moment we made the decision to live there, it was as if a protective spiritual veil had been lifted. In the following weeks, Richard's parents had to turn down at least five viewings from prospective buyers and there were three definite offers. That was truly bizarre – it was as if the bungalow had been sitting empty and waiting for us.

Miraculously, despite all the hurdles, everything was delivered in just a couple of weeks, much earlier than planned and well before our Christmas target. In less than four months of our initial meeting we were sharing our first home together. Nevertheless, I was extremely concerned about how my children would integrate with having to actually live with a new 'dad'.

My fears were unfounded as both children accepted Richard wholeheartedly into their lives as if it were the most natural thing in the world. Maybe it's because they saw me happy and settled, but we all assimilated into one new family unit almost overnight.

My new life encouraged an increased strength of character in myself. Having experienced a lifetime of reluctance in sharing my spiritual experiences for fear of being ostracised, my newfound confidence flourished beyond recognition. No longer did I put any personal restrictions on what I could talk about, allowing my true self to grow. For the first time, I was openly proud of my spiritual abilities.

By word of mouth alone, my days started to fill with clients from all over the country coming to see me for healing and guidance. People were content to wait weeks before they could see me and everyone loved their appointments in my new flower-filled home. Whenever I worked, it became like a portal to the spirit world, with, of course, Sam constantly by my side.

Being part of a newly formed couple, I became exposed to a new circle of friends and acquaintances. Whenever you meet someone new, it usually doesn't take much time before the conversation comes round to that familiar question, "And what do you do, Helen?"

There is nothing strange in this and I am sure you have been asked that question a thousand times. Previously I would just refer to myself as a housewife to avoid any misunderstanding my spiritual abilities might cause. However, I had now come to a stage in my life when I answered that question truthfully. I was beginning to realise I didn't need people's approval or their validation for my life to have value. In all honesty, I wanted to pinch myself each morning just to make sure I wasn't dreaming.

Interestingly, I did notice people's reactions to me were extremely diverse. For the most part, people had a genuine, healthy interest and were eager to know more. However, there were some who would look at me as if I was an alien or a demonic heretic, some were even downright rude.

People's attitude on hearing the words psychic – medium – clairvoyant – healer – spiritualist is very much polarised. No wonder innovative new descriptive titles are being adopted by the newer generation of spiritualists entering into the public domain to neutralise the feeling of prejudice. You hear titles like energy healer – angel card reader – aura reader – pathfinder – channeller. What people don't often realise is it's not the narrative of the spiritual title that's important, it is the progression of the spiritual ability that quantifies our differences.

As might be expected, there are always those people who say to me, "Oh! I don't believe in it."

This attitude I find most challenging, as I usually respond by asking, "What is the – it – you don't believe in? Are you saying you don't believe in an afterlife or are you saying you accept there is an afterlife, but you don't believe anyone can communicate with it? These are two totally different stances." This can open a chink for learning in the most closed minds.

Although Richard was busy with his own business, he became a constant source of encouragement and support towards every aspect of my work, giving practical help whenever he could. He learned very quickly when we were out together socially that if anybody showed an interest in my work, I could sit for hours and tell people their life stories and reunite them with their lost relatives. Sometimes I would even stand behind a chair and spend the time healing all manner of afflictions. With pride he would sit patiently, watching and listening to every word, oblivious of the time.

Quite often during these social occasions, the window to the spirit dimension will open up wide and very profound phenomena will take place. I rarely shy away from these impromptu meetings as I believe they are not random but somehow orchestrated from the spirit dimension to help someone in true need.

One of my newfound passions was enjoying good food at some of the nearby restaurants. Often, these occasions were a catalyst for impromptu encounters with complete strangers. On one such occasion, we were out to dinner at the Bodysgallen Hall Country House Hotel near Llandudno.

After dinner we were sitting by the open fire in the oak-clad drawing room, sunk deep into an opulent sofa, sipping cream-laced coffee from pure white china cups and nibbling on an assortment of home-made chocolates – the ones you can always find room for, even when you couldn't eat another thing. Three men who had also dined there earlier, asked if they could join us for a nightcap and kindly offered to buy a brandy. We graciously accepted.

Not surprisingly the conversation soon evolved to the question, "And what do you do, Helen?" Obviously, I had heard all the puerile remarks before: "Can I have next week's football pool's winners?", "You must have seen me coming?", and "Who is going to win the Grand National?" I had learned such disparaging remarks are made out of nervous ignorance. It isn't in my nature to be rude, so I discovered it was easier to laugh along as if nobody had ever thought to ask these same amusing questions ever before.

However, on this occasion, the more I absorbed their ignorant remarks, the more it fed their desire to berate me as if somehow I deserved their contempt. It never ceases to amaze me that people think they have the right to judge a stranger so harshly based on their perception of what they believe are the stereotype traits of a spiritual medium.

Sceptics always seem to want to substantiate their opinion by challenging me into failure. Thankfully, I long ago lost any inclination to be provoked into proving my worth.

Sam stood behind the men and I knew by his manner that these three men were in need of some spiritual enlightenment, whether they realised it or not. So when they predictably asked what I might see for them, I was able to respond with the intent of furthering their spiritual education, not for my own self-indulgence.

Following my own protocol, I asked the men's permission to talk openly about what the spirit dimension was telling me. I suppose they believed that I would reply with some vague generalities or feebly attempt to read their body language. Perhaps they thought at worst it would be something for them to laugh about later, as if I were the after-dinner entertainment.

Eager for me to fail, their permission was readily granted.

Although Sam never seems to become angry, I could sense he harboured a type of discomfort at the way these men were making me feel with their cavalier attitude and how they were trivialising my spiritual abilities. It's not that Sam doesn't have a sense of humour, but when ignorance is the source of disparaging remarks towards me, I have noticed he will impart some sort of wisdom that will positively inspire the antagonist to question their own perceptions.

However, tonight it seemed these men had much to learn as Sam had brought through another spirit to communicate. I had learned long ago that fighting my battles was not on Sam's agenda, so I knew the visitor was for the men's benefit not mine.

He was slightly taller than Sam, with clear, pale skin, dressed in a simple white tunic with a green sash around his midriff. His face was strikingly beautiful with eyes that sparkled a bright emerald green, similar in shade to that of his cummerbund. His presence radiated calm. In that serenity, my own clarity of spiritual thought seemed to be heightened. The men were oblivious to our spiritual visitors, but Richard pointed out to them the way the pupils of my eyes had dilated, a sign that a strong link with the spirit world was developing. He had noticed this physical response to my spiritual activity very soon after we had become a couple. Actually, he had noticed there were times during my altered states when my eyes changed colour from blue to green. Words were not spoken to me, but the spirit became as one with my mind, so I could give voice to his spiritual purpose.

After a good sip of brandy and a smile on my face, I relayed to the nearest stranger what the spirit visitor was allowing me to sense, "You, my dear, are a mathematical genius. You are employed as a top researcher by the British government and I can see quite clearly that you have also written textbooks used in educational establishments nationwide."

I paused, and then addressed all three men, "You are all part of the scientific community and at the height of your careers."

It always amazes me how people's initial mocking attitude can be crushed in an instant. The sneering men were silenced by this one declaration, their scientific minds questioning the source of this correct and profound information. All three men, hiding their embarrassment, were now perched on the edge of the sofa's squashy cushions like ten year old schoolchildren learning for the first time the brilliance of the sum of the angles within a triangle always equals 180 degrees.

To the second man I described in detail his role as an important physicist, also working on government projects similar to his two associates. To the third man I spoke of complications arising because of his Iraqi origins and that of his Iranian wife. I expressed my concern and stressed the importance of him helping his family flee from their homeland. All their lives would be in danger because of his connection with the British government and his involvement with the petroleum industry. (This was said almost three years before the 1990 Gulf War, when Iraq was an uninteresting faraway country to most of us and not in our normal day-to-day consciousness, as it is today.)

The spiritual messages flowed for over two hours until the early hours of the morning. My finale came as I calmly told them that they were all working on a top-secret project for the British government. I explained that it was of importance, not only for this country but for the whole world. I began to explain to them in great detail how our planet was covered by a protective shell, which was being destroyed at an alarming rate. This protective covering was already breaking over Europe far in excess of what their associates had originally predicted. In consequence, they were working on a massive project to manufacture an artificial protective shield for our earth's atmosphere. Perhaps in the 21st century, such a conversation might not be as profound, but in 1987, reference to the breaking of the ozone layer was certainly not in lay-use nor in anybody's general vocabulary. At that time, I don't think ordinary folk like me knew we even had one!

If you could have seen the look on their scientific faces. The man nearest spluttered out, "You should have no knowledge of these projects, they are Top Secret and protected by government order. If you were not just a young lady sitting here in Wales, we could have you silenced."

I had said what needed to be said and I could say no more. The visiting spirit bowed his head and walked calmly out of the room. Sam remained vigilant by my side. Totally enthralled by everything they had witnessed, the men expressed a newfound respect for my spiritual abilities.

At the end of the evening we parted as new friends and they each gave me their business cards. I knew we would never meet again as my role in their lives had been fulfilled. Their own extraordinary lives had been opened to another dimension they hadn't previously considered had any factual substance. I had empowered them in a way their conventional lives could not, and I had faith they would use this knowledge to benefit all of us in their research.

People often ask why the collective consciousness from the spirit dimension doesn't involve itself with global phenomena, but it does. However, while the mainstream still considers the nature of my lifework to be questionable or even fraudulent, they negate the positive contribution of this knowledgeable resource.

Weeks after this memorable night, Richard and I had our first Christmas together that included celebrations with my parents, who for the first time felt truly welcome in my home. This was a lovely new experience for me.

We were all blissfully happy, with fresh hopes for the New Year ahead.

Welcome to 1988.

5

Goodbye Daddy

"Some see death as an end,
I know it's only the beginning."
~Helen Parry Jones~

The phone rang. It was the morning of 18th February. The date is forever etched in my mind.

My father lay critically ill in Abergele Chest Hospital, and my mother and I had been put on death-watch alert … yet again. Now my father was fifty years of age, thoughts of my childhood premonitions haunted me on a daily basis.

Richard dropped me off at the hospital entrance so I could hurry to be at my father's side while he parked the car. On walking inside, I was greeted by the familiar smell of death. Heading to my father's room, I noticed there was a small girl, no older than ten or eleven, standing alongside the double doors that separated the corridors. She smiled compassionately, and intuitively I knew she was from the spirit world. Her energy was different to those normally visiting me as she radiated a light that seemed so pure it penetrated the essence of my very being, causing me to feel overwhelmed with the purest unconditional love.

Our minds became as one so I could hear her voice clearly. She explained that her energy was more than a spiritual being and was showing herself as a small girl for my father's acceptance. She said her presence would resolve his inner struggle so he could be led effortlessly into the spiritual dimension. She reassured me that it was not her role to control destiny, but to facilitate it.

Her appearance was so beautiful. She wore a simple, pure white dress, which for some reason had an abundance of material that pooled on the floor behind her, far more than necessary for such a small child. It was as though she was dressing up in a woman's ball gown.

Her long, glossy black hair hung in soft curls down to her waist and was adorned with tiny flowers. I was curious to know how they could stay in place, but the closer I looked, it seemed the petals vibrated with an energy that almost gave them an individual iridescence. Also, there was a distinctive scent around her; it was possible to discern the individual fragrances of lavender, apple and rose.

I noticed that in her hand she held a mirror, an apple and a rose, but I had no idea why. However, the spirit world often uses signs and symbols to help in communication. Although these symbols held no meaning for me, perhaps they had significance for my father at a time when he might eventually see her. I had no way of knowing.

Despite her childlike appearance, there was an air of strength about her and a profound wisdom. I heard her voice again directly into my mind as if she was replying to a specific question as to her identity, "I have been called by many names, but in reality I am more a source or presence than an entity."

The child joined me on my walk into my father's room. The smell of death became more pungent. Once I reached his bedside, the child escort disappeared.

I was astonished this visitation was concentrated into seconds of linear time, almost as if time had stood still during our encounter. This was the first time I had come across a spirit apparition I could nether identify as a Guide or Angel.

My mother was already at Dad's side as she had arrived ahead of me. The noise of the life-saving equipment was all too familiar. However, his breathing was so strained, even his legs had turned purple through the lack of oxygen in his blood, and his hands felt cold to the touch. This terrible disease had been slowly killing my father for many years and had cheated me of a normal life with him.

He would never accept spiritual healing from me, so I used my absent healing abilities to do what I could for him from a distance. On the number of occasions my father should have died in recent years, I believe the absent healing I administered had extended his life. I couldn't help but feel how much suffering this one man had experienced and conceded perhaps it was now time to let him go. For years my father had demonstrated he was a fighter, so I prayed he was not prepared to surrender to death … not today. But I realised it was now out of my hands.

This was no time for self-pity, as Mum and I needed to be strong for each other, and especially for my father. Mum's eyes were already swollen with stress and tears.

During that afternoon my Aunty Joan came over to join Richard in offering support to my mum and me. Now there were four of us at the bedside vigil … waiting.

By the end of the second day, despite being totally exhausted by the many visitors that came, Dad seemed no worse and was possibly even a little stronger. Many of Dad's family had been to visit believing this might be their last opportunity to see him alive. It had been a very busy day, so I begged Mum to go home and rest for a few hours, but she refused. She had neither left Dad's side nor had she slept. She was shattered.

Nevertheless, after a family discussion, we decided I should go to Liverpool the next day for a private doctor's appointment that had been made a few weeks prior. Although my father was critical, for the moment he was stable. Optimistically we all agreed he had pulled through similar situations before.

Routine tests showed I had developed a gynaecological problem, which Mum was adamant I shouldn't leave and was best attended to as soon as possible.

The morning of the third day, Richard and I called in early to see my dad and take some essentials for my mother before we left for Liverpool. My appointment was for ten thirty a.m., so we all felt I would be back by early afternoon. Fortunately, my father was no worse, so Mum gave the green light I could be excused for a few hours.

My visit to Liverpool went as planned. However, on our way back, as we approached the Chester area on the M56, Richard's mobile phone rang. It was the hospital.

The nurse was solemn, "I have been trying to call you, but your phone was dead. Your dad has had another panic attack and all he keeps asking for is you. He's so ill, I don't know if he can take much more. Please come as soon as you can."

I retched and I could taste the result in my mouth. Richard, sensing the urgency had accelerated. He assured me we would be at the hospital in less than an hour. However, by the tone in the nurse's voice, I doubted my dad could wait that long. I was fraught with guilt and the tension made me tremble. I so much wanted to be there for him at the end.

Richard reached over and held my hand to comfort me.

"I didn't think it would be today," I said. "Do you remember the message we had from Dad's guide before Christmas last year?

She said we'd know when it was Dad's time to pass over as we would have to cross over water."

There was a pause and Richard replied, "Well, she's right. We've just had to drive through the Mersey Tunnel under the river. It might not be the ocean you envisaged, but it is still a fair expanse of water and we've had to cross it to return home."

Richard was correct. Another prophesy was unfolding just as predicted. As soon as we arrived at the hospital, we rushed into Dad's room. What I saw was absolutely breathtaking.

In a crescent shape around my father's bed were eight girls of similar age, all holding hands. At one end of the arc stood my father's childlike guide still dressed in her white linen style suit and at the other end was the girl with the flowing white train who had greeted me in the corridor two days before. Draped around the crescent of children was one long garland of daisies. The decorative swag was thicker than any I had ever seen and was adorned by thousands of tiny daisy heads in brilliant white and yellow. It was truly beautiful. I was surprised the children could hold what seemed like a very heavy adornment with such ease.

My attention was drawn to the spiritual presence standing at the foot of my father's bed. He was very tall, and was dressed in a fine, gold swath of cloth that touched the floor, and he had what looked like a purple cape around his head. I say the cloth was golden, but it could have been a very fine translucent material that looked gold as a result of the very bright energy this spiritual essence illuminated. A belt created from similar material secured a long sabre-type sword made from a metal as shiny as any mirror I had ever seen.

As with many spiritual visions, there was a symbolism in what I could see. In this instance, the sword represented the spiritual ability to sever the chord that connected my father's spirit to his earthly body, and thereafter to cut through the darkness to take him back into the light. His presence was intimidating, but there was no sense of threat or retribution, his purpose was to ease the journey to the spirit dimension with pure love and compassion. His head was bowed in such a way the shadows created by the head cape made it hard to see his features, even when he turned towards me. I knew without any doubt this was an Angel of Death, as faceless as ever because death is a natural transition not a destructive being.

Suddenly I felt angry; I didn't want death to take my father.

Mum's cheeks were swollen and her eyes bloodshot from a combination of sleep deprivation and days of crying. She beckoned me to come straight to the bedside where Aunty Joan was sitting. She moved back a little so I could sit down next to my father.

Mum spoke softly to me, "Your dad has been asking for you all morning. He's been waiting. I think it's his time to go, but he won't leave until he has seen you. He keeps saying he needs to speak to you."

We had been at this point so many times before only to have him miraculously return. But today my hands were naturally cool, devoid of any healing energy, and I knew without some healing there would be no return for my father this time.

I took Dad's hand and whispered calming words to him. I could see his spiritual chord reach out from his chest, it was stretched thin and near to breaking point. He had begun to break free from his physical body.

Years ago, in my childhood, I remembered cutting the spiritual cord of my beloved Nana Ada helping her to pass over into the spirit world more peacefully, a spiritual procedure I had now done many times. But my Nana Ada was old and had experienced a long and full life. This was my dad – he was a young man cheated of life by a progressive illness. How could I choose right here and now to let him go, never to touch or see him again in this world? This was one call I was not prepared to take. If the Angel of Death wanted to use his sword to cut short my father's life, he would have no help from me.

Sam moved beside me and placed a hand on my shoulder to comfort me. "It's futile, my chile," he said with true compassion. "Your father's path is secured."

Reluctantly, I was beginning to accept my dad's time to leave us was imminent.

I felt helpless. Offering a lifetime of love, I kissed Dad's hand and remarkably he tried to speak, but the lack of breath muted his voice. I beckoned Mum to lean in and together we desperately tried to hear his final words. Summoning all his strength, he whispered, "I can see them, Helen ... I can see all the children with flowers ... I can see all the little boat children that have come for me ... they are so beautiful."

I now realised the purpose of the childlike apparitions was to bring calm to my father, as for him children were not intimidating or fearful. Having them instilling peace and inner tranquility gave him the capacity he needed to pass into the spiritual dimension with ease.

A faint, thin smile appeared on his face and a solitary tear gathered in the corner of his eye. "Look after your Mum," he said.

We held eye contact for as long as he could. "Love you." He paused for another short gasp of air, and with absolute sincerity he said, "I am sorry". There seemed to be a lifetime of regret in that momentary plea.

After all those years of denial, finally my father had seen what I had always seen. His eyes turned to look at my mother for one last time and his shallow gasps for life just stopped.

I heard my mother inhale deeply and then she sobbed uncontrollably.

I looked up to see Dad's spiritual body elevate from the bed, stand hand in hand with his childlike guide and then join hands with the other spirit children. Together they all walked through the window as if it were an open door into the hospital garden and beyond where I could see him being greeted by a small gathering of people. Their faces were very vague and faint, but I am sure I recognised my father's parents, Granddad Stanley and Grandma Lilly, amongst them.

Within a moment, they all faded away leaving only Sam in the room. He wiped a tear from his face. "I do not weep for your father, Helen," he said. "I weep for you."

The clock on the wall read ten minutes to two.

My daddy was gone.

Transition:

The empty vessel of my father's body lay still and motionless on the hospital bed. Although I had dealt with death all my life, this was the first time I was witness to a passing. The pain was immense. The four of us hugged each other for comfort and we cried openly together in our grief.

Then I needed to be alone, just for few moments, to reflect and collect my strength. I walked outside into the hospital garden and sat on a bench. If it was cold, I couldn't feel it as every part of my body was numb.

Not everyone is lucky enough to bear witness to the spirit dimension as I do. That clarity of understanding should have helped me to diminish the pain of grief at this desperately sad time. But if it did, then I can only imagine that other people's suffering must be unbearable. I felt lucky to have said a last goodbye to my father and be there for his final breath. For a multitude of reasons, many don't have that privilege. In some instances, being denied that moment can evoke all manner of negative emotions, adding to the pain.

Sam joined me and I asked him a question that I had never had cause to ask. "Although you speak to me about the spiritual dimension on a daily basis, you have never explained to me what happens at the moment we leave our physical body. I want to know what my father felt in that moment of passing."

Sam paused a moment then spoke, "As individuals, each of us will have a different account of how we pass and what happens once we reach the new dimension. Although I will speak about your father's specific passing, others might be slightly different, but there is a fundamental physiological similarity to each passing. As your father was taking his last breath, there was a change within his molecular structure. The elements of spiritual consciousness within the physical combine together in such a way that they are able to separate from the physical elements they were once part of. This is how the energy of consciousness has the ability to become an entity within its own dimension.

"At first, this process would have begun to feel like a tightness within him – like he was being pulled in two directions. This pulling sensation would gather and travel upward to his throat and then to the top of his head. Then, with a slight sensation of being catapulted upward and out of the physical body, the spiritual consciousness breaks free of the physical altogether. In that moment of the energy changing its form, it is so fiercely intense that the consciousness can experience what can only be described as a bright light ... but it isn't. In that instant, you feel more alive than ever before. This transition is instantaneous from a physical perspective, but it seems much longer to your consciousness as the life-force is still continuing. This process is no more stressful than a sudden rush of adrenaline. Your father would be more physically aware of his passing than, say, someone who is shot dead, because his death was slower. But in both cases there are the same sensations during the transition as the life-force continues, no matter what the physical circumstances.

"It is the initial progression after the transition that can seem different. It is this 'journey' those who have passed over refer to, and it is unique. In your father's case, he was taken by children to meet his family and thereafter on a symbolic boat journey to reach the spirit dimension. Even if you die alone, there is always someone to meet you after the transition, no one is ever on their 'journey' unattended. Often those who meet us are known to us, like a relative or friend, but not always. However, there is always a 'guide' participating in this 'journey'.

"As you know, your father's physical disease dies with his physical body, so there is no pain or suffering taken into the spiritual dimension. However, all his life experiences are imprinted within the consciousness and these transcend into the spiritual dimension. It may take some readjusting for him to realise he is free of his condition and its consequences. Now your father has transcended, he needs to adapt and accept his new environ. I have no idea how he will progress or adapt, or even how long it will take. Spiritual progression is not measured by linear time, but by your own development."

The need to be with my family overwhelmed me and I made my way back to the ward. I realised I had now learned how to bear the unbearable.

6

Grief

"Grief manifests from love."
~Helen Parry Jones~

My mum decided she wanted to die and join my father. Although she had cared for Dad for nearly twenty years, on the day of his passing, she was not emotionally prepared for his death. She was lost, and in her grief had sunk to such depths of despair, she was hard to reach in her isolation.

Mum now wanted to believe in an afterlife. However, when it came to listening to me talking about my spiritual sight, she seemed to still have a mental block at much of what I said. It wasn't that she was closed to the possibility of a spirit dimension, but that it was hard for her to accept that her daughter could possibly have the ability to communicate with it.

The catalyst for this willingness to believe in a spiritual dimension happened when we returned from the hospital to discover that a clock in her home and also in mine had stopped at ten minutes to two, the exact time my dad died. This was enough to catch everybody's attention.

I had witnessed many times how the presence of spiritual energy can interfere with other energies, like draining all the power out of batteries or making electrical items switch on and off. Despite my spiritual sight, I am not immune to grief. As a daughter in mourning, I was experiencing my own profound loss and yearned for my dad to speak to me. I had already pleaded with Sam to bring him, but all he said was that my father needed time to adjust to his new surroundings and was convalescing in his own way.

Sam had explained to me long ago that communication is an ability we can all develop in the spiritual dimension, however some people take longer to develop it than others. Some don't even feel the need to learn at all. Often, when those you love cannot communicate directly for whatever reason, they may send you signs or messages in other ways, like familiar smells or maybe in another form, like a feather, butterfly or bird – and in our case, by stopping the clocks.

I was experiencing first-hand how hard it is to accept that you can't just instantly summon whoever you want to communicate. The agony of such silence really does confirm how truly special it is to make spiritual contact with someone you dearly love, and it should never be undervalued or taken for granted.

Days later, I arrived home from the supermarket to be greeted by my dad's spiritual guide standing on my doorstep, still manifesting in her childlike form. I was so excited in the hope she had brought my father to visit me. With much wisdom in her voice she spoke, "Your father is safe. However, when he arrived, emotionally he felt he was weak because he had been fighting a lifetime of illness. Now it is difficult for him to accept his new condition free from disease. He has much to learn."

The guide smiled kindly and I knew she could sense my profound sadness. "Be assured he will visit soon alongside me, but only to observe." She turned and walked into my house as though the locked door was open, leaving behind a fragrance of roses.

The next day at my dad's funeral, true to her word, I could see him standing next to his coffin, watching and listening to his eulogies. Beside him was his childlike guide completely focused on him.

I concentrated all my thoughts on trying to speak to him. However, it wasn't until he left that he turned to look directly into my eyes. In that instant, I felt a lifetime of love radiate from him into my very essence. I didn't want that feeling to go, but as he faded away, my heart felt empty again.

I cried openly, not only for my loss, but also for Mum left bereft beside me. If only she could have seen him … just for a few seconds. She was inconsolable and seemed numb. I wasn't sure if she even registered the funeral as her eyes were dull and distant, doubtless recollecting the past.

In the aftermath, my mum became increasingly introverted. Of course, we tried whatever family get-together we could to cheer her up, but she had to find her own way to move forward and adapt to life without her husband. It was going to be a tough journey, but it was one I needed to help her through.

With love and understanding, as a family I knew we would get through this. We had to! However, no matter what your problems are, life continues and tomorrow always comes.

Bereavement and Grief – A personal observation:
Grief is a natural response to loss.

Loss comes in many forms and is not only associated with death. For many, the most intense grief comes from the loss of someone very dear. There is no right or wrong way to grieve. It is the most intense emotion living beings have to deal with. Even animals experience grief, nevertheless as humans our complicated psychology and behavioural patterns allow us to express this in many different forms. I have witnessed that the following are universal properties each one of us experience:

1. Denial and isolation
2. Anger
3. Bargaining
4. Depression
5. Acceptance

Those suffering don't necessarily go through all these stages, some skip stages or experience several stages collectively; it is totally dependent on the individual. Although there are psychological guidelines, it needs a lot of experience to assess the grieving process. Everyone will experience something.

As a professional therapist, I apply my type of healing therapy in many ways to help a person in grief. I have learned that it all depends on the individual's coping mechanism, as everyone has their own way to emotionally and intellectually express and accept.

Healing can happen gradually at first, as grief cannot be rushed. There is no timetable to grief. Some feel stronger within weeks or months, for others it may take years. For healing to emerge, the person needs to face the grief and actively deal with it.

As a therapist, I have encountered people with many tragic losses resulting in all manner of stress, depression and inability to lead what they consider to be a 'normal' life. Grief is not only confined to losing a loved one to death, it can be felt for any loss; for example, loss through breakdown of relationships, loss of a job or business, loss of good health, loss of a home or a way of life.

Many feel frightened, sad and lonely after their loss, which of course is a natural reaction. Crying is never a weakness, but some can try to put up a protective shield in front of friends and family. I personally feel anyone demonstrating feelings to others they love is a strength and is something to be encouraged.

Unfortunately, internalising the pain of grief can cause physical illness and sometimes this can eventually turn into something called 'complicated grief'. This is where the person becomes so depressed, or so guilty, they can develop suicidal thoughts and consider their own demise as the only option out of their situation.

There is no neat way to put grief into a box. Grief is like a rollercoaster where special events trigger memories which in turn compounds the grief. Feelings of loneliness, hopelessness or worthlessness sometimes emerge. This along with an inability to function at home, work or school can disrupt a normal routine.

Those who try to suppress their grief by drinking too much alcohol or by taking drugs to specifically induce a false euphoria will without doubt come crashing down, often with more serious complications. I always advise that it is beneficial to prepare emotionally for an anniversary, family reunions, birthdays or any other triggers that might remind you of your departed loved one. Prepare by remembering them, talking about shared past experiences, I actively encourage keeping their memory alive. Sharing with those you love not only brings the family unit together, but can stop the internal bitterness some feel in their grief.

Often caregivers who have nursed a person for a long time are more at risk of depression. They often blame themselves and feel they "should have" done this, or think "if only" I had done more. In these cases, a forgiveness of themselves is needed. Grief is a complicated process and should never be underestimated.

7

Fear

"Don't confuse danger with fear.
Fear is a choice, danger can harm you."
~Helen Parry Jones~

Days later, there was a knock on my front door. Answering it, a middle-aged man politely introduced himself as David Radcliffe, a journalist from the *Daily Mirror*. Apparently, he had heard about my spiritual abilities and searched me out.

Although I was grieving for the loss of my father, there was no way I could turn Radcliffe away as it was such a miserably wet and windy morning. So I invited him in as he appeared freezing cold. After sitting him down at my kitchen table, I made him tea and toast, which he readily accepted. After exchanging pleasantries, he went straight into the purpose of his visit – the newspaper wanted to do an in-depth double-page feature.

At first I was very excited at the prospect of sharing my extraordinary life interacting with the spiritual dimension and being regularly tutored by my guide Sam. Radcliffe listened in awe as I recollected one story after another, some about healing miracles others about spirit encounters. He agreed there was enough material to fill his newspaper ten times and more.

But then he dropped a bombshell. This story was to be focused on my romantic love story with Richard, and the personal conflict caused by our relationship within our circle of friends and family.

What a disappointment! And why?

Every family had its disharmonies, especially so soon after divorce, but it certainly was not our intent to exploit that for the sake of publicity. This was my first encounter with the press and I was a little unsure how to respond to their agenda. Naïvely, I believed the press would welcome the opportunity to research my abilities for a positive and informative feature, not just dismiss them outright.

Why was the spiritual truth so unpalatable? Even to this day, I really don't understand people's reluctance to accept it.

I wanted no part in Radcliffe's agenda and so we politely said our farewells.

Days later, the *Daily Mirror* published the headline 'Ace! Love is on the cards'. This was my first national press. Fortunately for us, without our input, the proposed two-page feature about conflict was stunted to a few columns.

With much surprise, a week or so later I was contacted by Mary Frances, a features writer from *Woman's Own* magazine, requesting an interview. After spending all my life hiding my abilities from my parents and family, I was excited by this newfound interest and at the prospect of having a public platform to finally express myself.

Can you imagine how nervous I was when Mary finally knocked on my door for our meeting?

The interview went for around three hours. We spoke about everything I could remember that had ever happened to me. She was fascinated about how Sam tutored my spiritual development from an early age, especially about my childhood healing stories where I explained how Sam had taught me to discern illness by showing me *ticks* and *crosses* over a picture of a skeleton – wherever the ticks appeared that area was okay and wherever the crosses appeared there was a problem.

She listened with fascination when I explained how I could sense illness inside people's bodies, identify broken bones and specifically see the particular organs where there was a problem – rather like having x-ray eyes! In many instances, I can sense a condition brewing that hasn't yet manifested itself and even the residual of old problems recovered. She seemed amazed at the number of letters I showed her from clients stating how my healing had improved their health and the many life-changing experiences people had had from having a spiritual sitting with me. Genuinely, she seemed absolutely enthralled.

At the end of the interview, Mary explained it was normal procedure for me to check the feature prior to publication for factual inaccuracies, although I couldn't change what was written. However, when it arrived for checking, I was so disappointed. Yet again it focused on my romantic meeting with Richard and not about my spiritual abilities. Feeling very frustrated I phoned Mary and confronted her, only to learn of the very strict media regulations precluding the showcasing of a spiritual medium. I couldn't think of another profession that was so ostracised.

Naturally I felt this was outright censorship. All Mary could say was that her hands were tied and she had to write about my work within a different context – they had to have an angle, and in my case it could only be made palatable through my new romance. Ultimately, I had swapped experiencing my father's intolerance of my abilities to that of the media's. And over the years, when it has come to expressing my capabilities, they have proved themselves to be dictatorial, full of prejudice and very powerful in quashing my standing in the public's eye.

I began to wonder how people would ever hear the truth about living on in the spirit dimension, and how the collective consciousness can benefit us at many levels throughout our lives. If the media were against me, and the establishment had a huge intolerance towards me, how could my lone voice ever be heard?

I felt I had been forced to become Britain's best-kept secret! So I decided that if the media were not going to help me share my voice with a global audience, I had to do it alone. The only alternative was to see people in groups; the larger the better. So I organised my first theatre-sized assembly.

At the time, it seemed a good idea to also use the assembly as a way of raising funds for the Abergele Chest Hospital, as a memorial for my father. I knew how desperate they were for some equipment on the ward where he had died.

I found the venue by chance. Richard's family were exceptionally good customers at the Bod Erw Hotel Restaurant, and the proprietor Tony had a good relationship with them. So on hearing my dilemma, he offered their function room.

To my astonishment, as soon as a few posters were put in the local area, the tickets started to sell fast. Naturally I was thrilled.

A couple of weeks before the event, Tony's wife Sue cornered Richard's parents over their lunch. In no uncertain terms, she told them that my booking had been cancelled and furthermore she didn't want me to set foot in there ever again as she was horrified at the prospect of a clairvoyant medium being on her premises.

To be honest, I would have loved to have been a fly on the wall as my proud future in-laws immediately rose out of their seats, left enough money on the table to cover their bill and walked out.

Richard's father told me, "I wasn't having that woman disrespect you in that ridiculous way. They will certainly miss our daily custom long before we would ever miss them. We can eat anywhere!"

This was the first time I had been so personally shunned because of my spiritual abilities. What was so terrible about me? Why would somebody want to ban me from their premises? Was it her fear of my communicating with another dimension or maybe it was her fear of me discovering some grave, private secret? I will never know.

Nevertheless, I was left with a problem. I was in a panic – my tickets were selling fast and I didn't have a venue.

Sam assured me that all would be well.

How right he was! A couple of nights later, Richard and I were dining out at the Talardy Hotel, directly opposite the Bod Erw. I had become quite friendly with Alex and Karen, the Talardy owners, as we were regular customers. When we were there, Karen loved chatting to me about my abilities and was overjoyed when I gave her spiritual messages from her family.

On this particular evening our dinner was interrupted when Sam appeared to me with an instantly recognisable spirit visitor. I turned to Richard, "You'll never guess whose walking towards us."

With curiosity, Richard leaned forward and demanded, "Go on, who is it?"

I responded, "It's Eric Morecambe!"

"What on earth does he want?" Richard enquired, intrigued.

For readers who are too young or not familiar with British television, Eric Morecambe was an English comedian who together with Ernie Wise formed a double act that dominated British entertainment from the 1960s until Eric suddenly died in 1984.

Eric spoke briefly about his family and then said something strange, which I repeated word for word, "He says that his friend was turned away from here". Then he just walked away giving us one of his famous little dance hops.

Always the entertainer, I thought.

A few minutes later, Karen came over with our food. "You will never guess who has just visited. Eric Morecambe! He told us his friend was turned away from here," I said.

Karen's jaw dropped. "That's amazing, yes, Des O'Conner came here recently without a reservation and wanted a room, but we were fully booked, so we had to turn him away."

It just goes to show that the earthly world and the spirit world are really just a thought apart.

Sam stepped forward and prompted me about my venue problem. So I told Karen how Sue from the Bod had cancelled my booking and banned me from ever going there again. Karen knew Sue quite well and was shocked by her conduct. Without any hesitation, she came to my rescue and offered me the hotel's nightclub. We all agreed the venue wasn't the most ideal place to have a spiritual meeting, but as I had already sold a substantial amount of the tickets, my chances of finding a better venue in the timeframe were small.

About a week or so later, on a cold November night, I held my very first "Evening of Clairvoyance", in aid of the Abergele Chest Hospital.

On the night, the auditorium was full. Standing at the side, I was stricken with fear at the sight of about 250 people anxiously waiting to hear from their loved ones. To be honest, I was scared in case no one from the spirit world actually turned up to say anything.

I shouldn't have worried as Sam appeared with a multitude of spirit visitors all wanting to speak. In no time at all, Richard finished giving a very eloquent introduction and I walked into the auditorium to a round of applause.

I am often asked how I select a person from a large audience to give them a spiritual message. As a general rule, I can see a glow over the person's head so I know who the spirit wants to address. This technique can be marred when the stage lighting is too strong or when people are sitting very close together, so it is not an easy task.

When communicating, the messages pass through me rather than my mind fully processing the information and then repeating it. As the process is instantaneous, the essence of the message is less contaminated by my own personality and consequently more accurate.

Still to this day it amazes me how life-changing it can be even to hear just a few reassuring words from our loved ones in spirit. Just knowing they are still near us can often bring closure and help us move forward with our lives on many levels.

As a surprise for my audience, I had brought in a bucket of fresh flowers on the request of people from the spirit world. Can you imagine, a sort of inter-dimensional floral delivery service!

In no time at all, a middle-aged lady stepped forward from the crowd of patiently waiting spirit visitors. She offered some personal details about herself and asked me to find her daughter Jeannie and give her the delicately wrapped solitary red poppy from my flower bucket.

Holding the solitary poppy up in the air, I called out, "I am looking for a daughter whose mother died just one year ago. The daughter has recently moved house, and her mother is saying although she is not here with you she remains very much a part of your life. This daughter is definitely here …" I paused, "… and her name is Jeannie."

There was a brief silence and a then a young woman stood up and said, "I am Jeannie!" Her face beamed with delight. I could see her Mum in spirit wade through the audience just to be close to her.

Jeannie continued, "Before Mum died last year, one day she left a single red poppy for me on my doorstep."

What a moment!

Jeannie's Mum relayed one fact after another about shared memories and what her daughter had been up to in the last few days. Soon after, an elderly gentleman in spirit stepped forward and told me the small bunch of freesias were for his wife Margery. I reached into the bucket and pulled them out.

"Where's Margery?" I asked. "Come on, where are you, Margery? Your husband's here in spirit. He says he is Irish and I am listening to him say you buried him 'without his bloody hat', but he is now saying, 'Margery – I have found my hat!'"

A little voice from the back of the audience shouted out in reply, "Thank goodness for that!"

The audience burst out laughing. That is what is so wonderful about these spiritual presentations, there is always a happy atmosphere and a room full of laughter.

The communication continued. "Your husband's saying your favourite flowers have always been freesias, and he hasn't forgotten."

If that wasn't enough proof for Margery, her husband continued by saying they had a close friend called Margaret and that her family originated from Stockport – to which Margery agreed. The true joy on her face was priceless.

Throughout the evening I was continually bombarded with messages, one after the other, and the audience were euphoric. However, without any warning there was a moment when I sensed the energy all around me change. Sam moved from across the room to stand really close to me. Our minds are so in tune, he sensed my concern and reassured me of my safety.

Something was about to happen and my skin broke out in goosebumps.

Seconds later, a spiritual presence materialised beside Sam. As the vision emerged, I could see it was a tall woman wearing a very simple white gown, fashioned similar to a nun's habit, with the addition of a bright, blue sash tied around her waist. Not only did she have a beautiful face, I felt a strong sense of compassion and nurturing ability radiate from her, far beyond anything I had ever experienced before. Her presence made me feel reverence towards her.

The woman showed me the head of a large red rose cradled in the palm of her left hand. Suddenly the petals transformed into what looked like bright, red blood dripping through her fingers. I interpreted this symbolism to represent a violent death.

In my mind, I could sense the woman talk to me saying her role was that of a protector. This worried me, as I was curious to know why at this time I would need her individual protection. She stretched out her right arm and instantly I could clearly see two young teenage girls in spirit standing beside me hand in hand. Shockingly, I recognised the younger girl as Anna Humphries, the missing fifteen year old schoolgirl from Penley, North Wales. Over the past few days the spirit of Anna had visited me at home several times in the vain hope I could help her in some way.

The disappearance of Anna was a mystery that was constantly being speculated about in the media, especially as no material facts had been discovered. So, as I started to explain who and what I could see, the room became electric with anticipation.

When I announced that Anna was here tonight because she had definitely been murdered, the audience gasped.

I paused for a moment to let them settle.

This revelation was a most powerful moment, as at that time everyone was hoping that Anna would be found safe and reunited with her parents.

Anna introduced the other girl to me as Pauline Reade, who had been murdered twenty-five years prior in 1963, a victim of the Moors murderers. I continued by explaining Pauline's presence was to help Anna adapt to her circumstances of dying from a sexually motivated murder, not dissimilar to her own.

I asked Anna why she had come. She told me there was a person in the audience that could help solve her murder. Naturally, at first I thought it was a member of her family or a friend she wanted to speak with, and I asked the audience if anyone knew her. But no matter how hard I tried, nobody wanted to associate themselves with this girl. Time and time again I confronted the audience to find someone who would validate her. There was something important to be said, but it seemed no one wanted to hear.

It was in that moment of persistent denial the energies all around me changed. I began to feel isolated and filled with frustration. Intuitively, Sam moved so close to me I could almost touch him, so I knew that I needed his strength in some way. The audience listened as I explained how the atmosphere was changing around me. The tension in the room became almost palpable.

Anna stretched out her hand as if she wanted me to hold it. However, I just stood there looking at her. The aura of the unusually tall woman behind her seemed to brighten and become as one with Anna's.

She spoke out to her ward, "Now you can touch."

As instructed, Anna stepped forward away from Pauline and touched my arm. At that moment, my very being filled with absolute terror. I bellowed out the most horrific scream from the pit of my stomach and almost collapsed to my knees. I became petrified with fear and outright revulsion. Not only did I feel my throat being gripped as though being strangled, but my whole body felt violated and my loins physically hurt as if stabbed by a knife. Nausea overwhelmed me and my racing heart wanted to burst from my chest. The very life seemed to drain out of me, my legs became weak and I started to collapse. Richard ran onto the stage to catch me.

Witnessing these dramatic events, the audience had worked itself into an absolute frenzy. Never before had a spiritual presence affected me like this. At that moment, Anna released my arm and pointed to a man in the audience. As she let go, the sensation of physical pain and being violated instantly disappeared. She shouted out, "He can help me!"

Without any hesitation, I pointed directly at a smartly dressed middle-aged man, "Anna is telling me you can help her. It's you. It's definitely you!"

Looking positively shaken, he shuffled in his chair and looked bewildered. He continued to deny any link with her.

Anna was so decisive, I became adamant this man was not going to dismiss her so quickly.

I asked, "Please, sir, this girl is insisting that she needs to speak to you."

The man too insisted, almost as an apology to the audience, that he was only there by default because his wife's friend had let her down at the last minute, and he came only because his wife didn't want to come here alone.

No matter how he tried to avoid the association, I begged the man to think hard why Anna had been so adamant.

His wife kept prodding him with her elbow and leaned over to whisper in his ear. Eventually, he reluctantly identified himself as being with the CID department of the North Wales Police and that he was associated with Anna Humphries' case.

The audience gasped again at this dramatic revelation.

As I continued to speak, the audience fell silent. Anna explained how her dead body had been abandoned down an embankment of a large river, under leaves and a fallen tree. She insisted the police were looking for her in the wrong place, they needed to search about forty miles from her home.

There was more. Anna told the audience how she kicked the car windscreen and smashed the glass while trying to fight her attacker, how she was strangled with her own underwear and how she was locked into the boot of the murderer's car loosely covered by a blanket. As if she hadn't given enough information about her situation, she told us her murderer's name was 'John'.

No sooner had I said this, the detective raced over to me waving his arms, saying, "Stop, stop, I need you to stop! You are saying far too much about the case and I must speak with you in private – right now!"

My evening had come to a sudden halt. So Richard, sensing the seriousness of the situation, quickly stepped in and announced it was time for the intermission. The detective took me to the back of the auditorium, asked me to repeat everything and took dictation. He insisted I should say no more about Anna's disappearance to my audience, as it was still an ongoing missing person's investigation. He then left.

Days later, when Anna's body was found, it was announced on ITV *News at Ten.* The same words were used by the newsreader to describe the location of the body on the banks of the River Severn as I had told to the Talardy audience that night, almost word for word.

As a matter of fact, when they did eventually catch the murderer, his name turned out to be David John Evans, but he was known locally by his middle name of John. He had a previous conviction for rape. When Anna went missing, his mother became suspicious of her son. It was when a lorry driver recognised him in France that he was arrested. Some buttons and bloodstains along with shards of glass on his clothing and in his car helped prove he had killed Anna. Evans was found guilty of murder at Chester Crown Court and sentenced to thirty years in prison.

On the night I heard the news report that Anna's body had been found, Pauline revisited me in my home wanting to share her own experiences with me. She divulged how prior to her abduction, she was going to a local dance. It was on the way that Myra Hindley invited her into the car and subsequently took her to the Moors to be brutally murdered by Ian Brady. She told me how her family managed to find closure after her body had been found, despite being missing for over twenty years.

Tears flooded down my cheeks as this poor girl unfolded her story. I felt strangely humble that she had shared these experiences with me.

People often berate the spirit world for not giving information to help solve horrendous crimes, but in my experience when the spirit world brought Anna Humphries to speak with me that night, they actually did offer sound practical help.

I am aware how the information I communicate from the spirit world or the way I administer my healing can completely change a person's life, so it is vitally important that I utilise my gift with honesty and integrity. Even from an early age I have felt a huge responsibility in the way I deliver my abilities. However, on this occasion it seemed to be *me* that was affected by the spiritual communication. This was the first time I had been exposed to such evil intent and the absolute terror experienced prior to death – albeit in the controlled environment of my guide alongside me in the auditorium and the divine-like protector, who seemed to orchestrate and control the situation.

Sam suggested I meditate so that he could help me to understand and reconcile the experience. Fully relaxed, in my mind's eye, I saw Sam and the divine-like protector in front of me. Her entrancing smile seemed to cleanse all of my soul and I actually felt as if I was being blessed in some way and washed with a divine energy. This was a most memorable and wonderful healing experience that throughout my life, so far, has never been repeated.

Not surprisingly it had been a traumatic year for me in the aftermath of my father's passing, so Richard decided to take me away for a quick break, just the two of us, to Antigua in the Caribbean. I was so excited.

We arrived at the Halcyon Cove Hotel in Dickenson Bay in the dark. The air was heavy with humidity and filled with the relentless sound of the tree frogs croaking.

The early morning sunshine offered a cool breeze to complement the white sand and crystal-clear sea.

Truly, I was happy to be alive.

Although the tragedy of Anna remained prominent in my mind, nevertheless, we were here for me to relax and recuperate, so I was determined to enjoy my holiday.

The hotel breakfast was hosted on a wooden pier stretching out into the sea covered by a simple roof to protect the tables underneath, and it was there, on our first day, I met an elderly man in spirit dressed in a very worn shirt and ragged shorts. His skin was a deep ebony colour, very wrinkled and leather-like from years of sun exposure. His hair was short and white, as was the stubble on his face. Over his shoulder he carried a wooden rod with six fish hanging from a piece of string tied to the end. With a smile he introduced himself to me as Bart, a villager who had fished in this bay for as long as he could remember. He looked over, made eye contact with me and reached out to touch my arm. At that moment, with our consciousness joined, I felt I was in the presence of somebody more than just a simple fisherman, and then he spoke to me, "You'll know who I am soon-a-nuff."

His English was hard to understand as it was heavy with the local accent. The man nodded and bid his farewell, leaving me none the wiser as to his visit. Although I was curious, I knew from experience my encounters were never by chance and always had a purpose. Nevertheless, there was a part of me that wanted to switch off completely from any sort of spiritual communication to allow myself to be a young woman in love with her partner and, just for my week's holiday, lead a normal life oblivious to such things.

After a wonderful day, we dined that evening on the pier again. During dinner, Richard jokingly asked me about what I thought the friendly-looking young couple sitting next to us might do for a living. Without any hesitation, I felt one was a stockbroker and one a teacher. Automatically, we jumped to the conclusion the man would be in finance and the woman would be in education. After dinner, they looked over to us and introduced themselves as Jenny and Frank Rounder from New York and explained they were on honeymoon. We found ourselves at ease in their company and happily chatted away.

The conversation soon came around to asking about my profession. Rather than being shocked, they embraced my explanation and were intrigued to know if I could see what their vocations might be. They were tickled pink when I told them that one of them was a teacher and the other a stockbroker, however it was Jenny who was involved with the New York Stock Exchange and Frank who was a sports teacher.

Thereafter, we spent a wonderful week in their company and promised to keep in touch when we returned to our normal lives, as you often do on these occasions.

We arrived home and were soon embracing our second Christmas together, albeit the first without my dad. This was going to be a tough one, especially for my mum.

Since his funeral I had looked for him every day ... but he had never visited.

Together in the kitchen, we lit a candle and said a little prayer for him. I felt he was safe.

But then I thought, *Come on, Dad, where are you?*

8

Oh Ye of Little Faith

"All truth passes through three stages.
First, it is ridiculed.
Second, it is violently opposed.
Third, it is accepted as being self-evident."
~Arthur Schopenhauer~

The first anniversary of my father's death seemed to come around very quickly. Soon after, Mum decided to go to Hampshire to visit my Aunt Pam and Uncle John, Dad's brother. She felt being around his family and talking over old times for a week or so might be a good tonic and lift her morale. At the same time, we decided it would be a great idea to take the children on an impromptu winter break to Majorca to give us a boost too.

This holiday was particularly memorable; firstly because it was the first time we had been away as a new family, and secondly because it was on this occasion I learned a very valuable spiritual lesson, which I now fondly call 'The Majorcan Effect'.

People often ask me, if we are constantly surrounded by loved ones in spirit why don't I just tap people on their shoulder and give instant communication? Actually, that's what many of my spirit visitors would like me to do. However, from bitter experience I have learned that people are not receptive to being reunited unless such revelations are done in an atmosphere of prior mutual consent.

It was during a warm Spanish evening while I was sitting in the hotel lobby chatting with my family and having a cool drink that I noticed two mature ladies walk past and sit down on a nearby sofa. It was no surprise to me to see a man in spirit walking behind them.

We were immersed in our own conversation when suddenly the man in spirit came over and introduced himself to me as George, Mary's husband. He pointed to the lady wearing the plain yellow dress that he had just followed in.

Normally I can just block out the spirit world when I want to, but for some reason George was most persistent and he kept begging me to talk to his wife. Apparently, he had very recently passed into the spirit world and his wife wasn't really coping with his death. The stress had caused her health to deteriorate which was really worrying him. With great pride, he told me it was their fortieth wedding anniversary that day and this would be the first year he had not bought her a beautiful bouquet of flowers. They were the love of each other's lives, so would I please go over and tell her he hadn't forgotten.

Hearing the tenderness in his voice it became apparent just how much he truly loved her. To be honest, I was very touched by his persistence and immediately thought of my mother who was suffering her own grief and would have loved a spiritual message from Dad.

I explained the situation to Richard and asked, "What should I do? Should I go and talk to the lady? If I was in spirit and I had the chance to speak with you, I would do anything to give you a message."

Having such a strong bond between us, I expected Richard to encourage me to speak to her. But instead he took a sharp intake of breath and started to shake his head saying he thought it was a bad idea, as the woman would probably think I was a little crazy. How sad is it that just wanting to be thoughtful to others could be considered as a questionable act of sanity?

George was having none of that absurd talk and insisted that his wife would love to hear from him.

In the romance of the moment, I threw caution to the wind and told Richard that I was going to take up the challenge, and as if the spirit world had prompted Mary, she and her friend stood up and made for the ladies' powder room ... so I followed behind them.

As I entered the room, I couldn't help but notice a distinctive smell of Brut aftershave following me, a very popular aroma in its day. Intuitively, I realised this must be George's choice of fragrance and he was offering another affirmation of his presence.

Despite having butterflies in my stomach, I calmly approached the two ladies chatting at the washbasins. I was so excited at the thought of reuniting Mary with George. So, after quickly introducing myself as a spiritual healer and medium, I went on to talk about George's visitation and what he had said to me about their fortieth wedding anniversary today and his concerns about her health.

Mary's face turned to thunder and she ranted a barrage of verbal abuse at me at the top of her voice, "What do you want? Who's put you up to this? How dare you!"

She was very angry and continued to shout, "How have you managed to find such private things out about me? That's what you sort of people do, isn't it? You search out personal information, then take advantage and scam people out of their money, don't you?" She caused such a loud commotion that the receptionist came running to see what was happening.

By now, I was choking back my own tears. I kept repeating that I was genuine and wanted nothing more than to oblige George and let her know he was well.

George was very upset by his wife's reaction. This was definitely not the cosy wedding anniversary reunion he had planned. The other lady recognised that I was shaken by her friend's behaviour. She began to calm Mary down and quietly reassured her of the impossibility of a total stranger finding out so many personal details, especially as we were all on holiday.

Watching, the poor receptionist had no idea what was happening as her English was very limited. However, sensing the fire of the situation was burning out, she yelled a torrent of words in Spanish, which sounded rather aggressive, and then left.

With an overpowering sense of entitlement, Mary started to demand in a defiant and mocking tone that I should tell her more about what George had to say – if he was really there!

It was then Sam appeared alongside her. His aura appeared particularly bright and glowed with a vibrant intensity almost as though it had taken on a defence strategy of its own.

Sam looked deep into my eyes and spoke to me in a soft voice. "Repeat to this lady word for word what I am going to say to you. 'Why do you go to Lourdes to partake the Holy Water and yet you have no faith?'"

Mary paled on hearing these words and was struck speechless. Her eyes filled with tears, "How do you know I am going to Lourdes?" she demanded. "I am flying out to France straight away after returning home from here."

Sam advised me to say no more, just to turn around and leave. So I did.

This lady was about to travel to Lourdes to search out and experience the spiritual, and yet it was right there with her in the ladies' toilet but she was too blind to see it.

So now you know why, from that day on, I don't tell anyone what I can see unless there is mutual consent and a genuine need to hear what the spirit world has to say. Even then, it is certainly not on instant demand no matter how much we may want the spiritual contact.

In contrast, just by being asked to pass on spiritual messages even with mutual consent, doesn't necessarily mean that the messages I deliver will be believed, no matter how accurate it might be. Some people are totally dismissive of anything spiritual.

One such encounter happened to me soon after our return home from our Majorcan experience.

We were invited to the VIP lounge at the Talardy Hotel's nightclub by the owners, Karen and Alex. In true 80's style, the Talardy was where the under thirty-fives liked to come, dress to impress and be seen drinking expensive drinks. This was one of those occasions where the champagne flowed alongside boisterous conversation, and I could let my hair down.

Karen introduced me to her friends, reminiscing about the many spiritual occurrences she had experienced. As I mingled with the guests, everyone seemed to be open to my gift – with the exception of two young men who kept openly chuckling about me in a disparaging manner. Never phased by such behaviour, and prompted by Sam, I purposely initiated a conversation with them.

They introduced themselves as Ivor and Darren. Ivor, the smaller of the two men, was well-built with dark, cropped hair. He announced his scepticism in my abilities, as if challenging me to prove myself to him. I don't pick up the gauntlet every time I am challenged, that would be a little too self-indulgent. On the contrary, I will only take the challenge when there is someone in genuine need and when requested by my guides to do so in service to the spirit world.

Unbeknownst to Ivor, there was a very muscular looking young man in spirit standing alongside him. The spirit visitor identified himself as Allen. He explained he was a close friend of Ivor and he wanted to chat with him about his death – about how he died – it was very important.

I was still reeling from the fiasco in Majorca, so I didn't want a repeat performance in front of Karen's guests. Sensing my dilemma, Allen in spirit suggested I talk to Darren about girlfriends. Naturally I had no idea why, but as Sam was supervising the events, I was confident that this was the right thing to do. As intended, the topic broke the ice between us, and Darren started to flick back his thick, floppy blonde hair and playfully flirt a little with me. He mockingly asked if I could tell him anything about his future love life. Sceptic or otherwise, he became very interested and wanted to hear what I had to say.

Without any hesitation I started, "There is someone in spirit here standing beside you both, he says he is a friend of Ivor." The two men looked at each other with raised eyebrows, tongues in their cheeks and doubt in their eyes.

I continued, "He is asking why are you with this girlfriend of yours? She is nothing but trouble. In fact, he says she is quite violent with you, and in your heart you know she is not the right girl. So he is asking you again, 'Why are you still with her?'"

This obviously had an impact, as Darren's pale cheeks reddened with embarrassment, and his eyes filled ever so slightly.

There was more. "You need to decide if you want to stay in this current relationship, because very soon you will meet someone who is potentially the new love of your life. I can see this new love as being a little older than you, and you will find her to be very challenging at times. She is without doubt very glamorous and has a vibrant personality. I would say she is due to make her entrance into your life in about seven months. You need to be free to date her without the cloud of a previous relationship hanging over you, otherwise you might lose her. In your eyes, no other woman will ever measure up to her incredible qualities." I took a deep breath and looked Darren right in the eye, "So … be prepared!"

He acknowledged he had been dating his current girlfriend for a long time, and was considering breaking it off due to her aggressive behaviour towards him. You could tell he was intrigued how I knew this information, but his friend Ivor stubbornly insisted one of the others must have inadvertently shared this personal information in conversation earlier. This is a common misconception amongst the dogmatic sceptics.

Even if Darren seemingly had little faith in my words, I believe he wanted them to be true.

In the process of spiritual communication, I empathise so strongly with the spirit, I can tangibly feel their emotional and physical pain at the moment of their passing. That link can be so profound at times I can be aware of every aspect of their consciousness at the moment of death. Consequently, there was no doubt in my mind that Allen had taken his own life. Furthermore, I knew he was frustrated at Ivor's wanton dismissal of my abilities and desperately wanted him to pay attention as he had something important to tell him.

"Allen is telling me that he telephoned you on the night of his passing. This was the last call he ever made. I have the feeling you didn't want to be disturbed, so you just ignored his call. You knew it was him, as you listened to him leaving a message on your answering machine. Allen is telling me that the next day, when you heard he had committed suicide, you felt extremely guilty, as you believed if you had answered his call, you might have said something to have stopped him killing himself."

Darren listened, totally spellbound. Rather bewildered, he spoke out to his friend, "Is that what happened?" It was almost as if he needed to hear his friend deny it. Instead, Ivor nodded reluctantly, confirming everything to be true.

Both men looked shocked. I was very aware how completely mind-blowing this could be for someone who had never had this type of experience before. But despite this proof, Ivor was still utterly convinced that my messages were fraudulent and somehow I had managed to discover this information in conversation with the other guests.

Fortunately, Allen was determined to prove his existence. I continued, "He is telling me when he was alive he was very interested in fitness and bodybuilding. Actually, as I look at him here, I have to admit he looks extremely fit and muscularly strong."

Ivor and Darren thought it would be the ultimate proof of his presence if he would use his strength to move something physical. Apparently, when he was alive he was very happy to display his physical strength.

"Proof?" I protested. "Hasn't the poor man said enough to prove he is here and very much alive in the spirit world?"

To be honest, I had never seen objects being moved before in this way, so I was doubtful that it was even possible.

It was then Ivor made the demand, "Ask him to open the fire door!"

The gauntlet was thrown.

Not far away from us in the corner of the VIP lounge was a heavy metal fire door. These doors can be hard enough to open at the best of times, so for a spirit visitor to open them was a tall order.

I was just going to tell Ivor he was being rather unreasonable to expect such a physical manifestation, when Sam intervened and attracted my attention. Intuitively, I knew the spirit world was going to attempt this massive feat ... but why?

Nevertheless, as I am always eager to push my own boundaries of spiritual communication I agreed to try, but was reluctant to offer any hope of it working. I explained it is hard enough to achieve a strong link for verbal communication, never mind expecting physical objects to move about to order. I really had no idea what would happen.

Then, for some reason Sam knelt down as if carrying out a meditational ritual of sorts. It seemed as though he might be invoking a higher energy to channel through him. As the ritual progressed, I witnessed a glow behind my guide. Due to the bright intensity, I could sense this was a highly evolved presence.

Sam looked directly at me and explained, "At this moment there is an opportunity for untold spiritual progression, not only for Allen but also for Ivor. Allen carries so much guilt because he feels that he has burdened his friend by seeking his help before committing suicide, and Ivor feels guilt for turning his back on his friend in his darkest hour. Both guilts are unfounded, but nonetheless they are real and very destructive. Allen is genuine in his quest for reconciliation and spiritual growth, so I have asked for guidance from a higher realm. This spiritual entity is the catalyst for much healing to take place. I believe that Allen demonstrating he lives on in the spirit world through this physical act of strength will further his progression, and also it will be a life-changing spiritual experience for Ivor."

No sooner had Sam said this, I watched Allen push the large, heavy door, and slowly it swung open, to about forty-five degrees.

We all gasped. Even I was shocked, and I watched him actually do it.

The two men were clearly shaken by this and started to nervously shuffle as if trying to plan an escape. However, for Ivor this wasn't enough as he assumed the door might have been left slightly open and a draught might have made the door swing open. Actually, Darren could not believe that Ivor was being so dismissive as they were both freaked out by the experience.

Ivor walked over to the door, slammed it closed and demanded it should be opened again.

Another very long minute passed. The four of us stood staring at a firmly closed door; there was no movement whatsoever.

Noticing that the two men were smirking at the lack of activity, I tried to explain a second attempt to physically open a closed door would probably be impossible. The two men beside me had all but given up on a repeat performance. Then, without any warning, the heavy metal door clicked and opened again, albeit this time by only about fifteen degrees. But nonetheless it opened for a second time!

This proved too much for them, and like terrified schoolchildren they both ran out of the VIP lounge.

I have come across ardent sceptics all my life, there are some people for whom, no matter how much proof you present, it is never enough. Their argument is you might have known the person, heard or read about them, spoken to other friends about them … and the one I love the most – you might have researched them. As if I don't have better things to do with my time than target specific individuals and research their dead friends in infinite detail! With that degree of investigative skill, financial commitment and patience, I would be better suited opening a professional detective agency.

There are sceptics who accuse me of 'cold reading', a technique whereby one person attempts to determine details about another by analysing their body language and physical appearance. In my opinion, that type of skill is best left to the performing stage mentalists who try to mimic spiritual communication in an attempt to debunk it.

Anybody with a modicum of sense would wonder if I practiced any trickery, how could I have successfully worked openly in the public eye as a professional therapist for over thirty years, especially these days with the freedom of expression on the internet. Why would I even want to devote my whole life to something so meaningless and false, exposing my whole family to disgrace? Actually, as a resourceful woman, I could have quite easily chosen another profession and excelled elsewhere if I wasn't totally committed to what I do.

When I have encountered aggressive criticism, it has been from people who don't even know me, not from my client base. However, I am not conceited enough to believe I please all of my clients all of the time, who can, no matter what your profession?

Recognising how some people can harshly judge me, you can understand why I sometimes have to be very careful who I tell about what I can spiritually see to avoid incredulity, criticism and being thought a little batty or, at worst, an outright deceiver. Nevertheless, in this book it is my purpose to reveal to you the absolute truth about my life. Therefore, it is with a sense of reservation I share with you how a long-term spiritual acquaintance started with a deceased musical icon despite my fear of igniting any scepticism in your mind. However, the truth is the truth, and I cannot change my life history just for public convenience or palatability.

It was soon after my experience at the Talardy Hotel, I was at home vacuuming the lounge carpet when I became aware of a spiritual presence in the room. I am used to sensing spirit around me, so at first I ignored the intrusion as I was far too busy with my housework.

Refusing to be ignored, I felt a tap on the back of my shoulder so physical, it was as if a person was standing behind me. Shaken, I turned around to face my visitor. It was a fully formed spiritual apparition of a man. He started to wave his hand in a defiant 'Stop' signal and exclaimed in a distinct Liverpudlian accent, 'Shut that bloody thing off'.

I couldn't believe my eyes! This man, a true legend, was standing right there in my home.

I nervously reached down to turn off the vacuum cleaner.

"Get a pen and paper and a tape recorder," he demanded, as if I was some sort of personal assistant.

Sensing I was rather awestruck, he announced, "Yep girl, it is me, I am John Lennon. Now hurry, go get a pen and some paper and hum this tune."

In haste, I searched around, but I just ended up fumbling through my cupboards while he sang to me. I didn't know what to focus on first, his celebrity, the tune, finding the stationary or trying to remember the words!

All went silent and I looked around, he was gone.

The tune was still running through my head and I kept singing the words. This was madness. Eventually, I found a pen and paper, and wrote down everything I could remember.

After this occurrence, the door to celebrities seemed to open wide and all manner of personalities came calling. *Why me?* I kept thinking. *Why them?*

The grief and emotional trauma of celebrities is no different to our own. Also, when the famous are in the next dimension, they share the same status and ability to progress as you or me. The problem for me is when I talk openly and honestly about speaking to celebrities in spirit, it can often seem incredible to the listener and an open invitation to be humiliated by the media. So, despite their life being more privileged than our own, do I just ignore them to avoid contention, or do I listen to them?

One such encounter happened soon after the Lennon appearance, during a weekend break at the famous Glen Eagles Hotel in Scotland. The hotel is very stately in appearance and well-known for being patronised by some of the world's most important people. I really do enjoy visiting such places as they are a unique environment for meeting extraordinary characters from both this world and the world of spirit.

One evening we decided to have a romantic dinner in the main hotel restaurant. For some reason, after we had been escorted to our table, I felt very uncomfortable. I don't mean the chairs were hard, it was more of an emotional feeling. Maybe it was all the beautiful people dressed in their finery. Perhaps it was the way our waiters kept fussing and fiddling with everything on the table, realigning the cutlery so there was a specific distance between each piece. It might even have been how annoying it was that our waiter kept on changing our empty ashtray every five minutes, despite us telling him we were non-smokers. Or maybe it was the noise of the many flambé trolleys as they trafficked around the tables stopping occasionally to fry yet another gourmet dish.

How stuffy … how pretentious. I needed fresh air – I felt I had to leave the restaurant … immediately.

It was then I saw a spiritual glow at the restaurant entrance. At first, I couldn't make out the body shape. Despite the restaurant being full of people, I knew from experience the spirit visitor was going to approach us. As the stranger came close, I recognised who it was by his distinct profile.

I looked straight at Richard, "You'll never guess who's going to join us."

Richard had now learned to play the guessing game perfectly, and gave up almost immediately.

I couldn't contain myself anymore, "It's Sir Winston Churchill!"

Churchill smiled very graciously and I felt this large figure of a man wanted to put me at ease. "Helen, my dear, you seem a little unsettled," Churchill announced with vigour. "I have eaten here many times, in fact this is one of my favourite restaurants. There is no reason whatsoever why you shouldn't have a wonderful time. I want you to imagine that this room is the stage, the restaurant is the backdrop of scenery and all the waiters and other diners are the actors. It is their job tonight to entertain you. So, sit back, relax and enjoy the show they are about to perform. Their performance tonight is for your sole enjoyment."

Since that time, I have dined in some of the finest restaurants. When I have felt a little intimidated, Churchill's priceless advice has always stood true.

Actually, I have developed quite a soft spot for Churchill after learning that when he was alive he was no stranger to the world of spiritual communication. When he was a powerful man in politics he wrote a memo to the then home secretary, Herbert Morrison, complaining about the misuse of court resources on the 'obsolete tomfoolery' of the charge of vagrancy and fraudulent mediumship that resulted in the nine-month imprisonment of the famous medium Helen Duncan in 1944.

Also, after the Second World War, Churchill was instrumental in legalising spiritualism as a religion in the UK, as a way of legitimately decriminalising the activities of many good mediums who simply had the natural ability to communicate with the world of spirit.

Although Churchill has never revisited me, throughout my life I have never been short of interesting people, renowned or otherwise, visiting from the spirit world.

9

Butterflies and Blessings

"Behold the beauty of a butterfly, it's here for the shortest of time."
~Helen Parry Jones~

Now that Richard's and my divorces had come through, we were free to marry and I couldn't help wondering what my own father would think of my forthcoming wedding. My dad had still not communicated with me. He was a man of few words during his life and this trait certainly remained true now.

You see, those in spirit do not change their personalities overnight. In fact, when people first enter the spirit world, some like to communicate as quickly as possible to try to ease the pain of those they have left behind. However, some may have to wait to develop these skills. Some find it too difficult and some don't bother at all! It seems that when you enter spirit, you have to draw on your inner self and ask yourself if you want to achieve this task and only then can others help you to develop the ability.

Dad was never good at conveying how he felt, instead he bottled everything up inside him. If a person was remote or quiet when alive, then that part of their personality will continue in the spirit world until they have learned how to communicate their feelings more openly, and it seemed my father was no different. In spite of that, I so much wanted his blessing for my marriage. Having had my first wedding in a church, ecclesiastical protocol restricted me to a having a civil ceremony. Richard was not prepared to allow our most special day to be lacklustre, so he suggested a flower-filled Caribbean wedding in Jamaica. In 1989, such occasions were not commonplace as the legalities were daunting, but this was no deterrent for Richard.

As a means of a more traditional celebration with friends and family, we organised a blessing ceremony at the beautiful Marble Church in Bodelwyddan to be held on our return.

On the day, summer was at its height and the church seemed to glisten white in the June sunshine. To record the day's events, Richard's parents engaged a videographer, Maurice Grey and his newly wed wife Margaret. To our surprise they were both of pensionable age.

About a week later, Maurice telephoned to say our video was ready for collection. I was excited to experience our blessing all over again and so we made arrangements to call at their home.

The doorbell chimed and we were warmly welcomed as if we were old friends. As we walked into their hallway, a cluster of spirit visitors trailed in behind me all eager to communicate with our hosts. I was a little disconcerted by the clarity of their presence as I hadn't come to hold a spiritual assemblage, just to simply collect our video.

Maurice invited us to sit in front of their television for a short viewing of his work, while Margaret rushed into the kitchen to make us a pot of tea. It became apparent these pensioners had inexhaustible energy levels.

No sooner had I taken the first sip of tea than I was being spiritually addressed by a kind old lady who said her name was Dorothy, and asked if she could please speak to her daughter Margaret.

What do I do now? I thought.

Spirit visitors can often be very persistent and it can be emotionally difficult to blank them out when they are offering so much love for their living family. All the same, I do try never to break my rule of offering unsolicited messages, no matter how hard it might be.

But coincidentally and without any prompting, Margaret started to talk about her own spiritual opinions. She announced, "Elsie, your mother-in-law, told me that you were psychic, but throughout my years I have yet to meet a truly genuine spiritualist."

I felt slightly bewildered and wasn't quite sure if I should take offence at her remark.

After a short pause she continued, "Maurice has always been the 'believer' in the family, ever since an Indian guru accurately told him his whole life story when he was stationed in India as a young army officer."

Maurice smiled the largest of smiles, extending his flamboyant military moustache right across his face. The spirit of Dorothy kept prompting me to speak to her daughter, so I decided that there was now an atmosphere of mutual consent to talk about such things.

After a short intake of breath, I announced, "Do you realise that this room is full of spirit visitors?"

Margaret looked genuinely shocked and started shaking her head, "No, I didn't realise, Helen."

I continued, "Well, they all walked in with me when you opened the front door. In fact, I have a lady here telling me her name is Dorothy and she would like to speak to you. She says you are her daughter."

The colour drained from Margaret's cheeks and I thought she was going to faint. She sat for a moment not saying a word, and then smiled, "Oh yes! That is my mother."

Dorothy held up the most stunning bunch of roses for me to see and although Margaret could not see them, when I described them to her she cried out with joy.

Dorothy cheerfully said, "I love roses so very much."

She told me how Margaret had secretly put similar red roses inside her casket to accompany her on her journey into the spirit world.

Margaret replied, "Helen, that's amazing. I was the only person to know that I asked the funeral director to put some into her casket and he did so only moments before he closed the lid. In fact, there were no other roses at her funeral."

It was apparent that Margaret was shaken by this revelation and tears of joy rolled down her cheeks.

Dorothy in spirit then proceeded to tell me all about her years as a nurse and how she was fondly called Florence Nightingale by her patients, as she was so dedicated to her work, just like the famous Crimean War nurse. Then she insisted on talking about Margaret's wonderful performing cat who was with her in spirit. It went for 'walk-ies' when called, would beg for food when told, stood to attention when ordered, in fact it did tricks any circus act would find hard to follow.

Margaret was thrilled to hear her precious cat was safe with her mother. She reached for a photograph high on the book shelf to show me her dear pet 'Suki', who had sadly died a couple of years prior.

Maurice sat spellbound. Quietly he asked if I could sense anything for him. At that request and within an instant, another lady in spirit stepped forward. She wasn't as forthright as Dorothy and she just showed me a large bunch of violets which gave off the strongest scent.

I described what I could see to Maurice. "I have an elderly lady standing beside you. Although I sense a lot of love towards you, unfortunately she isn't saying her name. I feel she has been waiting a long time to experience this moment and for some reason she is offering me the most beautiful bunch of scented violets, more vibrant than I have ever seen before."

Maurice looked shaken, his cheeks reddened and his eyes welled up a little, "My mother's name was Violet."

Violet nodded and smiled.

Another lady appeared beside her and immediately started to tell me about what a wonderful husband Maurice had been. This lady was a better communicator and gave her name right away as Phyllis. As I said this name out loud, Maurice could not contain his emotions any longer and tears rolled down his weathered face.

She then offered me two names. I looked at Maurice and asked. "Who are Philip and Linda?"

He was too emotional to reply, so Margaret responded on his behalf, "They are Maurice's two children, they are adults now, of course."

Phyllis told me how she died and I articulated those feelings as best I could. "She is so grateful how you selflessly nursed her right through her illness up to the end. You mustn't worry about her as she is now strong and thriving, completely free of all illness and pain."

Watching me intently, Maurice gently nodded his head in affirmation.

I continued, "I believe she died of cancer. I have her age as forty-three."

Maurice just stared at me. There was an emptiness within him that truly needed to hear what I was saying, and I knew by hearing proof of Phyllis's survival, the pain of his loss was diminishing.

Phyllis relayed to me that despite the loving marriage they shared before her passing, how happy she was that Maurice had found such a wonderful wife in Margaret, and she was not jealous of his newfound love. She acknowledged that Maurice had devoted his life as a single parent to selflessly bring up the children. Now they were adults, she believed he deserved someone in his life to partner him.

Phyllis talked openly to me about Maurice's army days during the Second World War and his life in India as a British intelligence officer. Although I was sitting in my hosts' lounge, my spiritual eye was focused on life in wartime India in all its opulence over forty years before. I even described a grand, lavishly decorated formal dining room, and in the centre of its table I could see a large, brightly polished scaled model train going round and round upon an oval-shaped train-track.

As I explained my vision to Maurice, he laughed enthusiastically through his tears, "I know exactly what you mean. As an officer, I sometimes had the privilege of dining on this long table in a prince's palace. It had a broad-gauge railway track that went all around the centre of the table. The exquisitely engineered engine pulled carriages containing a cargo of cigars and liqueurs in crystal decanters. It truly was a magnificent sight."

While I was telling Maurice about his army days, a very stiff-looking man in an officer's uniform appeared behind him. I could sense an aversion from Violet towards this man, and yet I felt a marital bond between them. This discord was so strong that Violet chose to withdraw so not to influence her son.

I continued to interpret what I could spiritually see. "Your father is standing directly behind you. I sense he is genuinely seeking to be exonerated for his actions towards you and your mother whilst he was alive. He is here to ask your forgiveness. So as not to prejudice your response, your mother has left the room so you can make an independent decision."

For whatever reason, Maurice wanted nothing to do with his father; he was not ready to give his forgiveness. I didn't ask why. By refusing to accept his father, it blocked any energy his father had established to create a connection with me. So the link just ceased to exist. In an instant his father had gone.

Maurice slowly leaned forward in his chair and covered his eyes with his hands. After a deep breath, he started to gently sob into his palms. Margaret began to voice her concern at the prospect of what might happen in the spirit world to couples who marry after losing a beloved spouse. She loved Maurice dearly and perhaps felt a little jealous at the prospect that one day Maurice might be given a choice of partner.

"What will happen when Maurice and I die? Will he spend his time with Phyllis as man and wife, or will we be together? I have often wondered, and it really does worry me. I am so scared I won't be with Maurice afterwards."

Over the years, Sam had endeavoured to explain this to me on several occasions. I answered as best I could, "Some people believe that having a marriage certificate means that they are eternally bonded together, even after a loveless marriage in this earthly life. But that isn't so, as marriage is a man–made institution. My guide Sam assures me that it is the quality and integrity of your love that determines who you will be with in spirit. If we have enjoyed a loving relationship before we pass, then there is no reason not to continue that relationship once together in the spirit world, if that is what both parties sincerely want."

Margaret was quick to respond, "Yes, I can understand that, but what if you had a true love for both spouses? What happens then?"

I replied, "Our journey in the spirit world is about spiritual advancement. Part of that journey is to develop our ability to love at many levels far beyond the boundaries placed upon us here in the earthly dimension. It is the depth of love we feel towards each other that determines to what degree we will share one another's life and determines whether we spend an amount of time together in the spirit world – and of course it must be by mutual consent."

Margaret became a little frustrated. "But will I be with Maurice?"

I smiled reassuringly, "I am sure if you and Maurice want to be together, you will."

Margaret breathed a sigh of relief and smiled lovingly at Maurice.

There was no doubt in my mind that Margaret and Maurice were indeed totally committed to each other and that they would remain together when they entered the spirit world for as long as they thought necessary, because that was what they both wanted above all else.

What I didn't say was there might be a time when they choose to explore spiritual progression and enlightenment in a way that does not include the other. But that was their choice to make under circumstances that were possibly inconceivable to them at this time.

Loudly I declared a solitary word, "Butterflies!"

Quite often it happens that I just say one word that is so significant, it becomes a momentous occasion. This was one of those times.

After a short pause I reiterated, "Dorothy is saying to Margaret, 'Butterflies'."

Margaret rushed upstairs and minutes later came down with a very expensive-looking pale, blue dress. She showed me the tiny butterflies discreetly printed through it. This particular garment was very significant to these two newlyweds as it was her wedding dress, and as a result, butterflies became a symbol to represent the love they shared. Since that time, they made a point when they bought each other love tokens, they would in some way include butterflies.

Despite talking with the spirit world for most of the evening, we finally managed to view the edited video of our church blessing. Richard and I were thrilled at the result.

Eventually, in the late hours of the evening, we all shared hugs and kisses and said our goodbyes to our new friends. On leaving, Maurice hugged me and looked into my eyes, "Helen, never worry about sharing your spiritual sight with others, as excellence beats a path to every man's door!"

When I went to bed that night I could see Sam clearly standing beside me and his face radiated the purest love. He started to talk about spiritual signs and how beautiful they were when they are given.

Since I was a young girl, Sam has always explained that our guides, angels and indeed our own family in spirit are able to make contact with us in many guises including by offering signs. Nevertheless, sometimes we have a habit of putting these events down to coincidence or random activity.

Lying in the darkness, I closed my eyes and thought about the day's events. I recalled how important the butterfly symbol was to Maurice and Margaret, and how Dorothy had used it to prove she was still very much part of her daughter's life.

Many people have so many spiritual signs offered to them, so why couldn't one be given to my mother in her time of need? As I prepared for sleep, my mind drifted to thoughts about my mother and how concerned I was about her. I was particularly worried about how my mother's grief was affecting her health.

As if my prayers had been answered, the next morning a single white feather floated down out of the air right in front of my eyes. All my pillows were synthetic as was the quilt, so how did this solitary feather float down from above me? More to the point, why did this happen just at that moment?

Sam reminded me that the white feather represented the deliverance of a divine message. Apparently, on this occasion the feather was a representation of the dove and was to signify peace and love. Nevertheless, I couldn't understand why my spirit visitors didn't just speak to me directly instead of sending messages through feathers, or any other sign for that matter, just to attract my attention.

It was then that Sam reminded me, "Sometimes those in spirit have to adapt and learn new skills in order to verbally communicate directly. Such skills might take considerable time to develop, however for others it might be almost instant. You have had many experiences of this truth, particularly with the lack of communication from your father.

"You see, Helen, no matter what people believe or don't believe, irrespective of creed or culture, there is only one truth, and that is we all live on in the spiritual dimension. Such a realisation can be quite a shock to some and often takes some adaptation."

I lay pondering on the different 'signs' I had seen throughout my life. The hard part it seemed for most people was not actually seeing them, but accepting them as a form of spiritual communication.

During consultations with my clients I frequently warned them to look out for signs from their loved ones in spirit, not in a vague way, but by offering specific circumstances. Several specific occurrences come immediately to mind: butterflies in an airplane, a robin tapping the kitchen window in summer, ladybirds in a suitcase, a visit of a stray cat on a birthday, to name just a few instances.

Sam has often explained to me spiritual energy can be so strong it can have the effect of interfering with electrical items. Such surges of energy have been known to drain batteries, switch on TVs or radios and even effect telephones! I have on several occasions experienced flickering lights during a consultation when being visited by a spirit.

Sometimes it is possible to smell perfumes, flowers, cigarettes or cooking … in fact it could be any type of smell associated with the person you lost. These smells and other signs can demonstrate that those in spirit are often with us in the most unlikely of places.

I experience smells and signs almost as a daily occurrence. Actually, that previous evening I identified Maurice's mother to him through the distinctive scent and sight of the violets that were shown to me. I remembered the Brut aftershave worn by George in Majorca earlier in the year.

The list is endless!

For all that, spirit can also link into your thoughts, especially in times of need or stress. What's more, they can offer premonitions or warnings while you are dreaming. When asleep you are in an altered state and very susceptible to spiritual communication. I have had many experiences where people have learned of family situations like pregnancy, health issues or even infidelity, during sleep. Unfortunately, after waking up, it can be difficult to differentiate between what was a dream and what actually was a spiritual message.

Although more rare, it has been known for objects to be moved to attract our attention. Even in my own home I have witnessed a picture frame being knocked over and a kitchen chair slide across the floor.

There are times when we hear music related to a person in spirit at a location relevant to a special experience with them. These and other highly coincidental events can often be attributed to interaction with us by the spirit world.

In fact, spirit visitors have even been known to show themselves to someone with negligible spiritual awareness. I have met people who have seen a glimpse or reflection of a loved one in spirit. Some have reported they could feel them close even if they couldn't see them. People often try to pass off these experiences as wishful thinking or imagination, but most often they are not.

Just because you haven't had these experiences doesn't mean they do not happen to a multitude of people. Many ask me how they can connect with the spirit world as I do. Just wanting to connect isn't enough. However, we all possess some sort of spiritual awareness, just like all of us can sing, but to varying degrees of aptitude. Be that as it may, only a very few have that special ability to sound like Pavarotti or Adele.

When I have questioned Sam about my own special ability to spiritually communicate, he has always explained it is affected by the spirit's character and especially their ability to express themselves clearly in a normal conversation.

So many people find it difficult to converse in our own world, especially to strangers. So just because such people enter the spirit world does not instantly guarantee them eloquence, hence some new arrivals even have to learn the skill of simple verbal expression. Sometimes, though, if during a person's spiritual development they lack the ability to communicate straight away, a guide might possibly assist so deliver a sign or a spiritual message to those we love.

Also, Sam has always explained to me the quality of any spiritual communication can be adversely affected by many factors imposed consciously or unconsciously by the recipient, for instance, anger, bitterness, intolerance, confrontational and other negative attitudes. Each of these traits has an energy of its own which by its very nature will have an effect on my own energy. However, more importantly, the quality of the communication can also be enhanced substantially where the recipient demonstrates positive natural emotion and has a genuine loving attitude.

Sam reminded me, "So you see, it takes a great deal of energy to deliver the essence behind a spiritual message and to communicate it successfully to the recipient. Sometimes, it's far too easy for those receiving spiritual messages to pass them off, without understanding the mammoth effort undertaken from both realms to communicate."

Because of this, I have learned that the offering of a sign, like Margaret's butterflies, is a special way to give comfort and reassurance, not only to the person they once shared their life with, but also to the spirit individual offering the sign.

We cannot even begin to understand everything there is to know about life in the spirit realm, as our brains cannot yet comprehend the vast spiritual journey we have to undertake and where it will take us. It is beyond our understanding to know what levels of spiritual awareness we can achieve and how much we will want to progress within it. Such a journey is an on-going process of infinite possibilities. However, I have learned the journey of greater understanding through progression does not come as an automatic right, but is down to how much mindfulness we offer to pursue this challenge.

During my many conversations with Sam, I have witnessed from my earliest childhood the underlying message is that it is the birthright of every individual to demonstrate love.

Another continuing theme that seems to stride through all of my tutorials from Sam is that of humour. If this is an indicator of the essence of our soul, then the hereafter must be a very jolly place indeed!

As long as I have known Sam, he has never tired of explaining the spiritual world to me. My own personal and spiritual development has been through my daily interactions with him and through his unlimited patience.

10

Medium with the Message

*"The manner of our death may vary,
but our destination is the same."*
~Helen Parry Jones~

The doorbell rang at ten thirty. The journalist coming to interview me had arrived right on time.

After my limited experience with journalists, it became apparent I needed to be a little cautious before agreeing to an interview. I had quickly learned their bosses wanted to print controversy not credibility. So this morning my stomach was full of butterflies.

I answered the door to a well-dressed young woman in her early twenties, and judging by the spiritual light following right behind her, I knew this was going to be an important meeting. On this occasion, though, possibly more for her benefit than mine.

The young journalist's name was Anne Hadcroft, and it was obvious by her endearing manner she was in the very early stages of her career. After the usual politeness and obligatory cup of tea, she was eager to talk about my life experiences from childhood.

After hearing all about Sam and a few of the many spiritual stories that came to mind, she became very excited and asked if I could 'see' anything for her. This was the doubter's test of course.

I explained to Anne that spiritual communication was not like instant coffee that happens consistently on demand. However, due to my experience, I could usually offer a meaningful message of sorts when challenged. Nevertheless, for a profound message that is worthwhile and has some substance, the recipient really has to have a genuine need and not just be fishing out of idle interest. Fortunately, at that moment, an abundance of spirit visitors showed themselves to me. It was evident that Anne had a genuine reason to hear from the spirit world, not just to satisfy a journalist's sceptical curiosity.

Naturally, Sam wasn't far from my side. However, on this occasion there was a strong golden glow of a separate entity standing right beside him. For some reason, I couldn't make out any visible features as the apparition was more of a presence. Quite often with spiritual visions, it isn't always what you see, but what you can feel, and my feelings interpreted this glow as a healing angel. Then – wham – without any warning, a source of light blasted my vision and within seconds I became aware of Anne's family connecting from the spirit world as clear as any telephone conversation.

On a blank piece of paper, I wrote down all the names these spirit visitors were shouting at me, almost simultaneously. My spiritual senses tuned into one name in particular – "Bernard". As I wrote down this name, I started to circle it over and over again.

At that moment, a very smart-looking, jovial man stepped out from the melee of spirit visitors and walked over to Anne. A strong paternal love radiated from his presence. Our energies made a connection and I knew without doubt it was Bernard.

I smiled and looked Anne straight in the eye. "I have the name Bernard. Actually he is here in spirit standing right beside you, and he says he is your grandfather."

At this revelation, the young journalist looked like her heart had stopped in disbelief. Just that one name had shaken her to the core and the surprise was evident in her face. Although I am sure Anne didn't know what to expect, I am confident she did not think I would irrevocably change her whole belief system with just a name and one short sentence.

With absolute clarity Bernard offered me two more names, one being her father's and the other her brother's – both were living. At this proclamation, she became so emotional she could hardly hold back the tears. Anne was obviously very close to her grandfather and still ached because of her loss.

I continued, "Bernard is showing me a birthday cake and he is singing *happy birthday to you*, so I believe you have a birthday coming up. I don't feel it's today, but certainly it's imminent, most definitely this week."

Anne responded eagerly, "Helen, it's my birthday in five days' time!" She giggled with joy.

As so often happens with a positive open mind, Anne's disbelief had now turned into excitement and discovery. Her face lit up and she leaned forward in her chair so as not to miss anything her beloved grandfather Bernard might say to her. Even the description of his attire and personality was confirmed as accurate, reinforcing the fact that the empathy between people certainly extends after death. It's true to say that people are also recognised for their well-known sardonic wit or other personality traits as well as their appearance. In fact, quite often it is these traits that irrevocably proves a particular person is communicating.

Without warning, the golden glow that had been apparent to me throughout this meeting slowly started to take form. Its silhouette became clearer with every second. I had an awareness this healing Angel was there for my spiritual support so I could bring a true sense of closure for Anne on the loss of her beloved grandfather. As the light around the entity waned, its definition became a little clearer allowing the outline to become more discernible to me.

The form took on a more female appearance with long, golden, wavy hair that swayed back and forth as if caught in a gentle underwater current. Now, on reflection, I believe the movement was created by the strong energy that radiated from her very being. She seemed naked but for a single sash of iridescent cloth swathed over one side of her shoulder covering most of her torso. It looked as though it was there more for modesty than practicality or status. Truly, it was an astonishing sight.

Sam smiled and spoke to me, "When you share your spiritual gifts, do so through the faculty of healing. Always explain it is your role to manifest healing energy to mankind, even if it is only to one person at a time. Healing energy has its own consciousness which connects everyone, irrespective of their beliefs or backgrounds. Spiritual communication is a form of healing, as it balances the mind, making the physical stronger, creating a greater positivity in your daily lives."

After Sam gave me this message, all the spirit visitors that had gathered in my home that morning faded and vanished.

Anne's intimate conversation with her grandfather was now finished. However, we chatted a little while longer, mainly about the relevance of my healing work. Also, to empathise with her at a personal level, I talked about the recent passing of my father. Oh, how I wished he would communicate with me in some way – and I told Anne so, too.

Despite our similar sadness, we were happy in the knowledge that we *both* knew those we love are never far away from us. The easing of Anne's emotional pain was most certainly a monumental healing experience for her. She was so appreciative of what she had witnessed, she promised to write about her reunion with her grandfather. Her article must have been purposely slid past her editor's critical eye on a busy day as the composition about me was favourably accurate and very commendable. Thank you, Anne.

After the success of my Evening of Clairvoyance at the Talardy several months prior, it seemed a good idea to hold another charity event. The owners, Alex and Karen, were more than happy to oblige my new booking and became quite excited at the prospect of a second performance.

I felt a little more organised this time and had even commissioned our new friends, the Greys, to video the evening. Due to their own impromptu sitting with me at their home, they had become ardent fans of my work and wanted to help wherever they could in bringing the spiritual message across to as many people as possible. Also, I thought that making the video was a way of storing the evening's events for prosperity.

The late August date soon came around.

On the night, almost by word of mouth alone, the audience for my second Talardy evening had swelled to a staggering 450 people. The auditorium couldn't physically hold any more. But I would have loved to squeeze one more in, and that would have been my mother. Yet again, for a second time, I was so disappointed she chose not to attend.

Although she was taking a little more interest in my work, she hadn't yet found it in her heart to support me and be present at one of these large audiences. Maybe by coming and witnessing what comfort my spiritual awareness gave to complete strangers would in some way undermine a lifetime of non-belief in my ability.

Her compromise was to babysit for the children.

That night, I walked out to rapturous applause and it took me ages to wend my way through to my makeshift little stage area as people kept standing up and hugging me. The atmosphere was positively electric. It was at that moment I realised that although death affected us all in a very profound and powerful way, there are in fact so many scenarios to how we die – that specific moment we let go of this world and take our first step into the next – maybe no two are ever exactly the same.

It was with that realisation I gave my first message of the evening. A little boy identified himself as Philip and I described him as being about eight years old. As if by telepathy, the boy told me about the moments prior to his death. Simultaneously, I explained to the audience how he was playing by a railway line when he was killed. By offering the boy's name, age and the way he died, I soon found his mother in the audience.

As might be expected, she was distraught and openly cried. As a mother, I cannot imagine any loss worse than that of your own child, especially one so young, no matter what the circumstance. But despite the tears, she had specifically come to my clairvoyance evening to hear from him. She had come to hear that perhaps her little boy had not been robbed from her and disappeared into nothingness forever; she had come to hear that he lived on and had a meaningful happy life, albeit in another dimension.

Through spiritual communication and in her grief, she found comfort. Philip did that for his mother, and in doing so her tears of loss became tears of joy. Her eyes seemed to brighten and come alive at the prospect of having her son back, even for those few moments. Philip gave more detail about his death – how he died with water and electricity and how he hoped his Mum was not angry with him. His mother explained to the shocked audience her young son Philip died in a pool of water under an electric pylon.

This was one of many reunions that night.

Unlike Philip's mother, sometimes at my evenings the recipients can be slow to acknowledge the message that is directed at them. I suppose identifying yourself and speaking out in front of a crowd can be pretty daunting for most people, so quite often I have to work very hard in giving copious amounts of details before the recipient will actually admit the message is for them. It can be quite frustrating for me as I don't have the luxury of time to allow the message to evolve and I will have to move on as I have a crowd of spirit visitors all vying for my attention to be next in line. This can then leave the audience with the feeling the information was incorrect or not applicable, rather than realising the recipient was too embarrassed or unwilling to speak out to me.

Also, it is often not recognised how much effort those in spirit have to make to deliver their message. Sometimes people dismiss the complexity of accurately giving a meaningful message from the spirit world far too easily.

Nevertheless, the most memorable spiritual encounter for me that night was with a good-looking young man in his late twenties, smartly dressed in an army officer's uniform. As was normal during these large group situations, a spiritual glow hovered amongst the audience guiding me towards the recipients of the messages. On this occasion, the glow seemed to settle over a group of three people sitting at the back. Through the bright stage lights shining directly at me, it was hard to define any facial features and most certainly not those sitting at the back. Nevertheless, I focused on the glow as best I could. My spirit visitor spoke for the first time, "Please speak with them. My family has suffered more than enough."

It was quite normal for those in spirit to recognise the suffering of loved ones that are left behind. However, I felt his concern seemed to reach a much deeper level of pain. I could discern this man had passed over with much anguish, and so I wondered how he had died.

No sooner had I put forward this question to him in my thoughts, the man answered, "Bang! And I was gone."

I repeated these words to the audience.

Without thinking, I put my hand up towards my face to shield it from the intensity of the stage lights. With my eyes squinting I pointed to the trio of people at the back who I thought might be the family of this young man in spirit.

I paused for about half a minute. The atmosphere in the auditorium was so intense it was almost tangible. There was complete silence. To those looking on it must have seemed as if I was resting, but the reality was in those moments I was emotionally experiencing the soldier's passing. I could sense everything about his violent death. I knew the soldier wanted his story to be told. It was now my role to relay this and yet somehow temper the realism out of respect for his family and to protect their memory.

Listening to his voice, I continued to repeat what he was saying, "We didn't know what hit us."

I continued, "I see this man as tall, about six foot with dark hair. He says he was married with two children and was serving as an officer with the British army in Northern Ireland. He says his name is Danny."

I paused, the group of three that I was addressing were turning a deaf ear to my descriptions. I thought, how much detail do I have to give to evoke a positive response?

With a sharp intake of breath, I gave up the final detail before moving on. "While on duty, he was blown up by a bomb."

The room gave a resounding sigh, amplifying the tension and anticipation.

This was detailed information that was hard to deny. The small group started to nod their heads and mutter quietly amongst themselves. One of them spoke out, "Yes, we know who this man is."

At long last, I thought to myself.

I asked, "Is his mother here? Or maybe his brother or a sister? Danny really wants to speak to them. It's so important to him."

One of the group replied, "No, but we do know them."

Thankfully I was now given the opportunity to speak to his mother, albeit indirectly. I audibly exhaled with relief as I felt this reunion was going to be a life-changing experience for the soldier's family.

Danny continued with his testimony, and I repeated out loud, "He says how much he is missing his wife and children, you must tell them how much he loves them. He wants you to promise me you will speak to his wife. This is important for him. Please say that he visits her and the children often and kisses them all while sleeping. The love he feels for them all is immense."

The recipients nodded.

Although the lights hindered my vision, I could see many in the audience were moved to tears at the soldier's words. It was hard not to be.

"Danny is telling me his mother has still not accepted the circumstances of his death. She must let this go as it is causing her so much mental suffering. There is so much going on in her head she finds it hard to even sleep at night. He is saying she believes the British government are endeavouring to do a cover up about his death. She has spent years digging around the authorities trying to find answers. He says she must stop this, as it is bringing her nothing but tears and upset. No amount of compensation can help with her turmoil. The true details of his actual death will never emerge, *ever*. She must stop looking for answers she will never find."

The recipients confirmed they believed what I was saying to be true.

"What matters to him is that his family must know he has no memory of pain or suffering and that he is whole again."

I have had many servicemen who have been killed in action visit me from the spirit world, and I cannot remember one of them showing any regret in losing their life in military service. Naturally they have the pain of not being with their families and obviously don't want to have been taken over so early in their life. However, the common consensus was their job in the armed forces was their chosen vocation and every one of them would have given their lives for their comrades in service. They all realised the risk and that possible death was part of the job.

However, the families of servicemen I see can sometimes want to hold someone else responsible for the death of their loved one. This I believe is an understandable and natural response to their grief. As in Danny's situation, he was trying to explain to his family that it was normal and proper to grieve for losing him, but not for grieving at the way or the circumstances in which he died. It held no importance.

The soldier looked into my eyes and smiled, I repeated his words. "He says to tell you he is still as handsome as you all remember him!"

His remark brought a levity to a profound divulgence.

Danny was a very brave man and he was proud to lead his men and serve his country and do the job he was trained to do. My encounter with him had a sincere effect on me and I was equally proud to help his family in some way to make sense of the most tragic of circumstances. The encounter with Danny even inspired London-based journalist Pam Riva to write to me and say that in her nineteen years of being on the newspapers staff, 'I have never heard such a wealth of splendid survival evidence.'

After demonstrating such a strong and powerful spiritual reunion at one of my public evenings, you might ask if it is difficult for me to continue and keep the momentum flowing. Fortunately, Sam is consistently by my side to bolster me and always has another spirit waiting to speak to me.

It is also important to realise that a communication doesn't have to be intense to be profound for the recipient. In fact, one simple phrase could well be as meaningful and life-changing as an hour of detailed spiritual conversation. However, they all resonate the same message – we all survive death and no matter what happens to us here, we are whole and complete to start our new journey in the spirit dimension.

That evening, my next spirit visitor identified himself as John. As he stepped forward I couldn't believe my eyes as I actually knew him; he was an old neighbour of mine from about three years prior when I lived in St Asaph with my first husband. I didn't know him as a friend, he was somebody I would recognise in the street and just nod a 'good morning' to when passing. And here he was in spirit wanting to communicate through me!

With the joining of minds, he told me he wanted to speak to his wife Elizabeth. He had never communicated before, in fact he explained how he had found expressing himself a difficult process when he was alive and how he would often keep his feelings very much to himself, especially from his wife.

John spoke openly about his love for his wife and the circumstances of a childless marriage, also about their beloved black Labrador. He even spoke about his complex job in a glass manufacturing company and how his father was a doctor. By describing John's life so specifically in this way and of course saying he was an old neighbour of mine, a lady in the audience waved her hand in the air in recognition. Unfortunately, it wasn't his wife but a close family friend, who identified herself as Sheila. She confirmed what I was saying about John's life and family to be true.

Without my realising, I had one of those moments whereby I didn't recognise what I was looking at even though I had seen it countless times before. It wasn't until I had nearly finished talking with Sheila that I recognised John's spiritual essence had that telltale sign of a specific traumatic death.

I paused and looked at Sam. He knew how progressed I had become at spiritual communication and that I could withstand the most challenging encounters. There was no need for him to intervene, he just looked right at me and smiled reassuringly.

John must have realised my recognition of his irregular passing and so he started to talk about his own death in detail. He explained how he had suffered a nervous breakdown which resulted in him finally committing suicide.

On hearing this, the audience started to shuffle in their chairs. The act of suicide always causes a mixed reaction amongst any group of people. My audience was no different.

John spoke candidly to me about his suicide and why he took his own life. It was evident in the manner he spoke and with his clarity of thought that he had recognised the reasons why he had committed suicide, come to terms with what he had done and was now making normal progress in the spirit world.

Naturally I feel any loss of life is tragic, however I am a little uneasy when certain religious groups want to brand suicide victims as evil doers and want to banish them to an eternity of their specific brand of hell. Irrespective of your religious belief, in my experience suicide victims pass to the same dimension as those passing under natural circumstances.

Actually, over the last 2000 years, many cultures have considered suicide to be an act of honour in certain situations or even a respectful duty expected of you in specific circumstances.

Sam and I had spoken about this many years before when I was in my early teens. I had heard members of my family whisper about a relative who had committed suicide by jumping from a bridge; quite the family scandal, apparently. All the adults would avoid talking about it when I was listening as if they were trying to protect me in some way.

At the time, when I questioned Sam about this subject, he explained to me there were so many reasons that people chose to end their own life, and most of the time such an action is usually made when the mind is afflicted in some way.

Sam explained the sadness of suicide is that we often feel it could have been avoided. However, the truth is many deaths are a result of not having the right form of therapy. That is why so many who enter the spirit world firstly need to address the fundamental reason, no matter what the cause, why they had these tendencies and ultimately why they took their own life. They have to go through their own individual learning progression associated to their needs. He explained it was even possible for a suicide to take place out of love for others and he described how a terminally ill person may voluntary end their own life to save their family untold suffering and mental anguish. He asked me if I would hold a mentally ill person responsible for their actions and punish them? He questioned would I punish a person for loving me so much and they wanted to save me from a situation that would mentally scar me forever?

Sam explained to me in such circumstances it is not a matter of right or wrong, but more a matter of the quality of the intent of your conduct. In my teenage years this explanation went over my head, but as I matured, so the understanding of making decisions based upon good intent cultivated in my developing mind.

Obviously, there are times when the act of suicide does have ill intent. There are suicides committed to purposely make others suffer or even to specifically ruin someone's life. In such circumstances, the spirit world always offers the opportunity for redemption. However, for those who choose to follow a darker path, they have their own specific journey to pursue.

Later on, the Talardy evening came to an end. Naturally I was physically exhausted but spiritually elated after the event, and happy that so many had managed to give messages to their loved ones.

Despite an invitation, the local press never came. I was disappointed, not for myself, but for the spirit world who work so hard to reach out to us in the name of love. The one spiritual conscience to which we all belong has so much to offer to enhance our lives and yet our earthly communicators – the media – actively undermine and invalidate their message.

11

A Leap of Faith

*"There are times when to cross the unknown
it requires the courage to take a leap of faith."
~Helen Parry Jones~*

One of the most endearing qualities I find about Richard is his propensity to laugh. He has a great sense of humour and often has me in stitches for hours. We both love comedians of all genres, and one of our favourite comedians at that time was Jasper Carrott. We vowed if he ever came to a theatre within driving distance of our home, we would buy tickets to see him live on stage.

Then one day I read in the local newspaper he was coming to Blackpool. By coincidence, he was on that same night, so in reality we had left it very late to book anything. Nevertheless, I rang the box office to try for some tickets. All sold out – had been for weeks. We had missed our chance!

No sooner had I put the telephone down, a woman's voice from spirit caught my ear. I looked around to see if I could see or sense the spirit communicator more clearly, but all I could hear was her voice.

"Hello, my dear," she said in a soothing manner. "If you travel to Blackpool tonight, there will be two tickets waiting for you to see Jasper Carrott."

"But they're all sold out," I replied in my mind.

"Take a leap of faith and go. They will be waiting for you," she responded.

That was bizarre, I thought. I told Richard what had happened.

Always looking on the bright side he announced, "Well, I say we just go! I know it's probably a three-hour drive, but if it turns out to be a wasted journey, what is the worst-case scenario – we can have a walk on the pier, eat some chips, have a game of prize bingo and come home with a stick of Blackpool rock!"

Although that wouldn't be our idea of the greatest night out, we both agreed there is no shame in strolling the promenade and joining in with some traditional British seaside fun.

On arriving in Blackpool, we drove past the theatre and were disheartened to see a massive crowd slowly making their way inside. There was no way we were going to get tickets. I felt guilty for suggesting a 220-mile round trip on the hopeless expectation of there being tickets available to a sold-out performance.

Reassuringly Richard said, "Don't worry about this, Helen. If we can't get in, we'll still enjoy our time together doing something tonight."

If he wasn't driving, I would have hugged him for being such a love!

After parking the car, we arrived at the box office at seven p.m. Although there were crowds of people lining up to get in, nobody was actually queuing up for tickets, which demoralised us even more; if there were any cancellations they would have been snapped up by now as the show was starting in only thirty minutes.

At the box office, Richard asked the ticket lady if there had been any cancellations.

She smiled, "Yes there have. It's most unusual, we have just had four seats handed back … they're front stalls."

She showed us the seating plan and offered us the choice.

At that moment, my spiritual senses were alerted and once again I heard the lady's voice from spirit that had prompted this adventure. "You see! I told you they would be waiting."

This was becoming a real mystery, I thought to myself. "Who are you?" I asked.

She replied, "You will know very soon, my dear."

Once in the auditorium we found our seats. We were only about six rows back from the stage, centre aisle location. We couldn't have had a better position if we had booked one year in advance! What's more, the other two empty seats were the two directly in front of us, so we had an unimpaired view of the stage.

About an hour into Carrott's performance, the lady's voice from spirit returned. I could hear her so clearly as though she was bent down low and whispering into my ear.

"You see that stage, my dear, well I have appeared on there many times. Very soon, you will be on similar stages in front of audiences as big as this. Any moment now he is going to talk about me and you will know who I am."

In the next breath, Jasper Carrott started to joke about the late medium Doris Stokes holding séances on the stage he was now standing on. He started to mock her and imitate the stereotype of a demonstrating medium.

The audience was howling with laughter, but what they didn't realise was that the famous Doris Stokes had joined them that very night. As Carrott said her name, her spirit form appeared next to me in the aisle, it was as if she was there in person and standing proud. She just smiled at me, then walked towards the stage and after a few steps she slowly faded and disappeared.

After the performance, to finish off our truly spontaneous adventure and in the spirit of Blackpool, we drove along the famous illuminations before making the long journey home.

So our leap of faith proved successful … was there ever really any doubt?

Life was hectic.

Richard was almost ready to open a new shop in Shrewsbury in time for the Christmas period. It was a huge two-floored building once occupied by Top Shop. He suggested I go with him on the two-hour drive on the pretext of needing my help, but I think he really just wanted my company and I was happy to oblige.

When we arrived, the decorators were working away and progress was being made. Richard introduced them to me as Ken, who I recognised from previously doing some odd jobs for the family, and a much younger man called David. Time was money, so the men were working late on overtime rate to try and meet Richard's deadlines.

When I travelled to Richard's shops with him, I tried to keep very much in the background as this was his domain, not mine. On this occasion, though, I felt quite useful as he needed to bounce some ideas around about where best to erect the shop fittings to maximise footfall.

Then out of the blue, I felt a tap on my shoulder and without any warning there was an old lady in spirit standing right in front of me. The clarity of the apparition was so strong that I almost thought she had wandered in off the street.

I immediately turned to Richard and explained, "You'll never believe this, but I have a lady standing right beside me. She says her name is Ruby and she is the mother of the older painter. She wants to talk to Ken."

Richard sighed deeply and started to run his fingers through his hair. All of a sudden, he looked very stressed.

"No, Helen! Please … not now. These men are on an hourly rate and if you start talking to them, I know we are going to be here for hours and nothing will get done!"

From experience, he knew once I gave messages, people could sit and listen for hours. He dreaded this might be a long *down tools* period, and at his expense!

I looked at Richard sympathetically, "But Ruby is being very specific, she says it is very important she speaks with her son."

Since my Majorcan experience, what options did I have? Was I willing to ignore my own golden rule?

Just to break the ice, I walked over to the two decorators and informally admired their work. I looked straight at Ken and without any hesitation I asked him if the name Ruby was significant to him. If it wasn't, I vowed in my mind to walk away and say no more about it. After all, it was just a name, nothing more!

His face paled and seemed to age ten years. He carefully placed his brush onto the open paint tin. His partner just looked on with bewilderment.

He replied, "Yes. That was my mother's name. Why do you ask?"

Thankfully, Ken didn't dismiss me outright. And now his question needed an honest reply.

He stood and listened as I explained how I could see the spirit world and more importantly his mother. David, however, fidgeted and giggled like a naughty schoolboy. He seemed very surprised his friend was standing quietly and being so attentive to what I was saying.

Ken remarked, "Only my wife, her parents and I knew my mother's name because she was always known by her second name to everyone. In fact, my own son didn't even know it!"

Ruby was so excited that she now had Ken's attention. She was in a mood to talk, and it was my role to deliver her message and fulfil the purpose of her visit.

I said, "Ruby is telling me she is worried about your health, and has been for a while. She feels you really need to have a check-up at the doctor."

Ken nodded. "Yes, that's true. Lately I have felt quite poorly."

Ruby showed me a baby girl in her arms, I knew this represented the loss of an infant. No matter how many times I have to tell the parents, it is never easy for me to talk about the death of a precious child. "Your mother says she is looking after your little girl and you must never worry about her as she is well cared for. Mum says that you lost her in what the doctors now call a cot death."

Ken swallowed deeply and I could tell by his demeanour he was shaken to the core. He nodded again. "We were devastated when it happened. My wife and I never really got over it."

I continued, "Who is Betty? Ruby says she is a relative of yours and very fond of you. She is sending you her love."

Ken smiled a little as if remembering pleasant memories. "Yes, she was my cousin. We were good friends when we were much younger. She was a bit older than me and I remember her often taking me to the pictures for company."

I explained to Ken how Ruby was small in stature but very large in personality and so it was very hard not to instantly warm to her.

"Your Mum tells me she wasn't much of a cook, but she was brilliant at cleaning. She is telling me she wishes she could get started on this place as she feels it's absolutely filthy."

Ken burst out laughing, "That's my mother to a T! My mum wasn't the best of cooks, I can tell you. But she was always on her knees with a bucket of hot, soapy water scrubbing everything clean."

I noticed the other painter, David, was now standing there with his mouth slightly open, almost gawping, staring at me. Throughout this reunion he hadn't said a word.

Ruby was still full of conversation, which I dutifully kept on relaying, "Do you remember Jim? Mum is telling me he has a bad heart and wants you to go and visit him. It is important you make the effort. Apparently, he has been thinking about you a great deal, especially about the old days."

Ken nodded knowingly. "I will, Helen. I believe he hasn't been well, so I promise to visit him soon. I feel quite guilty as I haven't seen him for years."

"Mum says it's important to tell you that despite what you think and what mistakes you have made, your father is very proud of you."

At the mention of his father, Ken's eyes welled up as if he was ready to cry. After taking a deep breath to compose himself, he added, "My father was a very wealthy self-made man, but despite all my efforts I always seemed to fail at business, and so I had to become a tradesman. It has always worried me what my father would make of me and my life. I wanted to fill his shoes, but as much as I tried, I never could. I always felt I lived in his shadow. You don't know how much that means to me to know he has some pride in me."

And so Ruby went on. As we stood in the large, empty shop, she reminisced with her son about their lives. She spoke about many things, the most memorable being their family's Yorkshire roots, the exact date of his wedding anniversary, his son's birthday and also that of his wife. To say Ken was utterly astonished would be an understatement.

Then, out of the blue, Ruby said, "As David is a friend of yours, so he is a friend of mine too."

For a moment I observed there was a great shift in energy around Ruby, and for no apparent reason Sam appeared beside her. He smiled reassuringly and explained, "Sometimes those in spirit need a helping hand. That doesn't mean by prompting them to deliver a message, but rather to strengthen their resolve so they can fulfil their own intentions."

Sam's light seemed to glow stronger than usual and merged with my own energy. I could feel a change in vibration throughout my whole body as if a profound healing were about to take place as a result of the combination of our energies.

I continued to repeat Ruby's words. "I have this young man with me that needs to speak to David." She then pointed to a spirit person showing himself to me as if he were in his late teens. He sat on the staircase with his head bowed and both hands cupping his face. I could see he was sobbing uncontrollably.

I described the scene to David, but he just burst out laughing, almost disrespectfully. On reflection, I genuinely don't believe it was out of derision, but more as a nervous reaction to the profound communication he had been witnessing between his friend and Ruby. I could understand how emotionally difficult it must have been spending the last half hour hearing so much accurate information from Ken's mother who they believed had been dead and buried for years. Being an eyewitness to such an inconceivable conversation would be hard for the most steadfast sceptic to doubt.

Ruby turned to me and said that the young man was David's younger brother and he needed my help. She explained his name was Gareth and he was only just coming to terms with his own death.

I intuitively knew the combination of our energies was to bring healing to David and Gareth so they both could come to terms with his passing.

Processing all this information, I addressed David, "Ruby says she has brought your younger brother here to see you. His name is Gareth, he looks about nineteen years old."

David almost collapsed to the floor in shock at this revelation. "Helen that *was* my brother's name. He died when he was nineteen. How could you ever know that?" he asked in astonishment. He turned to look at his friend, "Did you tell her, Ken?"

Ken shook his head, looking a little baffled at why he even asked such a question.

David's face hardened. "If my brother's there, ask him how he died?"

Due to Gareth's emotional distress, I found it very hard to communicate directly with him, he was far too upset. However, with Sam's assistance, Ruby explained the circumstances of his passing.

I listened carefully and slowly revealed the shocking truth about his circumstances. "Gareth had fallen out with his girlfriend, they had a big argument and she split up with him. He was angry with her as he thought his life would be over without her, and he was angry towards his family for not understanding the pain he was going through. He felt you all trivialised his loss because he was just a teenager. So he wanted to show everyone how hurt he was … how he was suffering. It seems he wanted to punish you all in some way and make you suffer as he was suffering."

Sensing the tragedy of his death I became a little anxious about reliving this memory, so I asked David if he was sure that he wanted me to continue.

David scanned the room with a fraught expression as if he could somehow find his brother. With nothing for him to see, his focus returned to me and he asked me to continue.

After a sharp intake of breath, I divulged the shocking truth. "He found a gallon of petrol, drank some and poured the rest over his head and body. He then set fire to himself." I paused before making the final statement. "Gareth committed suicide by burning himself to death."

The colour drained from David's face. He crumpled onto the floor. He looked absolutely devastated and sobbed. We all looked at him in silence. It was hard to know what to say to comfort someone after such a revelation. I noticed that Richard and Ken were both very upset after listening to his story.

After a short while David composed himself. "I felt Gareth had done such an awful thing committing suicide that way. At the graveside when we were burying him I walked away in disgust because I was extremely angry with him, I felt he had brought shame onto the family and wasted his own life. Out of rage, from that day onwards, I have totally blanked Gareth from my mind."

Gareth had to hear this. Nevertheless, he was slowly taking control of his emotions and had stopped crying so I was able to spiritually tune in with him direct. The link was weak, but now I could at least feel and understand his trauma. By having a direct link, I could sense the true intent of his visitation, and there was a genuine yearning for healing. Healing comes in many forms, and today it was needed in the form of forgiveness and redemption for David and for Gareth.

I continued, "He thought everyone would be talking about him after his death, but instead nobody did. I feel he is showing true remorse for what he did. He is saying sorry and is asking for your forgiveness."

David nodded and cried openly. In that moment, he let go of so much rage. He asked me where Gareth was sitting as he wanted to be near him to see if he could *feel* him in some physical or emotional way. He walked up the stairs to where I was pointing and sat next to his brother's spirit. The brothers' love bond was as strong as ever.

The spiritual energy around me waned and the links weakened. We had been chatting now for almost an hour. It was time for the reunion to end. Ruby and Gareth said their goodbyes and

I saw them both climb the stairs to the next floor where they simply vanished in front of me.

The decorators seemed mentally exhausted from their spiritual encounters.

Richard was absolutely right … no more work was getting done tonight! The men decided to finish for the day and so we locked up and we all went home. Richard was disappointed his opening would be delayed another day, but when the spirit world made their presence known, he knew that would happen. However, I know it was a sacrifice Richard was happy to make.

From my perspective, it was a job well done!

What a night, I thought.

Soon after this encounter, David wrote a letter to say how he knew I was speaking with Gareth that evening and although he still missed his brother, he could now accept his death and think better of him. I was genuinely touched he had taken the time to write to me. I was so happy that Gareth was now at peace and that his family were coming to terms with his death and could move their lives forward.

As Sam has taught me, from the healing of just one person, many lives can be changed.

When I returned home and relaxed in my lounge, I thought more about the many reasons people choose to take their own life. In an attempt to try and help me understand how easy it is for the most loving person to be overwhelmed by darkness, Sam suggested he take me on a journey of enlightenment. Over the many years we had been together Sam had taken me on many of these ethereal excursions in order to further my spiritual development.

To take this journey, Sam asked me to breathe deeply, close my eyes and relax into a state of meditation. As I did so, within a matter of seconds I saw Sam standing next to me on the edge of a large, open field. Right in front of us was a wooden fence with a stile we had to climb over to get into the field.

Sam walked with me right across this field towards a forest that was visible far in the distance. The grassy surface was vibrantly green and it felt lush beneath my feet. I looked up and saw pale blue skies and I could feel warmth upon my face.

Within just a moment, we were at the forest. Sam led me across a fallen tree that bridged a stream of fast-running water separating the end of the field from the edge of the forest. For no apparent reason, I felt noticeably cooler.

Although I now stood amongst long green grass and colourful wild flowers, the inside of the forest looked dense and quite dark. Sam told me we were at the very edge of the 'darker realms' and he was going to take me just inside the perimeter so I could experience this place.

Sam had taught me long ago that the 'darker realms' is an existence within the spirit dimension that is a region whose boundaries are not geographically determined, but is differentiated by the spiritual entities that occupy that space. These entities share similar characteristics of energy that tend to only think about what they want, what they desire, what they can do to cause suffering. They do not think about how they can help or how they can contribute to others.

Within that realm, spirit evolves in their own specific way, focusing on what they can take, rather than what they can give. It could be said the occupants shared what we term 'darker tendencies'. By its very essence, it creates its own division in the spiritual realm, whereas the mainstream spirit world is filled with light and general good intentions, the darker realms express varying degrees of degradation dependent on the dereliction of the consciousness of its occupants.

Despite this, it does not mean that everyone is purposely evil within the darker realms, in fact many are there as they are more misguided or have failed to grasp the fundamental notion of benevolence. However, nobody is confined to that place and everyone is free to rid themselves of its depravity.

On the peripheral edge of this realm it might be that you would notice that things are unkempt and decaying as there is no care given to the surroundings. As you go deeper, its wretchedness can reach levels that are incomprehensible to orthodox attitudes.

Sam presented me with a long-hooded cloak and said I should wear it. I asked what its purpose was, and he told me it was to obscure my bright aura. He explained that if the entities in this place sensed my strong aura, they might want to connect with me and try to drain my strong energy for their own quenching.

I asked Sam why he did not need similar protection and he explained he had visited the darker realms many times for his own spiritual development and was much experienced in dealing with its inhabitants.

Sam led me down a path through the forest. It soon became difficult to walk as the path was covered with dead leaves, tiny twigs and branches that had fallen from the trees. They seemed dry and lifeless, and heard them crunching as I trod on them. There was a definite chill in the air so I looked up to find the light, but the density of the trees was stopping it from penetrating to the ground. The atmosphere smelt damp and musty.

It became colder as we walked even deeper into the forest and I noticed the branches were intertwined, reducing the light further. The path was hard to navigate as the ground became very uneven and the dead undergrowth slippery under my feet. At times it was so thick, I almost stumbled to the ground.

I asked Sam if we had gone deep enough down this path as it was hard to walk. He smiled and said we were only just on the edge of the forest, but I shouldn't be concerned as despite the obstacles, the path would become easier the deeper we walked into the darkness. Somewhat further in he stopped and told me we had gone far enough. He asked me to look around and tell him what I could see.

This place looked and felt very unpleasant and in my opinion had earned its name. The leafless trees were tall and dense, only allowing minimal light to penetrate. I told him everything looked dead, and I was very cold. Then my nostrils became irritated by the odour of rotting vegetation.

I looked ahead of me and could see a small cottage, it seemed dilapidated and covered in dead undergrowth. I asked Sam why anybody would build a place here. He replied it was once beautiful with flower-filled gardens and surrounded by green fields. He explained the forest had overwhelmed this place and choked all of the vegetation and smothered the cottage.

I followed Sam towards the cottage. He opened the door and walked inside. The room looked unkempt and the dust was as thick as a layer of sand. The air was so dank it seemed to crawl over your skin. Even the fabric of the furniture looked rotten and ready to crumble. The whole essence of the place was lifeless through many years of neglect.

Sam spoke to me and explained this was once a happy place full of children's laughter and warm, homely smells. I asked what had happened to make it like this. He pointed and asked me to observe.

There was a lady sitting in a rocking chair gently moving it back and forth. She had rocked so much it had worn a groove in the floor. Her face was fraught with grief and her eyes seemed empty.

We watched her get up and walk over to a bureau. With tears rolling down her cheeks, she took out a photograph from a small drawer, looked at it for a while and then put it back. She then returned to her chair to rock once again.

Sam explained that she had three sons and the oldest died when he was twelve years old. She wanted him back so badly she lived her life completely immersed in her memories. Her other children grew up and left home not having the love and care they desperately wanted from their mother. In her grief, she did not notice time passing or anything happening around her. She had spent all her time questioning why he died and was totally immersed in thoughts of an imaginary life that should have been shared with her other two boys.

I asked why she was in the darker realms as obviously she was not evil but just in need of help. Sam looked at me, and I knew by the compassion in his face that help was always there for her, but she never wanted it. It was her choice to be in that place. She could leave at any time. But the longer she remained, the more the forest engulfed her. Sam explained in this place there are many souls wandering in the darkness by choice despite the many paths that will take them out.

I questioned that surely when she entered the spirit world a guide would have explained her son lived on and that the two could be reunited? And at that time her suffering would be at an end and the grief she suffered would go.

Sam explained that at any time she could go and be part of her son's life as it was now in the spirit world. However, she had always been totally focused on the life she felt cheated of. She would not leave her imagined memories of how she wanted her life to have been.

I felt angry and demanded that Sam and I should help her. We should take her hand right now and lead her from this desperate place to be with all her family in spirit.

Sam explained many had tried only to leave in frustration.

Now my mind was questioning the countless variations of this one simple quandary.

I asked what if a person is so ill in depression they are mentally unstable and don't understand what is happening to them? Sam explained in such cases the illness would be cured and then the person could make their choice with true clarity – but even then, people often choose not to change. There was a truth about this I had to reluctantly accept. Having experienced low points in my own life, I knew that the only person who could help me move forward from my adversities was myself, despite the clarity of good advice from others.

I asked if this lady had committed suicide.

Sam replied by saying despite what people might believe, it's not important how anyone dies, that has never been an issue. Death just is!

What's important to accept and understand is that circumstances can never be changed. Once this has been accepted you can move forward and have a productive future.

I thought about what Sam was telling me and yet my mind filled with many more questions.

My tutorial now finished, Sam quickly led me out of that place and back across the stream.

Thankfully, this dark journey was over – I opened my eyes.

Despite being in my own reality, my mind was preoccupied with thoughts of the troubled woman. It was hard to reconcile she was there by choice and could not be led away other than by her own doing.

I knew that one answer would lead to another question, and so this was going to be the start of another important spiritual tutorial about the 'Darker Realms'.

But not today please, Sam!

12

The Clock Ticks

"To know the true value of life
makes you richer than you could possibly know."
~Helen Parry Jones~

As any mother will know, quiet moments alone are rare and very much appreciated. In my case, I find these precious moments invaluable. These are when I can detach from everyday stresses and be free to 'open up' to a deeper level of consciousness and understanding for my own spiritual development.

During one of these meditations, under Sam's guidance, a lady visited me from spirit who said her name was Dian Fossey. Although this lady was a complete stranger to me, there was a strong honesty about her that I liked. Her feelings ran deep and I knew that despite her life in the spiritual dimension, she had unfinished work here in ours.

For whatever reason, she sat lost in her thoughts, with her legs crossed on the floor of my lounge thinking what to say to me. This lady seemed to ooze patience. I waited for her to collect her thoughts and speak. She looked in her early fifties, but I could have mistaken her for being a little older than she was as her hair was unkempt and her skin weathered by the sun.

Who is this lady? Why is she here? I thought to myself

She finally spoke to me, precise, and to the point, "I was in Africa and part of a group of three people studying primates. The evil against them has to stop. You will be able to speak out about this for me one day."

Fossey then went on to explain in a very direct manner that she had been murdered because she had upset some powerful and violent people. I found this revelation shocking and asked her why she was contacting me. She answered softly, "I have come because you have a spiritual understanding about why we should care about the environment. And in time, you will use your platform to bring awareness of man's continual destruction of life."

She was right about so much. I feel it is so important that each of us recognise the rights of every living being and have respect for our environment, but I was unsure how I would ever have a strong enough platform to promote such large-scale awareness.

It was then she started to talk to me of her particular love of gorillas. "There are about 600 mountain gorillas left in this world. My lifework endures and I am continuing to protect them. Over time their numbers will grow, however they will remain a critically endangered species. Despite that, the populations of all gorillas are diminishing and their future is most concerning. Their plight is understood and well documented, and yet the same blunders continue to destroy them. Many animal species could disappear during your generation if great care is not taken to ensure they are protected."

Fossey's warning went further. "Giraffes need special attention as their population will be almost halved over the next forty years. If giraffes become extinct, simultaneously the imbalances within the planet will have catastrophic consequences from which there might be no return. As the last giraffe falls, so the Serengeti ecosystem will be ravaged by dust and laid to waste."

This was truly a bleak outlook I hoped I would never have to witness, but it must be within the bounds of possibility as the spirit world were going to great lengths to promote the prospect. Understandably, animals don't have a voice and so their future is reliant upon the work of conservationists who struggle on their behalf. But it mystified me how she thought I could help, especially as there are many important and high-profile agencies specialising in such work.

However, I was no stranger to the concept of conservation as Sam had explained to me in my teenage years that by preserving the rain forests and the animals that live within it, we are in fact preserving man's place on earth. The corporate logging companies and developers as well as poachers, strip these areas of everything, reducing the natural habitats for thousands of animals to barren wasteland unable to sustain life. Without the rainforests, our own survival would be in doubt as its very existence is instrumental in the balance of the planet's ecology.

For as long as I can remember, Sam has expressed his fears about our world and the future we will have unless we pay attention to the conservation of the planet. He shows great concern when there are many people with real power that choose to do nothing about this situation purely for personal gain. I get very frustrated when it is said to me if the spiritual consciousness can see catastrophes happening why don't they warn us.

They do ... and by way of giving them a voice, I am now warning you!

On this specific occasion through Dian Fossey, the spirit world was offering ecological warnings with gigantic consequences.

Richard arrived home with the children. As the energy changed within my home, Fossey faded and disappeared.

That was it, my peace and quiet over. Time to make tea!

I spoke to Richard about Fossey's visit and he was equally curious as to why this stranger would appear in our home.

A few days later, we were walking along the promenade in Rhos-On-Sea. On many occasions we ended our strolls with a coffee at Nino's Cafe overlooking the harbour and sometimes had a browse in the second-hand book shop next door. This time, while I was paying for my little pile of paperbacks, Richard added an old *National Geographic* magazine to the stack. Apparently he liked the photo on the front – and it was only thirty pence!

Later that evening, Richard was flicking through the magazine. He laughed, "You are not going to believe what's here. It's a feature about that lady you were talking about the other day. There's a picture of her with some gorillas. Apparently she was murdered in Africa about five years ago in 1985. You will have to read this as it's very interesting."

This was the first time either of us had read anything about Dian Fossey. As I opened the pages, there she was in full-colour photographs sitting with her gorilla family. Don't forget there was no such thing as the worldwide web back then giving instant access to the world's knowledge at the press of a computer button, so our own general knowledge was restricted to the limitations of our own research and preferred reading.

Once again, I was encountering a remarkable concurrence of events without any apparent connection that could not be passed off as mere coincidence. Without doubt, the spontaneous purchase of the *National Geographic* magazine directly after my Fossey visit had to be prompted by spiritual intervention.

Another remarkable coincidence was about to unfold, the standard of which could only be attributed to spiritual intervention.

Outside, the Welsh winter rain was relentlessly pelting down. Inside, I was snuggled up with Richard on the sofa watching television, when out of the blue a spirit visitor appeared.

He stood with one hand on the fireplace mantle and the other on his hip. I noticed how tall he seemed and although middle-aged he was very handsome in his impeccably tailored suit, crisp white shirt and a formal tie.

I recognised this man. His iconic features gave no doubt as to who he was. And here he was in our lounge of all places. This was completely bizarre.

Without taking my eyes off him, I prodded Richard's side. "You are not going to believe whose standing over there!"

After being by my side for just over two years, Richard was well accustomed to that paradoxical phrase.

Excitedly I exclaimed, "It's J. F. Kennedy!"

He smiled, winked, gave a humorous salute and said, "I'll be seein' ya kid!" And then he was gone.

I was shocked. Why would he say that to me? More to the point, why did he come to speak to me at all?

The only situation I could link to his manifestation was that we were planning a holiday to California, USA, for the end of January.

But why JFK?

I was very aware that sometimes messages from the spirit world could take a while to evolve, so I would just have to be patient and wait and see what unfolded. Nevertheless, I was mystified at what this was all about.

That was not the only mystery that presented itself to me during the run up to that Christmas.

Strangely, each time I gave a sitting to a person living in my local area, there was an underlying message about copious amounts of water in their homes. At first I thought we were due a harsh winter freeze and that water tanks and pipes must be bursting in everyone's homes. Whatever the cause, the same wet warning kept trending throughout my messages.

Meanwhile, a couple of days later, an American business lady named Suzzie Preston travelled up from London to see me. After her appointment, she was so amazed with her sitting she wanted her boyfriend to fly in from the States to see me. Apparently he held an extremely high-ranking military position.

Suzzie was an interesting person, full of energy and verve. She was the CEO of her own airline company based in America and had come to the UK to vie for contracts to fly our military overseas.

I mentioned to her we were going to California after Christmas and she became ultra-excited in that special way only Americans can.

"While you are in the States, I insist you come out to Dallas to see me."

My geography has never been a strong point and so in the spirit of the infectious excitement, I agreed to what seemed a reasonable request. Surely it can't be that far to drive from Los Angeles to Dallas. At the time, I didn't realise this was about a 1,500-mile journey!

Then her excitement really erupted. "Better still, I have a personal friend high up in the Dallas police department, I am going to have a word with him to get you the permissions to do an outside event on JFK Memorial Plaza. You will definitely need a permit as it's a public monument, but as I know all the local top brass, I can get that for you. I can see it now, a big marquee on the grass and a thousand chairs. It'll be fantastic and they will love you! I've got contacts with the local TV station, they will do anything for me. That's definite then. And I won't take 'No' for an answer!"

Certainly being railroaded, and without really knowing what I was agreeing to or what it looked like, I willingly consented to appear in front of a thousand people on JFK Memorial Plaza!

Then, like a bolt of lightning it struck me. My visitation a few days prior. The words screamed in my head, "I'll be seein' ya kid!" The message from J. F. Kennedy!

True to her word, the next day she called Richard to discuss all the logistics and shared contact information. Apparently, the event was already being organised.

Richard had concerns as this was not the way we normally commit to arrangements. He didn't like leaving things to other people to organise, as he likes to know every little detail will fit together and run smoothly for me. In this case I had surrendered to Suzzie's entrepreneurial skills. However, at the end of the day, she was a CEO of a multi-million-dollar company – we couldn't argue with that!

Christmas arrived and the big winter freeze I was expecting had still not taken hold so I started to doubt my own prediction of water-filled homes. Despite my concerns, I was very excited to leave the winter problems behind as our trip to the States was fast approaching.

It wasn't until Peter Ackerman, a local shopkeeper of gentleman's clothing, came for an appointment did I make more sense of the mystery. Previously we had had several sittings together, but today was remarkably different.

As I began, Sam invited three other guides into the room. I say guides, but due to the bright intensity of their spiritual energy they may have been much higher progressed entities. As they stood before me, their energies seemed to merge as one as if they were joining for a single specific purpose.

Sam explained that their role was to offer protection to the local community from the effects of a large-scale disaster and to bring influence. I thought this sounded serious and began to be a little nervous as to what information I was about to encounter.

In my mind's eye I was being shown water coming through the walls of my home as though its strong brick structure was unable to hold it back. I realised this was more than just a tank bursting or a broken pipe, this was more like a river had overflowed.

Sam validated what I was seeing. There was going to be a flood. I was to tell Peter of a water disaster in his home and he would be well advised to increase his insurance. Naturally, he was very shocked and took my advice very seriously.

So from that moment onwards, all my local clients were advised to increase their home insurance. I even suggested to Richard we triple our own household policy and also rang my mother's insurance agent to make sure she had adequate flood cover on her home.

On the day of our departure to the States, I asked Richard if he had tripled our insurance like I asked. He said he hadn't, but he had increased it by fifty per cent. He thought the premiums were too expensive and the cover we had was probably sufficient, as we would never have to face a claim for the full amount. I was displeased to say the least. To appease me, he promised to further increase the policy again when we returned home.

For better or worse, our journey was now underway. California, here we come!

13

I'll Be Seein' Ya Kid!

"The greater our knowledge increases,
The more our ignorance unfolds."
~John F. Kennedy~

At the press of a button the bedroom curtains slowly opened and the Hollywood sunshine saturated our room.

After a long flight, we had arrived late the previous night only to discover that the hotel where we were booked, courtesy of our ticket vendor, was unbelievably rough. We couldn't get out of there quick enough.

Unfortunately, as this was a busy area, it proved very difficult to find a vacancy elsewhere. Eventually, in the early hours of the morning, we found what seemed to be the only room available on the Sunset Strip.

Even after only one shortened night, we had been seduced by the opulence of the St James's Club and it was going to be hard to leave. However, I could tell by the look on Richard's face, as much as we wanted to stay, a second night in our oversized oyster-shaped bed was not going to be a financial option.

All freshened up and a new day ahead of us, we checked into a hotel in another district, which was adequately luxurious and much more affordable. It was here I experienced my first encounter with the famous American customer service I had heard so much about.

As the bellboy showed us into our room, he openly exclaimed his dissatisfaction as it was far too hot and immediately rang reception to find one that had been pre-cooled for the guests' comfort. For that momentary inconvenience, we were given a complimentary cheese and fruit basket beautifully wrapped in coloured cellophane and a bottle of champagne on ice.

Now that's what I call service!

Needless to say, throughout our two-week holiday, my interaction with the spiritual dimension enabled me to experience an added element when discovering the Californian tourist sights. As unbelievable as it sounds, I met the eccentric Howard Hughes while exploring the *Spruce Goose* in its majestic domed hangar. When walking around the *Queen Mary* moored at Long Beach, I spoke with Allied soldiers who used the liner when it was a Second World War troopship, and I had a quick conversation with Judy Garland while walking down the Hollywood Walk of Fame. Perhaps the most challenging encounter was with some of the inmates of Alcatraz, the notorious prison island off San Francisco; I was so physically overwhelmed by their horrific experiences, we had to curtail our visit and leave that damned place to avoid me being physically sick.

As is the reality of life, our holiday came to an end far too quickly. It was time to fly out to Dallas for the J. F. Kennedy Plaza event that Suzzie Preston had instigated. On her recommendation, we checked in to the Adolphus, an historic hotel in the business district.

A really tough schedule lay ahead of us, as over the following week we had a long list of meetings to attend in order to finalise the arrangements. I was most concerned as the permit had still not been issued to use the Plaza and so a final date had yet to be confirmed. Nevertheless, I was assured not to worry as after some television and radio interviews the tickets would all be sold in a few days.

The butterflies had started and I was nervous – big time!

The following morning, we were collected by a senior police official who gave us a personal tour of the spotlessly clean city with its mixture of glass towers and grass parks. We felt very honoured.

During our journey, we stopped at some red traffic lights and I became very aware of a large, imposing building across the street. At that moment, I heard a lady's voice from spirit say that a huge fire had gutted the place years ago. I had a spiritual image of an impressive hotel burning furiously and people screaming in the street. Without hesitation, I announced to our official guide, "They had a big fire there years ago, didn't they?"

A little surprised and with curiosity in his voice, he replied, "Yes, they did, ma'am! It totally gutted the place."

I added, "It was a hotel at the time, wasn't it?"

With a nod of the head, he answered in a deep Texan drawl, "Yes, it was, ma'am! Was a burnt-out shell for years, but was demolished recently and that's the new building."

Richard looked at me and squeezed my hand in recognition of the officer's affirmation.

A little inquisitive, the policeman asked, "How did you know that, ma'am?"

I felt a bit embarrassed at the question, as he must have known why we were here and why he was showing us around. Having learned to be bolder during my stay in America, I replied, "Because of my psychic abilities! That's why I am here in Dallas."

He didn't reply, but I saw him take a long, hard look at me through his rear-view mirror.

We eventually drove around the J. F. Kennedy Memorial Plaza designed by Philip Johnson in 1970. I tried to picture how imposing a marquee would look erected on the grass with a backdrop of the surrounding massive white walls. I could see why Suzzie suggested this place as it would make an ideal venue.

I became so nervous and my heart pumped so hard, I thought I was going to be sick right there in the back of the policeman's car!

Richard leaned in towards me and whispered JFK's words in my ear, "I'll be seein' ya, kid!"

Together we laughed out loud. We were here … and it was happening.

My hope of winning the hearts of the people of Dallas was short-lived, however. Once again fate was about to bring more loss into my life.

During the evening of the 27th February, the telephone rang in our hotel room. It wasn't such a strange occurrence as we had been regularly keeping in touch with our families and it was more economical for them to call us rather than vice versa. Ralph, Richard's father, asked us to be prepared as there was some bad news. Richard's face paled.

Ralph asked, "Have you seen the news about what's been happening here?"

"No. Why?" Richard replied.

Ralph paused and then explained, "Yesterday the whole area was flooded. It's been an absolute nightmare. Your bungalow is totally gutted. Everything has gone. We tried to save some bits and pieces, but all the big stuff has been dragged outside and the looting has been rife. I'm sorry, son, but you haven't a home to come back to."

Immediately Richard asked about the children. They were both fine.

Ralph continued, "Our bungalow is safe because it's slightly higher than the neighbouring properties. However, Helen's Mum has been totally flooded out too. We have had a call from her, she has been evacuated and taken to the old Hoover factory with hundreds of other people. She said she was going to make plans to go and stay with her sister in Connah's Quay."

We couldn't believe the news. How could this happen? We lived at least a mile inland from the sea and there were no rivers nearby.

Ralph explained that miles of coastline were badly affected. Apparently, a catastrophic combination of high tides and extreme bad weather had caused the flooding. A tidal surge breached the sea wall and flooded inland causing streams and all the main drains to overflow. Any water damage to property was considered a contamination and a health hazard, and was to be treated accordingly. Thousands of homes were lost and there were fatalities.

After the initial shock Richard told his father we would call him back. We needed time to think.

Fortunately, Richard can be very pragmatic and with clarity of thought he suggested a plan of action. My maternal instincts overwhelmed me and I wanted to pack our bags and rush straight to the airport. Richard agreed we had no alternative but to go home on the first available plane, but suggested we needed to wait until the airline's ticket office opened the following morning and explain our emergency. Also, we had responsibilities to resolve in Dallas and an event to cancel.

The following morning, we made the necessary calls to everyone to cancel their contribution to the JFK event. All concerned were very sympathetic and obliging as images of the Welsh flood disaster were being shown on all the TV channels. Nobody penalised us in any way and even our airline ticket vendor managed to change our ticket without a penalty.

Once on the airplane, I put my head on Richard's shoulder and held his hand. He comforted me as I cried – I felt my life was in tatters.

Despite being surrounded by so much personal loss, I realised how lucky I was to have my husband beside me and that my children were safe. However, we had no idea what we were going to find when we returned home or where we were going to live. We just needed to get home now, find our children and regroup the family.

14

Tell Me There's a Heaven

"There is no death, only a change of worlds."
~Chief Seattle~

It was a steep climb up the narrow staircase to reach the recently vacated attic rooms. There didn't seem to be one empty hotel room on the North Wales coast. However, taking pity on us, the owners, Phil and Rose, were showing us their former living quarters at the Springfield Hotel as they had just moved out to live elsewhere.

I opened the door and in a giant mirror mounted on the wall facing me I saw the reflection of my father sitting in a chair smiling at me. I stared and refused to blink in case I lost the spiritual link.

I screamed out to Richard, "My dad's here!"

I turned to look around the room to find him, but the link was so fragile, in an instant he had gone.

This was a long awaited and euphoric moment for me. I was ecstatic! I had waited two years to hear from him. It was just a glimpse, but I knew he was trying to contact me, especially now when we were in so much need. I was overwhelmed with excitement. There was a time I irrationally felt my dad didn't want to come back and communicate with me for all sorts of ridiculous reasons. So seeing him, even for those few moments pushed away all the negative thoughts that had haunted me since his passing.

I couldn't wait to tell Mum that Dad had visited, looking healthy and happy, in the hope that she, too, would find it comforting.

This was a positive sign for me. Even though we had to drive a thirty-four-mile round trip to take the children to school, we took the rooms. For the foreseeable future, the Springfield Hotel was to become our new temporary home.

Since returning home from Dallas two days before, we had driven for miles looking for suitable accommodation and we had become accustomed to the 'No Vacancy' signs everywhere we went. Our insurance company had offered us a caravan on one of the holiday camps on the outskirts of Prestatyn. A caravan in winter ... and maybe for months? Not likely, Richard told them bluntly, and he became determined to find something more suitable for us.

Nothing could have truly prepared us for the devastation that greeted us on our homecoming. Everything touched by the flood water (a mixture of rainwater, seawater and sewage), was considered contaminated. Our cars had been towed away, most of our furniture was piled high in the garden waiting to be disposed of, and our former flower-filled home stood empty of everything but the scars of the flood.

Having found accommodation and rented a car, it was now time to get our financial affairs in order. Despite not tripling the insurance like I suggested, at least Richard had upped the policy by fifty per cent. Naturally, he was very upset about not listening to my warnings and felt very guilty not heeding the gravity of my prediction. I wondered how many more of my local clients had ignored my warnings from the spirit world to their own financial detriment.

Another task was to find a builder for our property repairs. By government instruction all flooded properties were required to have the interior plasterwork, up to a minimum of one meter, stripped from the walls and replaced. Also, all floors had to be treated or replaced depending on the construction materials. There was so much work in the area, it took weeks to even find a builder that would turn up to give a quote, and by the size of the estimates, they were blatantly profiteering from the disaster.

Despite the devastation to people's homes and their lives, there was a camaraderie of sorts in the community. Every day involved much emotional and physical effort by the community to strive towards the goal of restoring our homes. For our part, we tried to live as normally as possible.

One morning we were driving along Wellington Road in Rhyl and on the radio we heard for the first time a track called 'Tell Me There's A Heaven' by Chris Rea.

Then the chorus came ...

As we listened, the lyrics were so emotional, unexpectedly we both cried, as the words seemed to capture the very essence of my life's purpose. In that moment, I reflected how people responded and were physically moved when I gave them spiritual messages.

The sky was its usual wet grey-black and the rain pounded the windscreen with that unrelenting sound of bouncing pebbles. We were stationary in a long line of cars waiting at the traffic lights directly outside the police station opposite the Rhyl Town Hall.

I sensed that Sam was with us sitting in the rear of the car. His presence increased my spiritual senses, bringing an important spiritual message into focus without him even having to say a word.

I knew without any doubt what I had to do, and why I had to do it.

Embracing that inspiration, I called out to Richard, "Pull over and stop the car right here. That's it! I have to do what the music is saying and tell more people about the spirit world. Sam suggests I go inside the Town Hall right now and book the auditorium."

Without questioning, Richard pulled up onto the pavement directly outside the police station entrance. It wasn't the best place to illegally park, but I had told Richard to stop the car immediately and there wasn't anywhere else to go!

Forever the voice of balance, Richard responded, "Look, Helen, try by all means. But don't be disappointed if they say no, as you know what prejudice you get towards your gift."

I replied, "I really want to do this and speak out to people about the spirit world. Also, I want to do something to help the community in this crisis. I might not be able to create massive funds, but surely if I made some money to help the less fortunate, it is better than doing nothing."

And so the idea of 'An Evening with Helen Parry Jones' in aid of the North Wales Flood Disaster Fund – a local charity already in existence – was born.

Richard added, "I still don't think you are going to get much joy in renting the place!"

Undeterred by his pessimism, I jumped out of the car and ran over to the Town Hall to avoid getting drenched from the heavy rain. Once inside I asked for the booking office, and there and then I had a meeting with them about my proposition.

At first they were not going to allow me to rent the hall as they were unsure about 'this sort of thing' by 'your sort of people'. However, when I explained I was trying to raise funds for the North Wales Disaster Fund, they became a little less dismissive, but certainly not supportive. Reluctantly they agreed to rent me the auditorium at their normal full fee, but they were still unsure if anybody would bother turning up as they didn't feel there would be enough interest in the local area for 'this type of thing'. They were quite patronising towards me and clearly thought I was being very overconfident when I assured them I anticipated a strong turnout.

After the meeting I ran back to the car and with much excitement told Richard the good news. "I have booked the Town Hall for 27th March! That's only in a couple of weeks' time. Apparently, the auditorium holds about 350 people, so we might have to limit tickets." I smiled confidently. "Told you so! Sam told me they would rent it to me."

I leaned towards Richard and we hugged each other. At that moment, as if the spirit world were pleased, a chink of blue sky appeared in the dark rain clouds and a strong beam of sunlight came glaring through the windscreen. It was so bright we had to squint to protect our eyes. Half a minute later, the heavy clouds absorbed the ray of sunlight. Coincidence? Maybe. But to me, it was a positive sign that the spirit world was happy that the Town Hall was booked.

I became very excited at the prospect of organising a fundraising mini-tour and chatted about the logistics on the drive back to the Springfield.

Two weeks later, all the Rhyl tickets were sold, so we had a meeting with the Town Hall to see if some extra seats could be accommodated. We decided to build a little podium in the middle of the auditorium for me to stand on so fifty extra chairs could be put on the stage area. A little unconventional, but it at least disappointed a few less people.

This was a very busy period, we were trying to organise the reconstruction of our home, my mother's home, the business warehouses … then we had the long commute for the children's school and now trying to organise this mini-tour. No wonder we felt exhausted every night.

For no apparent reason, while relaxing on the evening of 15th March, a strange thing happened. Richard and I were lying under the bedcovers quietly watching a film on television when out of the blue I saw this rather distinguished old man join us from the spirit world.

At first I assumed it might be a relative or friend making contact, but it soon became apparent that he had no connection to either of us. My visitor seemed affable enough. His silver hair and beard were well-groomed as was his appearance – he was impeccably dressed like a true gentleman in a tweed three-piece suit, in the style of a previous generation.

Once I started to link with him at a spiritual level, I could sense this was a person with a highly developed intellect and a deep understanding of life.

Trying to be polite, I enquired as to his purpose at this late hour.

My spirit visitor robustly questioned me. "Do you not recognise me? Do you not know who I am?"

It was obvious he thought I should know him, but to be honest, I didn't have a clue who he was.

Then with much authority he declared, "I am George Bernard Shaw."

He paused as if the sound of his name might faze me in some way. Actually, it didn't and I was just puzzled.

To be honest, at that time, I knew nothing about Shaw other than remembering his name being bantered around during my schooldays.

Shaw continued, "I want you to write down what I am about to say to you."

It was then it became apparent to me at a spiritual level that his passion for writing transcended far beyond his earthly life.

While communicating with the spirit world, I have witnessed that it is not uncommon for them to continue with their life's work when passed over. By that I mean, health professionals might want to continue healing people, the truly gifted, creative people might want to continue in their craft and even inspire the living in whatever way they can. I have spoken to so many successful people who have openly said an innovative idea had come to them while dreaming – an ideal state for inter-dimensional communication.

Right now, Shaw wanted some of his creations to exist in the earthly dimension.

I shouted out to Richard, "Quick! Find a pen and some paper!"

Highly surprised, he jumped out of bed as if it was a matter of life or death. He ran around the bedroom, totally naked, scrabbling around the drawers and tabletops.

"Quick! Quick!" I screamed again, trying to bring some urgency to the situation, as I knew at any moment the spiritual link might be lost.

Noticing Richard was looking rather vexed, I explained, "George Bernard Shaw has just walked in and demanded I take dictation."

Richard was so used to my unusual encounters he didn't even look a little bewildered at the fact I had a Nobel Prize winner who had been dead for forty years making demands upon us at ten o'clock at night!

Sitting bolt upright, and with pen and paper in hand, I spent the next twenty minutes taking dictation from my spirit visitor.

Richard didn't know what to do or say, so he just lay in bed beside me and watched me write at incredible speed.

Then, as quickly as Shaw came, he just faded away and left.

To be honest we were both a little shocked at the nocturnal intrusion. We sat up for the next two hours excitedly reading and discussing what Shaw had written; there were six completed pieces. He never came back to visit me nor has he revealed any reason why he gave me the prose that evening.

The first one he dictated he named "Fruits Foreboding", and this was always my favourite. It reads:

Two apples on a tree were falling.
"Save me, save me," said one apple.
"Let me go," said the other apple.
I asked, "Why did you the first apple want to be saved?"
It answered, "So I may ripen and develop my full body, aroma
and delicate taste."
I said to the other apple, "Why did you the second apple want
to be let go?"
It answered, "Why wait when all I was going to do was drop.
It is evident that if I am falling in the first place,
then I have fulfilled my place here and I can grow no more.
Therefore it is far better that someone benefit from the limited
taste I already have rather than perish and ferment on the tree
where I can grow no more!"

Why Shaw gave me this prose is a mystery to me. However, I always felt it captured a certain aspect of life and death which seemed very appropriate to my vocation.

Soon after this occurrence, the 'HPJ Evening' at Rhyl Town Hall came around very quickly. Richard and his brother Robert were at the venue ensuring all the equipment worked correctly and that people were finding their seats in an orderly manner. For convenience, I was changing into my 'posh frock' at my in-laws, about a ten-minute drive away.

Mum had by now started to show more interest in my spiritual abilities since the success of my last Talardy event. Quite often when we met she would ask sensible questions about my work and listen intently to what I had to say. Her sceptical remarks had almost disappeared.

She had asked if she could come with me as she wanted to witness what I actually said to evoke such emotion in people on such a large scale. I was so happy that at last she wanted to show me some positive support.

Just before we left, I had a phone call from Richard to say it was all a bit chaotic as there was a long line of people forming outside who thought they could buy tickets on the night, not realising they were all sold out. Fortunately our friends Maurice and Margaret, the videographers, became self-appointed doormen and ushers. Without their help I don't think we would have been able to seat the ticket-holders and diffuse the frustration of the 'turn-ups' so successfully.

About fifteen minutes prior to starting, I parked the car in a nearby spot that had been reserved for me. Mum and I were shocked to see the long queue of people waiting to buy unavailable tickets and then another queue of ticket-holders trying to enter through the main entrance.

Richard was right, it was chaotic! Apparently, in the vain hope they might be accommodated when everyone had settled down, those waiting wouldn't leave, and some suggested they might be allowed to stand up at the back and watch.

Mum and I just sat in the car as I didn't know what to do. Previously we had planned for me to walk in through the main entrance, but now it was apparent this was not an option.

At that moment, noticing my arrival, a mass of people ran over and engulfed the car. There wasn't an inch of window that didn't have a nose pressed against it looking inside at me. Everybody was calling my name and trying to catch my attention. The noise was overwhelming. Even though I knew they didn't mean me any harm, I did feel rather frightened and by the look on my mother's face and the way she was gripping my arm, I knew she was absolutely petrified!

There wasn't an alternative, we had to leave the car. As we did, people shook my hand and gave me hugs … it was really lovely. To be honest, I was very surprised as I hadn't expected such a rapturous welcome. Everybody was very supportive in what they had to say and so it was hard to leave them. Even though I began to relax into the moment and wanted to stay longer, I saw one of the Town Hall clerks waving to me from a side door. I think he realised there was no way I was going to get away voluntarily, so he came over and managed to prise me and Mum away from the crowd and escorted us inside.

Eventually he managed to direct Mum to her seat, and show me into a little annex room where I waited for Richard to start the introduction for the evening's event. Over the loudspeaker I could hear his voice making the introduction. We had planned to commence the evening by dimming the lights and playing Chris Rea's 'Tell me There's A Heaven', which was the inspiration behind my mini-tour.

I made my way to the auditorium door ready to make my entrance. Reacting to the musical lyrics, I could feel myself becoming very emotional. As the final bars faded, my stress at seeing so many faces in the auditorium waned and my empathy with the spirit world dramatically escalated. I was aware much responsibility was on my shoulders and people's lives would be changed by what I said and how I said it. Going in front of a large audience is always demanding and more so when you don't even know what you are about to say! But Sam was by my side, so I knew all would be well.

For all these people I was about to offer irrevocable proof of survival after death, and for most of them it would be the very first time they would have had this most extraordinary and life-changing experience. I prayed that my visitors from the spirit world would not let me down at this crucial moment.

Richard proudly announced, "Please welcome your very own Helen Parry Jones!"

The lights came on, and I walked in and made my way to the podium through the audience.

No sooner was I amongst the people, I became aware how the music had physically moved everyone as people were still wiping tears from their faces. The love in the air was tangible and there was a need to touch hands with the audience as I walked through them. It was as if the people I touched knew beyond doubt I could feel their loss, and in return I felt the need to free them from their grief.

As I focussed on the spirit world, and with the help of Sam, the messages flooded through.

One reunion that stands out in my mind from that night was seeing a lone woman from the spirit world, showing herself as in her thirties, holding a well-worn teddy bear. She was cuddling it close to her, as would a small child needing the sense of security. It was an unusual sight to see a grown woman clutching at a teddy bear in this particular needy way. She pointed over to a lady nearby in the audience. With a sharp intake of breath, I realised that I recognised her as the headmistress of the school my children attended a couple of years before.

My mind went into overdrive! It becomes so much of a dilemma as to what I should do in moments like this. Is it acceptable to

179

give messages to people you have had previous contact with or is this considered 'cheating' in some way? It is true I had spoken to this woman previously in the context of her profession, but I knew absolutely nothing about her private life or her deceased relatives. So any information I gave would be as fresh as if she were a complete stranger. But would the other members of my audience realise this as a true reality or would they consider my words predetermined or somehow staged?

The woman in spirit had such a strong link with me, I knew she would not allow herself to be overlooked to appease any earthly criticism I might encounter. There was a determination within her and so as a solution to my problem, I openly established with the audience my prior relationship with the headmistress and that she knew me only through my children's school. Now I felt I had a clear conscience to deliver her message.

Still pointing at the headmistress, she announced, "This is my sister. She gave me this teddy. She helped me so much because I was slow to learn."

Naturally, I repeated this word for word. That was it, end of message, no name, no other detail … just that! The message seemed very disjointed and staccato.

On hearing these words, she immediately burst into tears. It felt so strange watching my children's old headmistress cry like this.

An elderly lady in the next seat put her arms around her shoulders to offer some comfort. She spoke clearly as if to explain to everyone about the situation. "It's my other daughter you're talking to, Helen. She died a few years ago having been mentally disabled all her life. My daughter Susan here would sit for hours with her patiently trying to teach her, right up to the time she died."

There was a reverent stillness in the auditorium.

She continued, "Susan gave her the teddy and she would cuddle it and carry it with her everywhere. She loved her bear that much, we even buried it with her when she passed over."

Such uncomplicated messages like this can be so very powerful and bring so much comfort to the most tragic of circumstances.

Another message I gave that evening reinforced the fact that sometimes death can be caused by the simplest of accidents that could often have been avoided.

A man in spirit appeared by my side and intuitively I knew he had experienced a most tragic death.

He explained, "I was picking my car up from the garage after a routine service. It was up on the ramp when I arrived, so I walked over to have a look at what was happening. As I walked behind the car, it rolled backwards off the ramp and crushed me to death."

With a death so specific, it didn't take me long to find the recipient. She identified herself as his daughter. I was unable to make out any of her facial features as she was sitting in the upstairs balcony. Nevertheless, she confirmed my account of how her father had died.

As my evening finished, Councillor Ron Davies, Mayor of Rhuddlan Borough Council, joined me on stage fully attired in his official regalia and congratulated me on a fabulous demonstration of survival evidence. This was a greatly appreciated gesture and one that I am still proud of today.

Nevertheless, despite the evening's success, Richard was disappointed for me as he had personally invited all the local newspapers. This was a fundraising event of local interest, important enough to be formerly attended by the mayor, however it seemed they wouldn't show up to record the evening as they didn't want to showcase my work in any positive way.

Naturally I was a little disappointed too, but it was dwarfed by the main triumph of the evening – having the full support of

Mum for the very first time. After struggling for acceptance from her for thirty years, attending my evening left no doubt in her mind that I could communicate with the spirit world and bring healing comfort to those who listen. After just one night she had become my biggest fan. I never doubted her love – ever – but now I felt she had faith in me. This truly was a major landmark experience for me.

That evening also proved to me beyond any doubt that it was the people who were my champion, not the media. That fact has remained with me throughout my life.

Based on the success of the Rhyl event, we applied to venues in Chester, Shrewsbury and Wolverhampton.

Hearing about our plans, Rose from the Springfield Hotel suggested using their large function rooms for an extra event. We thought this was a great idea, and it became our venue number two.

Also, we made a plan to drive down to Shrewsbury to discuss with the local newspapers and radio stations the possibility of doing a feature on the forthcoming events to support my fundraising for the Disaster Fund based upon the success in Rhyl.

On the day, Richard went into the newspaper's office alone and wasn't in there above five minutes. Returning to our car, he sat beside me and relayed how they had completely dismissed him and said they couldn't write anything to promote me or the fundraising event as it would contravene the 'Witchcraft and Fraudulent Mediums Act of 1951'.

We were both furious and spent the next few minutes berating the media in general, when suddenly the car started to rock violently and the buildings around us shook. We held onto each other and watched the road in front of us undulate as if it were waves of water. After a very long thirty seconds or so of shaking, it all stopped.

Apparently the earthquake registered a peak of 5.4 on the Richter scale and was the strongest to have struck the UK since 1984. The epicentre was in Clun, a small town a very short distance from where we were parked.

If I didn't know any better, or had it been a more unenlightened period, it might be said some divine deity might have been showing their wrath at the local community for turning down my spiritual request!

Fortunately, Steve Rhodes from Beacon Radio wasn't as close-minded as the newspapers and agreed to offer me a slot on his radio show. Although he was based in Wolverhampton, his audience stretched all over the Midlands and Shropshire. After a very successful interview on his show, the Shrewsbury venue tickets sold well.

Lastly, the most expensive and difficult venue to organise was the Wolverhampton Civic Hall. Their office was very reluctant to even take my booking as they hadn't heard of me and suggested I use one of the smaller hotels in the town. I really wanted to cater for a big turn-out and their auditorium could seat about 1,400 on the lower level and another 600 if the upper level was open. Saying how important it was to me to use the prestigious Civic's facilities, I managed to charm the booking clerk into making the booking, however it was with the compromise I could only hire the lower level.

The euphoria of booking the Civic Hall was short-lived as the following morning I had a letter from Chester City Council stating they had refused my application to hold my fundraising event, as it wasn't in the "public interest". They said they were concerned others in the community might be offended by my event.

You might think most adults are perfectly capable of deciding what events are appropriate for them to attend themselves. Surely such decisions are part of the journey of life? If you didn't want to watch me demonstrating my healing abilities or watching me communicate spiritual messages, you wouldn't actually come along and buy a ticket. My events weren't compulsory.

Richard was livid, and I can't repeat what he said here, but it was along the lines of if any other minority community had been denied the use of a public resource, the council might risk an expensive lawsuit. However, with a positive attitude, we embraced the prohibition as a new opportunity. We made an application to use the Chester Gateway Theatre and they were happy to open their doors to me. Actually, the theatre was much more suitable and I don't know why we didn't approach them in the first place!

Being banned by Chester Council was catnip for all the local press and they gorged on this news and wrote about it in abundance as if I was a scourge on society. Regardless, I was determined not to be disheartened and eagerly prepared for my next event at the Springfield Hotel.

I was always nervous before one of my evenings, more so this afternoon, as the *Sun* newspaper had sent their top journalist Jim Oldfield to report on my evening. I was under no illusion that he had come to report on the reason why people had flocked to see me; in fact, Oldfield had only come as a personal favour for his good friend – my photographer, Peter West. Based on the phenomenal response I had had, West felt that in his professional opinion I deserved the opportunity of some positive publicity.

Oldfield was a well-seasoned journalist, devoid of much sentiment and not particularly friendly. He had been interviewing me most of the afternoon, scribbling page after page of shorthand in his notebook. He had listened patiently to many of my spiritual anecdotes, but now it was time for him to become one too.

Right in front of me a glamorous looking lady in spirit appeared and stood beside Oldfield. Her face was instantly recognisable – it was like looking at one of my own family members in spirit. Here was the unmistakable presence of Pat Phoenix, aka Elsie Tanner from the long running British soap, *Coronation Street*, and it seemed she wanted a word with Oldfield. From her demeanour, I could sense this wasn't a reunion of past friendship but more for confrontation and resolution.

I explained to Oldfield what I saw. He didn't react at all to my statement – he didn't even make eye contact – he just continued to write.

Phoenix told me that she had died about four years prior of lung cancer and was angry with this journalist as he exposed her illness to the public. She reminisced how in temper she smacked his face for the intrusion on her private adversity. She continued to talk about the days leading up to her passing. He looked up from his pad and in that moment made strong eye contact with me and candidly announced without expression that he had exposed her illness in print. I had never met anyone who managed to maintain such an emotionless and deadpan expression.

After about two hours or so, Richard joined us to see how my interview was progressing. He could tell I was exhausted and was worried about me because I had to get ready as people were already arriving to take their seats for tonight's event.

Bringing the interview to a close, we all engaged in light conversation and Richard ordered some coffee. I was confident our meeting had gone well as I had shared with Oldfield enough spiritual anecdotes to write a really good feature.

Then, for no apparent reason, Oldfield took all his notes and ripped them up in front of us. My eyes welled up, and I had to try very hard not to burst into tears. I had been with this man all afternoon and exposed my heart to him; I couldn't believe what had just happened, and right before I was to go out in front of a live audience.

Looking at the shock on my face, he explained, "You strike me as a very genuine lady and I really have enjoyed my time with you. I know you are upset right now, but believe me I am doing you a great favour. I could write the most complimentary feature about you, and the paper would probably want to build you up for a short while. And then, at some time in the near future they will send me or another journalist with the order to destroy you. It's inevitable. This happens all the time and I really don't want that to happen to you, Helen."

My stomach was churning and I could feel the consequence of a lifetime's prejudice and bigotry trying to swamp all of my senses. Not only was I furious with him, but I was incensed by the way the media would never use its powerful voice to acknowledge and validate people with the genuine ability of spiritual sight. Only through acknowledgment and validation can society discern between the truly gifted and the fraudsters, and then calibrate the variation in competence of those that share similar spiritual abilities.

It was at that moment I realised I would spend my whole life working like an underground movement, forced to be disenfranchised and active away from the mainstream, having my name passed around by word of mouth from one person to another. Nevertheless, my inner self intuitively knew the wisdom of patience, and if longevity was my intention, this would be better served with strong roots that were established over time.

Oldfield turned to Richard, "I would like to give you some advice. Already you have experienced appalling prejudice against Helen, I recommend you keep a diary and continually record all these incidents."

Feeling very disappointed and emotionally distraught, we respectfully said our final goodbyes.

There was now an auditorium slowly filling to capacity. To add to my stress two policemen walked in to see what was happening as a section of the A55 dual carriageway was being used illegally as a car park. There was that much of a traffic backlog, they said they thought Tom Jones was appearing here tonight.

Sadly, Oldfield missed an incredible evening and a most memorable encounter that I am confident his media masters would have loved as a human-interest story – had it not been orchestrated by the spirit world! That night, two middle-aged ladies came to my event and despite being strangers, they randomly sat right next to each other. During the evening, I selected one of the ladies and reunited her with friends in spirit and relayed recent events in her life. A short while later, I selected the other lady and reunited her with friends and events.

It was then Sam brought forward several family members, and as is normal in these situations, they discussed family affairs. Whatever I said to the one lady, I kept repeating to the other lady next to her. I was simultaneously giving them both the same family information. To the audience it seemed I might be confused and indecisive with my selection of the appropriate recipient.

With help from Sam, I quickly realised what was happening here.

I needed to resolve this mystery. I confronted the two ladies and asked them if it were possible that unknowingly they might be related in some way. To be more specific, I announced that I had a lady in spirit standing behind them who said she was the birth mother of both ladies. I then went on to say that as young children they were separated from each other and as a result had totally different lives.

It was hard to comprehend – here I was in front of hundreds of people reuniting two sisters who had not had any contact for nearly fifty years. They looked at each other. The traumatic separation was evidently etched in their minds forever. However, in reunion there was such joy!

It was then the ladies filled in the missing pieces. They shared their recollections of being very young children and subsequently being separated. Growing up in new families, they stopped thinking about each other and their early memories were naturally almost erased, as our minds often do to protect us from such traumatic experiences.

I told the audience I felt like Cilla Black having a 'surprise surprise' reuniting moment during one of her television shows. The room embraced the comedy and erupted into laughter. It was amazing!

The success of Springfield left me on a high and I was now looking forward to the event in Wolverhampton. However, something was amiss and I couldn't put my finger on it. That part of me that sensed tragedy was trying to signal me. We had had enough disruption that year, so I dismissed the warning signs as me being overly sensitive. If there was something on the horizon, it would show itself soon enough.

15

As One Door Closes, Another Opens

"It is during our darkest moments
that we must focus to see the light."
~Aristotle~

There was a loud knock on my dressing room door and in walked
Peter West, my photographer. He had come with me tonight to
capture some of the emotions these evenings can inspire. With
much excitement he informed me, "You are not going to believe
this, Helen. I have just taken photographs of the people queueing
outside. It is so long it goes right around the theatre!"

Generally, Peter was unemotional about most things, so to see
him so exuberant caused me to feel even more nervous about my
evening at the Wolverhampton Civic Hall.

I had never been behind the scenes of a large venue and
definitely not one as large as this. For a moment I thought about
all the famous pop stars and comedians that might have sat in this
little dressing room and the vast entourage of people they might
have had to make sure their own show was successful. All I had
in my entourage was Richard and Sam. Despite it being only the
three of us, I felt we made a brilliant team!

Eventually it was time to take my position in the wings and wait for Richard to introduce me. I was determined to do my best for the spirit world tonight and reunite them with their loved ones. My introductory Chris Rea music slowly faded and with love in his eyes, Richard stretched out his arm and welcomed me on to the stage.

Quite often when focused on a particular task, we can lose all concept of time. Without realising, I had been giving one message after another for nearly two hours. The messages flowed through me between the two worlds, and the audience had been open and responsive, creating a sensational atmosphere.

I breathed deeply to reinforce my focus, and was reassured by Sam who was always standing no more than five paces away.

I pointed to a lady in the front row. The man in spirit standing near me on the stage assured me that she was his wife.

Confidently I announced, "I believe I have your husband here in spirit beside me."

Quite often people give me a blank look waiting for more information before they commit to an answer, and this lady was no different. I suppose it's understandable, as people want irrevocable proof the message is for them before they acknowledge the link. However, this can be very frustrating for me, as unless the link is spot on and finely tuned from the outset, I need the energy of a voice and even some natural emotion to build a viable spiritual connection.

In comparison, an artist doesn't complete his picture with one stroke of his brush, he slowly creates the image from the range of colours on his palette and the true likeness is limited by the range of colours available to him. Similarly, for me to build a strong spiritual connection, I need a range of emotions given to me by the recipient, so the more restrained the input of emotion

I receive, the more limited the spiritual connection. Conversely, the more apparent and positive the emotion, the stronger the link will become. It is only with much experience I make it seem so instant and effortless – just as a very experienced artist can create a true likeness with fewer and faster strokes of his brush.

There was no shortage of emotional energy from this lady so I continued to build her a very detailed picture. "Your husband died while outside, not in the hospital or in his home, he died well before his time … and he says his name is Kevin."

With such accurate information, the lady couldn't stall her affirmation any longer. She nodded, acknowledging what I was saying to be true. "Yes! My husband Kevin died outside when he was forty-five. You're right, he was far too young."

The link was strong, and Kevin in spirit was as clear to me as anyone in the audience. I continued, "He is telling me he didn't die of natural causes, it was something more sudden, he was here, then – *bam* – he was gone."

Again the lady nodded in confirmation.

There was more, much more, "Your husband is speaking of a Karen."

The lady quickly identified herself as Karen.

Kevin in spirit then explained in more detail how he died.

Sometimes death can be such a private affair for the family left behind. In fact, respecting privacy is a very important part of my work. While it is imperative that the recipient and I share complete honesty, in these public situations I have a duty of care to be careful what I say to avoid sounding irreverent. Specifically on such occasions, to avoid crossing the line of common decency, I keep asking permission before I reveal certain intimate facts.

I asked, "Are you sure you want me to say in front of everyone how he died?"

There was no hesitation in Karen's voice. Permission was granted. She wanted to know what was being said to me.

Slowly I repeated what I was being told so the recipient could stop me if it became too much for her. "Kevin is showing himself to me standing next to a tree."

Once again, I sought permission to continue. Karen nodded.

"He is holding a thick rope in his hand and he is throwing it over one of the stronger branches."

Again I paused. You could hear a pin drop, as the audience were so attentively silent.

I placed my hands around my throat to demonstrate how I felt, as if I were being strangled. "I can feel Kevin choking and gasping for breath. There is a rope around his neck. He is hanging himself from the tree."

As one, the audience gasped in horror.

Karen's bottom lip began to quiver, her chin crinkled and her eyes filled with tears. Within moments her cheeks began to gently blush and puff out ever so slightly. Wrapped up in the mood of the moment, tears started to gently roll down my own face. It never ceases to amaze how the tragedy of strangers can promote so much emotion in others.

Karen nodded, but never spoke.

To help diffuse the moment, I gave Karen some close family names and some details about the day-to-day activities in her home. Then I asked her if she knew why Kevin had committed suicide, as he genuinely seemed so sorry for his actions.

Rather than give me an answer, silently Karen looked me right in my eyes; she could see my tears, which seemed to comfort her in a strange way. Intuitively, I knew she didn't want to answer my question, but I felt she wanted me to continue.

Kevin spoke to me, but I hesitated before I repeated what he was saying. To the audience it might have seemed I was stalling or not receiving accurate communication. However, in reality he was deep in conversation with me explaining that he took his own life rather than make a decisive lifestyle choice. I paced up and down the small stage for a few moments as I needed time to process the intimacy of what Kevin was telling me so I could relay what I was hearing with some tact and sensitivity.

"Who's Mary to him? It's someone very close, someone he might have even loved or cared for in some way."

Up until now Karen had been able to place every piece of information and every single name given to her, but now she shook her head; she couldn't place the name. She was adamant that she didn't know anybody of that name, friend, relative or distant relative. What do you do when the recipient is so negative? I had spent about fifteen minutes talking to Karen about Kevin and everything had been spot on, so why now should this one name create such a powerful rejection? Such defiant refusals are often very frustrating as they give the impression the communication is incorrect or inaccurate when quite often this is not the case; I knew what I was saying to be accurate and true.

In the aftermath of this negative outburst, how could I bring this communication to a successful and dignified conclusion? Fortunately, Kevin in spirit knew Karen's friend sitting beside her, so I saw this as an opportunity to give her some spiritual messages which would bring this link to a positive end.

Inside, I knew this was not the last I was going to hear about Karen, Kevin and Mary.

Moving on, I soon became focused upon a communication with a young couple deep in the audience. Then simultaneously and without warning an unusually bright light appeared by the side of an elderly man in the front row directly before me. He looked so dignified with his thick silver hair, smartly dressed in a light grey suit, a crisp white shirt and tie.

After a couple of seconds the light manifested into a beautiful young woman. By the intensity of the light I knew this was no family relative but a presence of much spiritual progression. Her essence radiated such a powerful feeling of love it almost overwhelmed me into silent reverence. It took all of my concentration to keep my focus on delivering spiritual messages to the young couple.

She smiled at me, and at that moment the palms of my hands burned with healing energy of great intensity. Her arm reached out to the elderly man and although he didn't know it, she approached him and gently touched his head above his left eye. By sharing spiritual thought, I knew she wanted me to do the same. Then she disappeared.

As if nothing had happened, I continued talking to the young couple while at the same time walking down the stage steps to the elderly man on the front row. Right in full flow of talking to them, I stopped and looked deep into the man's eyes. I could feel his emotional exhaustion caused by years of physical pain.

"Oh, dear me!" I exclaimed. "I can feel such a stabbing pain over your left eye. You have suffered with this for over twenty years. We can't have this, can we?" I took one step towards him and stroked two fingers along the top of his left eyebrow as the spirit visitor had instructed. "There. It's gone now."

This action released the burning in my palms and they became cool again in an instant.

The man seized the moment to speak to me. "I had an operation there twenty years ago and had a growth removed. Since that time, I have suffered so much pain in that spot every day of my life."

All this took less than a minute; the encounter was over seconds after it started. The audience saw my actions, but were oblivious that a healing miracle had just occurred. I stepped back and continued to talk with the young couple as if nothing had happened.

As my evenings draw to a close, sometimes I open the floor to a 'question time' as people are naturally inquisitive about the afterlife. Quite often this may lead into more spiritual communication, especially when the question is about a specific loved one in the spirit world.

Out of the sea of waving hands I was drawn to a lady about ten rows back and pointed at her. Before she even had time to ask her question, I began speaking to her.

"I believe you have come this evening with two other friends, and each of you have recently lost someone very close to you."

She looked surprised at my bluntness, but nodded nonetheless.

"You three girls do so much together, I want to call you the Three Musketeers!"

The audience chuckled.

"Yes, that's so true!" she replied with so much excitement in her voice. Without hesitation she asked, "Do people with mental disabilities here in the living, have normal lives in the spirit world?"

It was evident to me why she asked that question, because by my side was a beautiful young lady in spirit whom I could sense had only recently passed over. She identified herself as Elizabeth and was the sister of one of the Musketeers. She told me that when she was living she was mentally disabled.

In such a moment, it is hard to decide what to do. Was this lady wanting a general response to her question, or did she want her friend to hear a spiritual message from her beloved sister? Might such a reunion be too emotional for her in an open platform? At such times, I have to make some tough decisions.

I explained to the audience that the pain from any illness is not taken into the spirit world. Neither are any mental or physical disabilities carried over. Life in spirit is free from any such earthly affliction. The only eternal effects on our spiritual life are the impressions made by our actions and by the way we lived our life here in the earthly dimension.

Elizabeth smiled at me and I could sense by her essence that she had been in spirit only a matter of weeks. Intuitively I knew she wanted to wait for another occasion before she reunited herself with her sister; tonight was neither the time nor place. I felt I would meet the Three Musketeers again!

Soon after question time, I brought the evening to a close. However, as I had become accustomed at these events, people stayed behind to have a private chat with me.

One lady introduced herself, she said her name was Mary. She repeated, "I'm Mary. You know – Mary. The Mary!" As she said her name, she lifted her eyebrows as if I should recognise her.

Then it clicked … Kevin, the suicide by hanging – *his* Mary.

Now I understood who she was, she wanted to tell me why she was talking to me.

Mary spoke candidly. "Kevin and I were very much in love. He told me he was going to leave his wife for me. Everything you said about his death was so accurate and I really wanted to speak out and say that I was the Mary he was asking about."

I could see the love in her eyes and the grief she carried in her heart. Holding Mary's hand I offered confirmation that Kevin loved her dearly.

Mary became most apologetic. "I could tell you were frustrated and I wanted to tell the audience you were on the mark. But I couldn't, I didn't want to hurt Karen, she has gone through enough. Actually, we have all been affected by Kevin's death! I am so sorry, Helen, for not speaking up."

I reassured her she had made the right decision in being discreet.

After my evenings, many people would stay behind to tell me they knew a certain message was for them, but they were too embarrassed or emotional to acknowledge what I was saying in front of the audience. They all had the expectation that now we were alone, I could try and get their relatives back for a chat. I cannot stress enough to people at these events that communication is not on demand on-the-spot. The opportunity needs to be taken in the moment, as when I have a clear link it flows through me and then afterwards it's gone! I am not saying I can't establish a new one, but that particular link has gone.

Eventually, as midnight passed, the security staff turned off all the lights and politely asked us to leave the building. I really don't mind staying behind after any event as I enjoy the personal contact with people, but I did resent the extra invoice from the management for about £500 for not being out on time, especially as it was less money for the charity!

The Civic Hall proved to me without doubt that the majority of people had a genuine desire to learn more about the spiritual dimension and how it could help our daily lives in so many positive ways. The mainstream media might well want to demonise and censor genuine spirit communicators, but the ordinary general public demonstrated their approval of me by buying tickets and attending these events in their droves.

After the success of the Shrewsbury event a week or so later, in a follow-up interview with a spiritual newspaper, I challenged the mainstream television companies to allow me to appear on prime-time television and they would have the hottest program since *Coronation Street*! Needless to say, the gauntlet, was thrown, was well and truly ignored.

By now we had been at the Springfield Hotel for almost three months. Trying to live a normal life from a hotel was very difficult – you couldn't even make yourself a piece of toast!

There didn't seem to be an end in sight to our homelessness. The repairs to our homes were almost static. The builders would turn up for about one day or so every two weeks to keep their contract active and when they completed a job it seemed shoddy and rushed. At this rate we felt we might be homeless for years.

During this time, my mother hadn't been very well as she had been suffering with a bad stomach. At first her doctor suggested she had a stomach bug in the aftermath of the floods, and when it persisted, he put it down to the stress of living away from home. I had my reservations, but under the circumstances such a diagnosis was plausible and I didn't have cause or the opportunity to look any deeper into the problem.

However, something niggled me, so I suggested that Mum have some hands-on healing from me. All she kept saying was there wasn't enough room at Joan's for my portable therapy couch and that she was fine enough.

However, the pain persisted and my spiritual alarm bells began to ring – very loud! It wasn't until I really put my foot down with her did she pressurise her doctor for a specialist appointment at the hospital.

Eventually, the doctor referred her to Mr Davies, a surgeon from Glan Clwyd Hospital. I was pleased with this choice as he had a good reputation for his medical vigilance and caring bedside manner. It might take six weeks for the appointment to come through, but at least she was in the medical system.

In the wake of the stresses forced upon us by being displaced from our home, Richard decided we needed our own space and we should get away for a while. He suggested going on holiday to a villa in Portugal for a month, as it was cheaper to rent than our hotel accommodation and it would most certainly boost our morale.

We agreed we should take Mum with us to give Aunty Joan a break from her long-term lodger. Also, a holiday with us might give Mum the pick-me-up she needed too. She wouldn't go for the month, but agreed to join us during our third week, for a seven-day break.

Soaking up the Portuguese sunshine and having some prime time together living in a family environment was what we all needed. Later, as planned, Mum arrived and readily joined in our family antics.

During her second night, and over a glass of wine outside on the terrace, my mother asked about Sam and whether there were any messages from spirit for her, especially from my dad.

Over the years, I had come to realise it was very difficult for me to offer a sitting to close friends and family as I tend to hold back what needs to be said. I suppose it's partly to do with trying to shield them from any unpleasant situations and partly because I might subconsciously reject certain spiritual feelings as not being relevant. With a stranger, I can offer information decisively as I have no preconception of their lives, and so the spiritual communication passes through me with clarity.

It was a daunting prospect trying to offer a sitting to my mother.

So, trying hard to disassociate myself from her, I managed to secure a weak spiritual link with my mother's grandparents. For whatever reason, the link was fragile and difficult to maintain.

However, Sam was there with us. He had his own agenda and wanted to address my mother's health. I sensed there was much to be said.

Almost casually I asked, "How's your health been, Mum? Sam's a little concerned about how you've been recently." Already I knew I was compromising what I really needed to say to her.

My mother explained, "To be honest, it's not been getting any better. There are days I feel quite rough, but there is nothing I can do until my appointment comes through from the hospital with Chris Davies."

With some urgency I replied, "Sam is suggesting you must see the specialist at the earliest opportunity. It's most important. Mum, you must listen! Meanwhile, he says you need to start having some hands-on healing from me, and there is no time like the present."

I never doubt Sam's advice. So under the evening moonlight, with my mother sitting on a white plastic patio chair, I laid my hands upon her. With some simple breathing exercises I soon had her fully relaxed. It was quite apparent to me from the colour of her aura that her problem was more than stress. To add to my concern, every time I placed my hands around her bowel area, I could spiritually sense a blockage of sorts and I experienced a stabbing pain as though someone had put a sharp blade into my stomach. Although I had my concerns of what it might be, I said nothing. My spiritual assessment would serve no purpose as she was already committed to see a specialist.

After the session, my mum felt uplifted and relaxed, in fact she commented that the pain she was experiencing earlier had gone. I knew that my healing session might be enough to relieve the pain, but on this occasion, it was not going to be enough to solve the problem; she needed urgent surgery. I couldn't rest easy until she had seen Mr Davies.

Early the next morning, I called his secretary from Portugal. At first she wasn't very helpful as there was an official appointments procedure to follow. On my insistence, I managed to speak to Mr Davies personally and without hesitation he agreed to examine my mother as a matter of urgency the day after she returned home.

Our last few days were so happy together. We played games, relaxed and laughed so much. Fortunately, Mum seemed to have very little discomfort. She even remarked that she doubted she needed to see the specialist after all. However, as we kissed goodbye at Faro Airport, I made her promise me that even if she felt better she must still go and get herself checked out with Mr Davies – just to put our minds at rest. She promised.

I telephoned Mum during the evening after her appointment to see how the meeting went. She didn't want to worry me, but Mr Davies had found a problem and he was going to take her down for exploratory surgery the following Tuesday. As it happened, that was the day we were flying home, so I reassured her with a bit of luck we might even be there before she went into the operating theatre.

On arrival into Manchester Airport, I rang the ward to check on my mother's situation. They informed me that she had been taken down for surgery earlier and she would probably be back on the ward within an hour.

I asked to speak to the ward sister and pleaded with her not to discuss anything with my mother about her condition until I arrived, as I wanted to be there for emotional support if there was anything seriously wrong. She agreed, as this seemed a reasonable request.

However, when we arrived at the hospital I found my mother quietly crying all alone in a side ward. The doctor on duty didn't think it was necessary to wait for my arrival to tell her they had found several cancerous growths.

Although I wasn't shocked at the findings, I just couldn't believe the doctor was so insensitive not to wait until we arrived before telling her such devastating news.

I held Mum's hand and we cried together. My heart was breaking for her, and I felt absolutely helpless.

Mr Davies eventually arrived on the ward to have a chat with us.

He apologised for his associate's insensitivity, but the damage was already done. With a pen and a simple piece of white paper he drew a little sketch to explain how the cancers had travelled throughout my mother's body and what he had done during surgery. The prognosis was not good but chemotherapy might help prolong her life.

We went outside and privately I asked him how much time my mother had; I felt I had a right to know.

Rather pessimistically he answered, "We never know exactly how long. But from experience based on your mother's condition, it is a matter of weeks, maybe months if she is lucky. Definitely not years, not even if all the treatments were successful."

This was devastating news.

I went back and sat with Mum. With strong resolution she announced, "Helen. I am not having chemotherapy. If I am going to die, I am not going to prolong my suffering."

As much as I wanted my mum to fight this illness, she had her own agenda. It seemed Mum was determined to spend what time she had left with her family doing the things she wanted to do and not having the trauma of one hospital treatment after the other. With or without medical intervention, the outcome was inevitable, she was terminally ill. I was shattered.

Silently we drove back to the Springfield. I hated leaving Mum all alone in the hospital.

Once back in our room I sat and sobbed. This news made fresh all the grief of losing my father less than two years prior.

Guilt overwhelmed me. If the cancers were so progressed, why hadn't I seen this coming long ago? Why had the spirit world blocked me in this way? For years they warned me of my father and prepared me for his passing. I was extremely confused.

I also couldn't understand why Mum wanted to decline medical treatment. Somehow I must instill some fight into her. She was a determined and stubborn woman, so why would she not want to battle her illness? I had so much love for my mum and I wasn't going to let her give up so easily.

After a while, I decided to close my eyes to meditate and ask the infinite wisdom of the universe for guidance in an attempt to make some sense of the day's events.

Everything was blank, nothing happened – perhaps I was too emotional.

But then, there must have been a draft or suchlike as a piece of paper wafted onto the floor. I picked it up, it was a section of the original prose from the George Bernard Shaw visitation back in March. For some reason, I was drawn to read these words on the page:

Why wait when all I was going to do was drop.
It is evident that if I am falling in the first place,
then I have fulfilled my place here and I can grow no more.
Therefore it is far better that someone benefit from the limited
taste I already have rather than perish and ferment on the tree
where I can grow no more!

I read it three times.

Maybe, just maybe, this was the answer to my question?

16

Floods of Tears ... Rivers of Hope

"Hope is a powerful energy that provides possibilities."
~Helen Parry Jones~

"Well you never saw that one coming did you, Sam?" My tone was extremely bitter and distinctly sarcastic. "How could you ever hide something like this from me?"

I was angry. Very angry!

No ... more than angry ... totally incensed. My stomach was churning, my heart was racing, my head felt weighted somehow and I was on the verge of screaming with rage. All I wanted to do was shout out loud and hit Sam hard with my fists. I was hurting, and I wanted him to feel my pain and sense my outrage.

But it was more than that. Throughout my life I had learned to trust Sam implicitly. Now I felt absolutely betrayed.

I was devastated, not only at the prospect of losing Mum, but at losing everything I believed and held steadfast in my spirit guide. Our relationship was now under question ... how could someone who was meant to transcendently love you, seemingly be so dismissively cruel?

The June dawn was breaking and I'd hardly slept. I had just spent the night tossing and turning, going over and over how

I could possibly have missed the signs of such a progressed terminal condition right under my nose. I was aware that Sam had suggested something was wrong two weeks ago in Portugal, but this was too little much too late.

"Why, Sam? Why?" I pleaded. "You Judas!" I snarled.

Sam remained silent. He looked calm, which irritated me even more. I felt it was his fault. I wanted him to take responsibility for this immeasurable emotional pain I was experiencing and suffer with me.

He walked over and sat on the end of my bed as he had done on so many occasions. When I was a child, I recognised this as a time for spiritual growth and learning. However, now I wanted no part in his teachings – ever!

Eventually he spoke to me. His tone was calm and compassionate but devoid of any type of apology. "Every day since your father passed into spirit, your mother has prayed to join him. She has pleaded night after night that if there was a world of spirit, we should spare her the misery of loneliness and allow them to be happy together."

I was shocked at this revelation. His words made me shiver and infuriated me. I didn't want excuses, I just wanted to know why such a life-changing happening had been hidden from me. "So now you are teaching me the spirit world just fulfils your wilful pleas? Are you saying just because she was feeling depressed and experiencing grief, you all decided she should die because she said she wanted to? How can such a decision be made when you are at your most vulnerable?"

Sam was resolute in his response. "No. It was nobody's decision for this to happen. I am only sharing with you what your mother wanted to create for herself. Free will and the power of creational thought is very potent. You know this. This truth is part of you and who you are."

My mind did not want to process the spiritual message Sam was endeavouring to give me; my anger wouldn't allow it. I was locked into just one thought, I wanted to play the blame game – and to blame Sam for her illness. All I could think, over and over in my mind, was why didn't Sam tell me; why didn't he just volunteer the information about her problem?

My snarls were unrelenting.

Eventually I quietened, and Sam spoke. "I did not volunteer the information about your mother because you didn't ask. This does not mean that it is your fault, or mine, it suggests that you did not need to know." He paused. "Your father had been pleading for help for years. You knew he was ill and you instinctively knew he needed your help. However, your father wanted his healing to originate from the conventional medical profession alone and would not accept alternatives. He wanted to be healed by doctors, not by you. Nevertheless, he did have the desire to be healed. Your mother has been praying for her own death. The spiritual consciousness was not granting her wish, she was trying to create her own destiny. Just as a positive thought can create a ripple of hope and well-being, so too much negative can create the opposite. I am not saying you can just wish yourself dead on a whim, but I am saying the power of negative thought can be very destructive at many levels."

This was a challenge for me to consider that potentially we are all so powerful as to create out of pure thought, but as Sam turned and smiled at me I knew his words had a sense of truth. I thought, maybe her desire to die helped to stimulate this illness from a genetic inclination and activated her cancer cells, or, more probably, it was her very heavy smoking habit since her teenage years, or maybe this illness had always been her destiny to experience.

Free will and destiny are two expressions that I often find to be quite contradictory.

Some spiritually minded people profess that life is subject to absolute destiny and our lives are mapped out at birth like some sort of movie script. They would argue that our only input is the quality of our performance, and therefore our freedom of choice is limited only to define the style and intensity of our unique rendition. Hence, no matter how well we perform the pre-ordained script, the plot with its grand finale remains exactly the same.

However, there are others who suggest that life is ours to create and mould depending on our life choices, and that we are completely in charge of our own future based upon those good or bad lifestyle selections.

Personally, I try not to look too deep into these contentious philosophies and instead try to enjoy each day for what it brings. Generally, I try to keep as positive as I can living a normal, mortal life. But there are moments when this is hard to do, and coming to terms with my mother's death wish was one of these difficult times.

Was her imminent death her choice or was she just fulfilling a preordained destiny? Either way, it was utterly devastating to face the outcome.

I felt helpless … and still very much at odds with Sam.

Later that morning after taking the children to school, Richard and I drove straight to the hospital to be with Mum. Fortunately, she was still in a private side ward and had recovered sufficiently to be propped up on the starched hospital pillows. However, sadness overwhelmed me at the realisation these were now my mother's last months of life.

I sat beside the bed and held her hand. Her body felt so cold.

I really wanted to pamper her, she deserved the very best, and right now she needed to be in her own home resting comfortably. Everything seemed to be against us: Dad's passing, the floods, the never-ending homelessness and now Mum's terminal illness. Right now, I really needed to create the ambience and comfort she deserved in her last months of life. However, all she wanted to talk about was getting back into her own home so that she could die in peace. She seemed to take much pleasure in the thought of having the opportunity of being with my father in spirit.

Being faced with death, Mum opened up her feelings and chatted frankly. She explained that now I had found happiness with Richard, there was no need for her to be around in order to be an emotional crutch for me. As far as she was concerned, her mothering role was now completed and she needed to follow her own path and go with her husband.

Her cold logic infuriated me. My mother was only fifty-two years old and she wanted to give up and leave us. It took all my resolve to hide my exasperation from her. How dare she think this way! I wasn't going to let her give up so easily. I loved her – she was my mum! She was also my children's grandmother. What was she thinking? We all wanted more time with her. I already felt robbed of my father and so I begged her to grasp at life and undergo chemotherapy or any other medical treatment. But she was resolute.

However, having had much experience with grief, I understood at such times people very often lose perception of their core values and can say what might be perceived as hurtful and bitter comments.

Nevertheless, even though her cancers were so prevalent, she did agree to have some healing from me to relieve her symptoms. At least if she had chosen to shorten what little time she had left with us, I was going to ensure she had an improved quality of life by giving her some intense sessions of spiritual healing.

It was then I looked across the inhospitable hospital room at my own husband; his eyes met mine and I could feel the love they radiated towards me. His love engulfed my very being, it had become the essence of my life. In that instant I knew why my mother wanted to be with my father. The understanding of her life-choice overwhelmed me, and all the misplaced anger and frustration towards her and Sam evaporated.

I understood completely the inconsequentiality of death.

Perhaps I had been too hard on Sam, and forgiveness flooded my heart.

In an instant he was there. Sam said, "The forgiveness you feel is for yourself. I am just the catalyst for your desire to forgive."

While Mum was convalescing in hospital after the operation, naturally I put all my work commitments on hold to be with her. However, amongst the many telephone messages that had accumulated on our answering machine during our absence in Portugal, there were two I couldn't delay responding to.

Firstly, our Antigua holiday friends from New York, Jenny and Frank Rounder, wanted to tell me Jenny's father had just been murdered and desperately wanted any help I could offer. And secondly, a lady named Maureen, who had attended my recent Shrewsbury event with her friend Trevaline Evans. Trevaline had mysteriously disappeared one lunchtime after walking out from her antique shop in Llangollen, North Wales on 16th June – officially missing or at worse, presumed murdered, please – please would I help?

Hearing about a murder at any time is shocking, however hearing about two simultaneously is absolutely horrendous. So much unsolicited death was surrounding me at one time.

Murder investigations are something I don't court and actively avoid, but I had a prior connection with these people before their tragedy. Under such circumstances I would never turn my back on a genuine request for help. However, on this occasion I had to consider my mother's needs too.

Respectfully, I returned the Rounders' phone call to express my condolences for their most tragic loss and find out what I could do to ease their pain.

Jenny was beside herself with grief as she explained that her father had been shot dead, seemingly for no apparent reason. She pleaded with me to try to communicate with him to shed some light on the motive and maybe even the murderer's identity. She couldn't understand why anyone would want to hurt her dad in any way.

As we were speaking, I became aware of a spiritual presence beside me which manifested into a middle-aged looking man. The spirit introduced himself as Nick, her father. Although in appearance his face looked rugged and his body was bulky in a strong muscular way, I could tell he was in a state of shock at being in the spirit world. He wore a navy-blue workman's overall that was styled like a pair of dungarees. Then for no apparent reason he pulled some glasses out of the chest pocket of the garment and placed them on his head and then removed them and put them back into the same pocket. Over the course of our time together he repeated this procedure many times.

Jenny confirmed that Nick was her father's name and my description fitted his appearance. She laughed at the glasses observation, as this was a recognisable habit of his, constantly putting on and taking off his glasses and placing them into his dungarees' pocket.

Within moments Nick started to tell me all about his death. Jenny listened intently, and I could hear in her voice she was becoming upset.

She interrupted me, "Helen, the police are investigating Dad's murder, I really want them to hear what you are saying about him. Can I call you back early afternoon tomorrow, your time, so you can talk to them too?"

True to her word, she called me back the following afternoon and a police officer was listening in on her extension. I was painfully aware that spirit does not come to order, and so was concerned that Jenny's telephone call might turn out to be fruitless.

My fears were unfounded as Sam dutifully appeared with Nick's spiritual presence alongside him. Without any hesitation, I was able to tune into him again, and he did not disappoint.

Suddenly I experienced a sharp burning sensation in my right side. I winced with the searing pain this spiritual feeling inflicted upon me, and in that moment I could sense Nick stumble to the ground. As if I was looking through his eyes, I saw a pair of long, female legs with red stiletto shoes. The woman started to walk away, but I couldn't see her face as her back was to me, however she was smartly dressed in a fashionably short skirt and blouse. I instinctively felt that possibly this was the murderer or murderer's accomplice. My eyes clouded over as I experienced the life force drain away from this dying man's body.

Nick clarified this spiritual vision by telling me he was shot at close range by a .45 calibre handgun, and the bullet ripped through his belly flesh into the wall behind him.

Feeling disorientated, I needed a few moments to gather my faculties before I described what I had just experienced. As I repeated this through the telephone, the police officer confirmed the size of the bullet to be a .45 and that there was a bullet casing found in the wall at the murder scene. He said there was no evidence of a woman being there, but welcomed this information as a possible line of enquiry.

For some strange reason, I kept seeing diamonds glistening before my eyes and I repeated several times the phrase 'bright diamonds', but somehow I knew this was a wrong interpretation. Then loudly I announced: "Diamond Bright! Dad is telling me he was involved with a business called Diamond Bright."

Jenny confirmed that years before when she was a young child, her dad had owned a small company of this name.

"Well, I feel his death has something to do with those years and the business associates he had at that time. Dad is showing me the back of a white yacht, I believe it is his. Written on the stern are three names, I can't make out what they say, but they all start with the letter J. But clearly I can see three large Js."

Jenny became excited. "Yes, for years he has owned a yacht! It's named after me and my two sisters. We all share the same initial, that's why you see the three Js!"

Nick went on to say that in those bygone days he went back and forth from New York to the state of Connecticut. Jenny confirmed what I was saying.

It was then I realised that Jenny's dad might well have been involved in some sort of courier service that might not be legal. This was a massive dilemma for me. Her father had been murdered and she was experiencing the natural grief associated with such a loss. Should I now shatter a lifetime of memories by suggesting that he had been involved in an underworld lifestyle she knew nothing about? What purpose would it serve to destroy her in this way as it certainly wouldn't bring her father back? Exposing any type of dubious associations would be subjecting Jenny and all her family to pointless pain. They all adored their father, to them he was the perfect dad and I didn't want to jeopardise the love of the good memories they all enjoyed together.

Do I have the duty to tell the full truth irrespective of consequences to those listening, or do I have the responsibility to protect them from information that would bring unnecessary suffering?

After an instant's consideration, I decided I had to say something, and blatant lying wasn't an option. "Dad is telling me that years ago he would often take risks in his business, some of which pushed the boundaries of what might be considered totally legitimate. He says his death had an association to some of his activities from that period."

In all honesty, I felt this gave a truthful overview without going into unnecessary and sordid details. Out of respect for my friends, I made the decision to bring the communication to a close, as to expose in more detail a possible criminal lifestyle that was unknown to them would be pointless and counterproductive in dealing with their grief. Not only that, the police were listening in too!

I found it unsettling that I was demonstrating the same protective characteristics in limiting the spiritual truth as Sam had shown towards me. Was I a terrible hypocrite, or was this the right choice to make? Is limiting or filtering the truth a characteristic we all demonstrate at some time or another in the name of love?

Nick had been very precise about where his murderer was based and I suggested to the police they send me a map of the vicinity so I might identify the location. The police went a step further and asked me to fly to New York to visit the murder scene with a view to becoming more proactive in the case, as all their leads so far in the investigation had become dead ends.

After careful consideration of all my family responsibilities, I declined the offer. Was this a missed opportunity of becoming a spiritual liaison with American law enforcement? I'll never know. But I do know that Jenny and her family, despite their loss, still had loving and dignified memories of their father.

My next telephone call was to Maureen, to discover what had happened to Trevaline and enquire how she felt I might be able to help.

Naturally, I offered my condolences to her and her friend's family on the disappearance and their probable loss. It was shocking to think that only a few weeks prior these two ladies had attended my Shrewsbury meeting. Apparently, while at the event, Trevaline said she felt she was going to have something to do with me in the near future. Based on this revelation, Maureen believed I might offer some constructive insight into the cause of her disappearance, especially as the police investigations had drawn a complete blank.

Maureen explained that Trevaline had a son in the police force and he specifically requested I become involved in order to throw some light on the situation. It seemed the only presenting facts were that she had left a note on her shop door to say she would be back in two minutes, and her handbag, purse and keys were casually left behind the counter. Naturally the longer she was missing, the more likely she had been murdered.

On my suggestion, Maureen gathered all the family members together to give each of them an individual sitting, as I felt their combined love link might help focus Trevaline to communicate – if she had passed over.

However, not every murder victim is as articulate as Nick from New York, and sometimes it takes a good while for any new spirit to adapt to their surroundings, especially after violent death. Taking this into consideration, a viable communication might be out of the question, but it was worth trying.

One thing was for certain, I would do my best!

We agreed to gather at the Evans' holiday home on the North Wales coast. On my arrival, the small lounge seemed full of people and the prospect of speaking with everyone about Trevaline's possible death was very daunting. There were also two detectives present and they asked me to record everything that was being said for them, even though they went to great lengths to keep saying my involvement was very "unofficial".

Before I started to speak with everyone privately, I asked the group to be truthful and open. I turned specifically to Trevaline's husband and said, "This is a very important question, and I want you to think very carefully before you answer, because what you say and how you answer this question is going to have consequences."

There was a long pause before I continued, "Were you happy with your wife?"

The husband looked at me pensively, then after a short while he nodded his head and said that they were very happily married.

When I speak to people their emotions are like tissue paper to me, I see right through them. And I knew without doubt this was not a truthful answer. It was then I made a very specific and shocking statement, I announced to everyone in the room that Trevaline's body would *never* be found.

Many hours were then spent interviewing everyone that volunteered to take part in this spiritual ensemble to try and gather some vital information that might help find Trevaline, dead or alive.

With no explanation, the husband was the only person to decline a private consultation with me. However, as I gathered more and more information through spiritual communication from the rest of the group, it became apparent that Trevaline and her husband were talking of divorce and were negotiating the sharing of monetary assets.

Throughout my interviews, two names were consistent; Garth and Trevor. At first I thought they were names of people involved in the mystery, but then I realised they were two villages a short distance apart in the vicinity of Llangollen. I believed this location was critical to the disappearance, and coincidentally it transpired there was a chemical factory in that vicinity where the husband worked.

It was so sad to see Trevaline's only son, a young man in his prime, trying to understand how and why his loving mother had just disappeared. By the end of the day I had gathered over five hours of recorded information which was handed over to the police – unofficially of course!

There must have been plenty of useful information as days later one of the police officers contacted me and asked if I would join in a hunt on the Welsh mountains in the vicinity of Llangollen in the hope that I might offer some more spiritual insight.

On the day, there were officers on the ground and a police helicopter overhead complete with specialised body detecting equipment. This invitation made me feel very much part of an organised search team – albeit unofficially!

To offer greater flexibility, I decided that Richard should drive me in our own car as this would enable me to better concentrate on focusing on the job in hand. We spent hours driving around to locations selected by the police in the hope I might offer some spiritual insight.

Were my spiritual feelings useful? Well, we never found Trevaline's body, but that was no surprise as I told everyone at my first meeting that her body would never be found!

This prediction stands true to the present day, over a quarter of a century later!

Nevertheless, with all the extensive amount of fresh information that I offered, it contributed towards a reconstruction of events that was filmed for the prime-time television program *Crimewatch*, in the hope it might prompt some additional memories from the public that could help solve the mystery.

These two very different murder victims demonstrate that spiritual communication is not a science, and how its success is affected by seemingly random factors and circumstances. It also clarifies that my role in these circumstances is limited to offer mutually consenting spiritual communication between two dimensions, not to interrogate the spiritual realm for hardcore answers – however important they might seem.

Only days after his death, Nick was eloquent, accurate and specific with his communication, in contrast to Trevaline who was unable to establish the most fundamental spiritual link with me. It is this disparity in results that unfortunately fuels the scepticism and criticism from the non-believer in anything spiritual. However, for the free-thinking individual, the lack of continuity in a uniform standard of spiritual communication should not be the basis to wantonly reject the existence of the spiritual dimension or its potential to help us in our daily lives.

During the week I was helping with the Trevaline investigation, my mother had started to recover from her operation and become much stronger. It was time for her to come out of hospital and she had no alternative but to move back in with Aunty Joan.

In fact, Mum's house was not going well. The building work was so bad, we had to bring everything to a standstill pending the outcome of a private surveyor's report we had instructed to itemise the catalogue of mistakes.

I was so upset that I couldn't offer her a home with me. With little progress from our own builders, I had no idea if we would be able to return home in her lifetime.

It was with this problem in mind I asked the spiritual consciousness for guidance on how to best resolve our homelessness. The answer became clear, we should look at moving into a new house altogether. And so Richard and I looked at new houses being built in Llandudno.

We spoke to Macbrydes, the builders, and they reassured us we could take possession and move in by October. Apparently, with a four-month build time, it was quicker to construct a new house than have the old one repaired!

Mindful of the doctor's prognosis that my mother would be lucky to be alive by Christmas, Richard and I decided to make the move, and contracts were signed. At least we had some light at the end of the tunnel. The whole process was made easier when Robert, Richard's brother, seeking his own independence, agreed to buy our bungalow from us, as he was more than willing to wait for the repairs to be completed, thus enabling our lives to progress forward.

We received more good news! The Talardy Hotel had two vacant rooms as the former occupants had fortunately moved back into their own homes. At least by changing hotels, we would be back in our local vicinity and drastically reduce school travelling times.

Meanwhile, I had to concentrate my energies on organising the Gateway Theatre, the September date of which was fast coming around, and thereafter a second appearance at the Wolverhampton Civic.

Fortunately, Richard had managed to secure me a couple of interviews on local radio stations to talk about my work and mention my upcoming events. However, it was emphasised that I was categorically forbidden to reunite the listeners with their loved ones through spiritual communication, as apparently this was prohibited by the Independent Broadcasters Association's regulations. For the broadcasters, this regulation was a commandment written in stone!

Despite having my spiritual abilities completely censored, the majority of listeners loved to hear me talk about my spiritual anecdotes with Sam and my other guides.

It was during one of these interviews with the popular DJ Steve Rhodes, I voiced to one of my callers some definite medical problems he was experiencing, pinpointing that he was stone deaf in his left ear, a problem that stemmed back to his early childhood. Naturally the caller was shocked as he knew there was no way I could have known about his disability. After he confirmed everything was true, a subsequent caller was put through to chastise me. Their criticism was I could have identified the previous caller's deafness by detecting the way he was holding the telephone receiver. How ridiculous! If it was the station's intent to undermine my spiritual abilities, measured by such inane remarks, it didn't seem to work!

I noticed that callers weren't randomly put through to speak to me on air; they were screened and selected to express a bias of opinion. So when I talked to a supporter of my work, it seemed the station would make sure there would be a line of confrontational callers to follow in an attempt to antagonise me and provide entertainment through our conflict.

On this same occasion, I actually experienced a death vendetta against me. A Born Again Christian was given the opportunity to attack me with a barrage of insults and openly stated that as I was a heretic, I should be publicly burnt at the stake as was Christian practice in years gone by. When asked by Rhodes if she meant figuratively speaking, she announced she believed I literally needed to be burnt to death! I was flabbergasted. How do you respond to that sort of bigoted opinion? More specifically, why would any responsible broadcaster want that or any other violent statement said to their guest?

In retaliation, and despite the gagging requirement put upon me, I defiantly reunited the next caller with her mother in the spirit world, as I felt this lovely lady was truly in need. Once I started to be so rebellious, I could see the telephone switchboard suddenly light up with callers and, according to the operators, they were all wanting me to reunite them with their own deceased loved ones.

My actions caused a right rumpus! Within seconds, about five radio personnel appeared at the studio window giving me signals to immediately stop or I would be unplugged! One even held a piece of card up reading, 'Stop it or we will cut you.'

Rhodes, despite being very concerned about upsetting his paymasters, was thrilled at the boost in caller traffic. In a rather cavalier manner, he stalled my unplugging and signalled to his team to keep the show going and the calls coming. However, I am convinced his intent was for showmanship rather than to help enlighten his listeners.

What was really wonderful, in the aftermath of the show, was that countless messages of love and support from the people came flooding into my office. I had given spiritual messages live on air, and the listeners loved it and they wanted more.

But, as usual, the media censors forbade it!

17

A Glass Half Full or Half Empty?

"The things you take for granted,
someone else might well be praying for"
~Author Unknown~

A healing thought for us from my Spirit Guide Sam:
When we are stressed with life's burdens and anger engrosses us,
help to keep us on the path of positivity and light.
Bring love and communication to us through open channels,
so we may receive higher energy to balance our lives.
Allow our minds to fill with love to fuel our hearts,
allow our lives to fill with determination, so we may be driven with
divine purpose.
In doing so, may we then achieve the positive outcomes we seek.
We send thanks to you, our guides, angels and the eternal spirit
consciousness,
so you will always protect and love us,
letting us share and bathe in your energy and light.

Quite often, people who know they are terminally ill talk about
making a 'bucket list' of things they want to experience before
they die. My mum was no different. When we talked about

this, she said she would really love the children to have a truly memorable experience with her, something special they would hold dear for the rest of their lives. After a family meeting, we all agreed that a trip to Disney World, Florida would be the ideal place. Even though Mum looked so well, we had no idea if she would have the stamina for such a long journey, nor did we know how much time she had left.

The cruelty of many cancers is that even after diagnosis, the sufferer can look and feel relatively normal, despite their body being a terminal time-bomb. Sometimes, sufferers are unaware they are stricken until the cancer grows into an unstoppable force. We all loved my mum beyond words, and I lived in hope she would fight the disease to stay with us longer. I pleaded with her to consider having some chemotherapy treatment, but she always said no as she just wanted to be with my dad – nothing was going to deter her.

Even so, in the weeks following my mother's terminal diagnosis, she did become increasingly curious about the spiritual and wanted answers. Despite knowing our time together was short, it was really lovely to chat openly with Mum about the spirit dimension and what she might expect when her journey there eventually began.

It wasn't long before she agreed to have some regular healing sessions from me. I relished the prospect of building up her strength to fight her illness. I was determined to do what I could to help her.

The doctors implied that Mum wouldn't make it to Christmas, but I reassured her that by focusing on positive goals, it would bring an enhanced quality of life. Hope, positivity and determination are strong medicines and should not be undervalued.

Respectful of her limitations, I asked Mum if we could arrange to go to Disney in the October, just before my return visit to the Wolverhampton Civic Hall on the 8th November. She was absolutely thrilled, as it was something for her and the children to look forward to.

Unfortunately, I could no longer offer private appointments from home, but Richard had recently converted the upstairs of his Rhyl shop into the most beautiful offices so we could jointly use them. They were ideal because they had their own entrance facing on to the main road, three large office rooms, a reception and a separate area that could be used for a waiting room.

My new offices became the ideal place to offer healing appointments to Mum and she welcomed the opportunity to begin her treatment.

"You have nothing to lose and everything to gain," I said, smiling into my mother's eyes as I stood over her while she lay horizontal on the therapy bed.

"What do I do?" Mum asked nervously.

"You don't have to do anything," I reassured her. "I just want you to close your eyes and relax. As you start to relax, I will lay my hands above your body so I can spiritually connect with your aura. Then I will ask you some questions, and I want you to tell me what you can feel or if you see any colours."

"What is an aura?" Mum asked.

I tried to offer a simple explanation. "It's like an energy overcoat that surrounds your body. The energy aura can change shape, it can vary in thickness around the body and contain many different colours that alter depending on your mood, your health, and what you're experiencing in life. At the moment, your aura is looking particularly thin and fragmented, which is because of your illness."

Mum was more than inquisitive. "And what do all the colours mean?"

I was hoping to do just a simple healing session, but this was fast turning into a spiritual tutorial! At least Mum was now taking a genuine interest in how I administered the spiritual healing to my clients.

"There is a common misconception that each colour has a specific meaning. Some people say that red *means* passion, yellow *means* optimism and purple *means* spirituality, but this is not the case, as you have to take into consideration that the different tones and shades of the same colour represent different meanings. So trying to establish a specific meaning for one colour really does oversimplify the matter. As my spiritual sight is very progressed, I am able to use the vast variation in colour tone and shade to assist in establishing a more accurate indication of your body's health and well-being."

Mum asked, "How can I see these colours with my eyes closed?"

I explained, "Quite often the healing can stimulate your own spiritual essence, so that your mind can sense the predominant colours of your aura more easily, especially with your eyes closed."

To prepare myself to give healing, I slowly took three deep breaths. I always start this way, so my brain intuitively knows that I am preparing for my altered state to channel the spiritual healing energy.

"Wow! That's some heat!" Mum said as I extended my hands over her face.

"Just open your eyes for a moment," I requested.

She saw that my hands were about ten inches away from her body.

"How can that be?" she said, surprised. "How can I feel so much heat when your hands are so far away?"

I looked down at my mother's beautiful face, as yet, it was not ravaged by the cancers within her. When you are young and in the prime of your life, it is not uncommon to feel your parents are immortal and they will always be there for you. It was difficult to believe that in a few months this awful illness would take my darling Mum away. I wanted to cry.

Quickly, I pulled myself together and answered her question as plainly as I could. "It's because there is so much healing energy radiating from my hands."

"Well, what will happen next?" she asked,

"Don't worry, there's nothing to fear," I said. "Your guides and angels are here by our side offering healing help to you."

A little unnerved, Mum turned her head to see if she could see anything.

I chuckled. "You aren't likely to see anything, but you will feel the powerful healing energy as it swamps through your body. It has a comforting feeling like someone has put a heated blanket around you."

I went on to explain that many people report they experience great warmth or even cold radiating from my hands, depending on whether positive or negative energy was being administered. My clients often think that negative energy is a bad energy, but when using it through the channel of healing, it is just used as a balance so that the positive energy doesn't become overly strong.

I knew my mother was feeling immense heat from my hands as her face was flushing bright red.

I continued, "The healing help that is administered through me from the spiritual dimension comes in many different forms. Whereas conventional medicine treats a specific area of your body, spiritual healing treats your whole body, your mind and your spirit. Generally, I am assisted by all manner of healing entities from the spirit world, depending on what my client needs."

With a puzzled look, Mum asked, "What do you mean you have healing entities helping you?"

"Well, I am the vessel or conduit that delivers the healing energy to my client from a very powerful source. There are many that visit me to assist while I am healing. Amongst them are medical doctors and other health workers who have lived an earthly life, as they still want to help and continue their life's work. For instance, Harry Edwards and Doctor Clarke are two such spirit people who attend with me on a very regular basis."

I could sense my mother becoming a little disconcerted at the thought of all these visitations happening around her, but she looked at me in total fascination.

"Doctor Clarke was introduced to me by Sam many years ago when I was a teenager. Apparently, when he was alive he was a medical practitioner in London. In recent years, Clarke has taken a major role in helping me with my healing work. Harry Edwards was, in his day, a very famous spiritual healer who in 1954 filled the Royal Albert Hall with his healing demonstrations. In 1955 he founded and was the first president of the National Federation of Spiritual Healers."

At this time, during the late 1980s and early 1990s, when I was actively healing a client, Edwards seemed to be always there working with me.

Watching my mother attentively listening to my every word, I became overwhelmed with emotion and gently stroked her cheek with the palm of my hand.

"Quite often angels attend during a healing session, but their energy is totally different than any other spiritual presence. Their role is to impart an emotional essence of sorts. They may bring compassion, forgiveness, humour, love, understanding – whatever it is that person in need requires at that time to help them progress through their current situation."

"I thought Sam was your guide and he did everything."

"Yes, he is my main guide, and he certainly helps me all the time, but there are many guides and angels who help us in our daily lives."

"So, who is my guide?"

Instantly my mother's guide walked forward from the corner of the room where she had been standing next to Sam. I had seen her countless times before and never far from my mother. To me, she appeared to be in her forties and had beautiful feminine features. She looked tenderly towards my mother and then to me, and identified herself as Rosalinda. Her presence was compassionate and caring.

I introduced my mother to her guide and I described in detail everything I could see about her. My mother seemed to find great comfort in knowing Rosalinda was always with her. There was true empathy in my mother's expression and I genuinely believed she wanted to experience more.

"Helen, can you help my illness in any way?" There was a plea in her voice and she searched my eyes for her answer.

With a deep breath, I began the task of making simple an answer of infinitely complex possibilities. "Firstly, you must understand spiritual healing is a way that a person can connect to their own natural spiritual energy, and by treating a person as a 'whole', it will encourage the mind, body and spirit to work together in unison, to encourage harmony within the whole being."

Mum seemed totally overwhelmed by my explanation.

"I can't explain everything I've learned in my lifetime during one healing session, we will probably need many more chats about how I can help you during the many stages of your illness."

Like my mother, many people in the past have turned to me for spiritual healing as a last resort, when every other health practitioner had given up on them. However, fortunately in more recent times, I have found that more people are asking to see me as a first resort in trying to balance their health.

To make the point, I explained to Mum. "I never advocate spiritual healing as being an alternative to conventional medicine,

I always suggest it is used alongside or as an adjunct to the conventional. That's why I really feel you should participate in the doctor's treatment plan alongside your healing sessions with me. And, Mum, be warned, no matter how well you feel after your healing sessions, you should never alter your medication unless told to do so by your doctor."

From my standpoint, my brand of healing is not territorial. It doesn't matter who or what makes the patient better, as long as they ultimately enjoy positive improvement in their health.

"Actually, Mum, I always stress that when participating in a course of healing sessions there is no guarantee or promise of cure in advance – spiritual healing is not a magic cure-all. It must conform to the physical and spiritual laws that govern each and every living being. Naturally, within the scope of these laws there is a great deal that can be achieved ranging from no help at all prior to your healing experience, to varying degrees of positive results and reaching up to a possible full hundred per cent cure."

And then my mother asked me the hardest question I could ever possibly answer. "Can you cure me, Helen?"

This was going to be a tough one to answer – a very tough one!

I knew the right answer was not a matter of whether I could totally heal someone or not, it was about understanding my specific role in the spiritual healing process. My mind was overloaded with thousands of words, and I searched for the right combination to reply to such a direct question from my own terminally ill mother.

"What I have learnt over the years is there is no known organic disease, irrespective of its cause, that cannot be helped in some way through the power of healing energy. Nevertheless, I am unable to change any congenital birth defects a person may have by making a new body part grow, but I can help the conditions associated with it. Likewise, as with any disease, there is a point from which there is no return and I can only manage the eventual outcome."

I could sense my mother trying to process what I was saying to her. "But, *can* you cure me, Helen?"

I looked down at my mother. I knew how progressed these cancers were within her and how they had taken hold of her whole body. My eyes filled with tears. I swallowed nervously as I knew a total cure was not my decision to make. I can never promise anything to anyone – that is not my role. Nevertheless, countless people have written to me and reported how they have improved or been totally cured after my healing sessions with them, even when their situation was dire. However, when the illness is debilitating or at worse imminently terminal like my mother's, there are times my healing sessions can only ease the pain and enhance the feeling of well-being. Even so, I have noticed at these times that even the most modest improvement achieved is a major accomplishment for the recipient – a miracle no less! Such changes can improve the quality of life substantially, to a level that we would otherwise take for granted.

During terminal illness, I can help significantly with coming to terms with the disease and perhaps ending the associated denial. I can also help someone to overcome the fear of death and to understand in a positive way the natural process of passing over into the spirit world.

I smiled at Mum and squeezed her hand lovingly. "What I can promise you is I will work as hard as I can to arrest the cancer growth, to control the pain and maximise your quality of life."

My answer fell short of offering a full cure, and my mother looked at me with realisation in her eyes.

"Your doctors have told you the seriousness of the problem, so for me it is going to be like turning back a very high tide. If you truly want to fight this illness, you will also have to do your part in the process, which will require you to participate in some absent healing to help boost your energy levels when I am not with you."

I could see my mother was trying desperately to figure out how to handle her own mortality.

"How do you know where to do the healing?"

I tried to reply as simply as I could. "When I am healing I can see right through people's bodies as if it is like tissue-thin layers of an onion. It is as if I can see or sense broken bones, diseased and malfunctioning organs, blood disorders, hormone imbalances, all sorts really, even illness that has been, or that is current, or that is going to happen."

She clearly found this information hard to process. So I asked her to once again close her eyes and relax.

During my healing sessions, I will place my hands on or above the problematic areas and more specifically on the various chakra points, of which there are seven major recognised chakras, however some fraternities recognise a total of fourteen. In my experience there are many more, generally not recognisable by the majority of other healers.

Having said that, more importantly is the network of energy paths which links together all these chakra points. Fundamentally, the chakra points are the gateway or portal linking into the aura. They act like funnels through which this energy network joins together the whole system, passing waves of energy through each chakra, and then through into the aura, an interconnection of physical and spiritual.

When our bodies are in equilibrium this continuous flow of energy encourages our body to maintain a healthy condition and will naturally rebalance the system for minor imbalances. However, when illness is more severe, the chakras can 'tighten up', or sometimes even 'close up', which results in the slowing down of any natural self-healing process. It is my role to stimulate the chakras to 'open up' back to their original condition and stimulate energy flow so the system will work more efficiently to naturally rebalance itself.

In reality I see a total mass of interconnected energy lines linking together the whole aura. This network is so prolific and complex I would need an experienced cartographer if I chose to plot them!

By spiritually accessing this network I can specifically 'tune into' the patients' blood, hormones, toxins, psychology, and complete physiology of their body to allow me a more comprehensive understanding of an individual's imbalance and needs.

As I reached my mother's stomach chakra, my hands tingled indicating to me there was pain radiating from this area. As this was a problematic area, my hands radiated more healing energy, which my mother felt in the form of increased heat. Through my spiritual sight I could see her liver was compromised with multiple tumours the doctors had yet to diagnose. I decided to keep this information to myself for the time being. Such knowledge served no purpose whatsoever to my mother at this time.

"Mum, I feel you are not telling me everything. I think you are in much more pain in this spot than you are saying. I can feel it radiating right around into your back, is that true?"

She burst into tears, and I knew I had hit the mark.

After a short while I could see by the relief on her face that the deep healing energy radiating from my hands was easing her pain.

After the session, Mum was calm and comforted. This was normal, as people regularly reported a sense of inner peace and strength in the aftermath of a spiritual healing session. She was excited by her experience and wanted to talk about everything that had happened! We had a great heart-to-heart talk about the spiritual.

I reminded her how I had tried my utmost to talk to my father about having some healing from me before he died. All of a sudden, she seemed to become an expert on healing. "Well, your healing would have been wasted on him as your dad had no faith in you or the healing, so it wouldn't have worked. Not only that, he wasn't at all religious!"

Such remarks really do expose the lack of true understanding of my spiritual work, and my mother was not the first to express their misunderstanding to me.

In an attempt to clarify, I made it clear that spiritual healing has no boundaries and it is open to everyone, regardless of age, sexual orientation, religion or culture. To demonstrate the point, I explained how I regularly healed sick animals and very young children, neither had any understanding what I was doing to them – so the healing either works or it doesn't. In such cases it cannot be a placebo, in the mind or just blind religious faith!

Obviously, no matter what type of therapy or medical treatment a person might receive, a strong positive attitude is always beneficial to any type of healing experience. However, for healing to actually work it's definitely not in any way an essential ingredient.

The day arrived for her to visit her oncologist in Liverpool and Mum had a sense of positivity about her as a result of her healing sessions. As we neared the Clatterbridge Hospital gates, I reminded her there was only so much that could be achieved with her healing and no matter what news she received from her CT scans, it was her quality of life that now mattered.

My mother's doctor worked efficiently, but was very emotionally detached from his patients. On the previous visit she was quite offended by the off-hand approach the consultant seemed to have when he talked to her about her illness. He announced in a matter-of-fact manner there was nothing more that could be done and there was no hope for her. He wasn't even sure she would be able to make the next monthly visit.

Having heard similar accounts from my other terminally ill clients, it seemed common practice at that time for medical practitioners to use such absolute expressions of profound negativity to explain an incurable condition.

So we were relieved when the receptionist informed us that Mum's original consultant was on holiday today. I hoped the stand-in would be a little kinder to her in his manner and more positive in his attitude.

Thankfully, the stand-in consultant seemed very pleased with my mother's progress, commenting that she was remarkably well considering his findings on her CT scan.

Mum was so pleased with her progress that she asked if she could have chemotherapy, believing she was now ready for the emotional commitment to the treatment.

The consultant informed her the window for chemotherapy had passed. Her tumours were abundant and he could only offer drugs to help with pain management. He explained he was amazed at her well-being and remarked that other patients in her position did not enjoy such long periods of relative good quality of life. He commented that whatever health regime she was following, it was having a definite positive effect on her welfare and she should keep it up.

So my mother's battle began – only instead of declaring war against her illness she was really making peace within herself, and so the outcome was joy, not stress. She started to learn to live with and face head-on the undeniable truth that she was soon to be leaving this earthly life. But so do we all – it's the most natural thing in the world that will happen to each and every one of us! It is not the time we are here that is important, but what we do with that time that counts.

My mum came to love her regular healing sessions with me and I noticed that after each one she would chat more openly about her experiences. She suddenly became softer, more adaptable, wanting to look deeper into the meaning of life. She talked of how she felt energised and focused on living. It was as if she was not ill at all. She seemed to look at what was important in her world, rather than looking at what was missing from her life. Never in my life had I seen her laugh so much, and everything and everybody became a joyful experience to her and she enjoyed every moment we were together.

Naturally, we shared many tears, but as the fear of her illness subsided, she adopted a more optimistic approach to life, and more than anything, she wanted to live.

She now had a chance to see how full her life really was.

For me, this was without doubt another healing miracle I was witnessing.

18

Three Minutes Please

"Start by doing what's necessary; then do what's possible;
and suddenly you are doing the impossible."
~Francis of Assisi~

"Three minutes please, Ms Parry Jones. Three minutes!"

This was it ...

Somehow the voice broadcast from the dressing-room intercom at the Chester Gateway Theatre seemed to be addressing someone else. However, it quickly dawned on me there were people actually sitting in the auditorium who had paid good money for their tickets to see me.

I recollected how Chester City Council had previously banned my event from the Town Hall to protect the local residents from me as if I was a threat to common decency, and yet here I was with my knees knocking waiting to face a sold-out auditorium.

Richard was by my side pumping me up with his energy and enthusiasm. Tonight was special, not only was this my home town, but it was the first occasion I had ever appeared in a traditional theatre.

It was time for me to leave the security of the dressing room and take up the position for my grand entrance. My heart was beating so hard I thought it was going to explode out of my chest. Nevertheless, I was very excited.

Richard walked out of the dressing room, turned quickly back to face me and gave me a smile.

"Break a leg!" he shouted in theatre tradition, our eyes met for a second of deep love.

The sound technician greeted me, identified himself as Tony, and hooked me up to the radio microphone system. He casually commented on the large mob that had gathered outside the entrance waving placards and large banners, attempting to block the entrance. Apparently, people had to physically jostle their way into the theatre through a barrage of insults from the chanting crowd. The cause of their protest was me and my God-given natural ability to communicate with the spirit world.

The troublemakers identified themselves as a group of Christians, and they felt it was their duty to denounce me as evil and demonic, and to protect others from my contamination by actively stopping them from seeing me. I didn't know whether I should be flattered or insulted that so many had gathered to make the protest. Fortunately, my audience were a robust lot and the picket line didn't stop a single person from joining my evening.

It seemed my home town was a city truly polarised – divided for or against me.

As I walked down the corridor to take up my entrance position in the front of house, the chanting grew louder. Never had I experienced so much malice towards me. Even though I was under pressure to start my evening on time, on impulse I decided to go outside to meet the crowd. After all, they didn't know me and had never witnessed my work, so I was curious to find out on what basis they felt I should be the target of their hatred.

As moral support, Tony my technician stood by as I bravely walked towards the chanting picket line. Banners and fists were shaken at me. Despite having copious amounts of adrenaline pumping around my body, I felt quite calm and fearless. In hindsight, I believe this was more from my naïvety rather than bravery.

As I approached them, the crowd jeered and hissed in unison as if I was the wicked witch making an appearance in a Christmas pantomime. I was appalled that my audience had to brave the same verbal abuse to enter the theatre.

It was difficult to make myself heard above the senseless bawling, but despite the noise, I offered two of their leaders the opportunity to join my audience. I suggested they might want to listen to me talk and experience the love my evenings inspire, and afterwards they could put their questions to me during the 'question time' so everyone could hear in a positive manner what they had to say.

Their stance was intransigent. My Christian critics refused this opportunity and instead continued to chant for my eternal damnation. The zealots' furore escalated and I genuinely started to fear for my welfare. Alarmed by the change in atmosphere, Tony took my arm and led me in fast retreat back into the theatre while the delirious crowd defiantly roared a new chant, "There's the devil! There's the devil! There's the devil!"

After listening to such base abuse, I must admit I felt alone and isolated. I so much wanted to cry, but I was determined not to be undermined by their behaviour.

Once safely back inside, their violent manner prompted me to question myself. I considered their opinions carefully in case they had any validity. I reasoned most religions promote an afterlife, so why is it not possible I could actually see it? Actually, it does not seem logical for one religion alone to have the monopoly on the spiritual realm, does it? That would be rather elitist, I felt. Would I consider the particular religious group to which you belong sufficient criteria for you to be considered a good or bad person? Surely good or bad comes from within an individual, not the religious creed they follow?

On balance, my rationality would not give their claims any credence.

Despite these questions going over in my mind, I realised countless wars had been fought and millions of lives pointlessly lost fighting over these same arguments. I doubted I could solve thousands of years of misguided religious dogma in one night.

After careful consideration and in simple reconciliation, I asked myself why I did what I did – the answer was crystal clear – love. By focusing on offering true love to people, I knew without any doubt I had a pure heart and my message was true.

Tony was now urging me to make my entrance as the start had already been delayed for too long.

My nerves started to take hold of me again and as a result of the protest outside, doubt crept into my mind. What if the messages didn't come through? What if I froze?

I took a deep breath and focused on Sam's loving smile which instantly filled my heart with strength and confidence. My faith in myself, my guides, angels and my God-given gifts, was as strong as ever.

In the background, the ranting rabble were still chanting for my blood.

"Get thee behind me Satan!" I commanded under my breath.

Sensing my nerves, a stage technician smiled and reassuringly squeezed my arm, "Don't pay any attention to that lot, they don't know what they're talking about. You are no more the devil than my own Mum! You are a lovely lady, Helen. Go out there and just show them what for."

He counted down my entry, "Three … two … one … go!"

I wanted my audience to expect the unexpected, so I entered from the rear of the auditorium, which naturally caused everyone's head to turn in surprise. As the spotlight highlighted my journey down the centre aisle, it felt like the night had taken on a dream-like quality. The applause from the audience sounded like a thousand galloping horses. Many stood up to greet me with hugs and handshakes as I walked past. Their loving welcome was what I needed right now to wipe clean the vile experience from the crowd outside.

On the stage ahead of me I could see a forest of fresh flowers and shrubs kindly donated for the evening by the world famous Grosvenor Garden Centre. It smelt as though everyone was sitting in a natural meadow rather than a packed auditorium.

No going back now, I told myself. I was on my own – but hopefully not for long.

Uncannily, the first person I laid eyes upon walking through the audience was the brother of the missing Trevaline Evans. This had now become a high-profile murder enquiry, especially in North Wales. I doubted there was a person in the audience that hadn't heard of the strange and tragic circumstances surrounding this case. However, the audience were not aware I had been working with the Welsh CID in connection with trying to find the missing body.

He caught my eye and smiled at me. I could sense his loss and the frustration he had to endure, as after so much police investigation his sister's body was still missing. I suppose he was hoping she might communicate with me that evening. But, as the investigation was so high profile and I knew the family quite well by now through my association with the search, it would not be appropriate to offer any messages in front of a large audience as it might seem like a publicity stunt. I didn't want to give my critics any cause to undermine my abilities. However, if Trevaline was to communicate, I would be sure to deliver the message to him privately afterwards.

Slowly I walked up the steps onto the stage.

As I took centre stage I could see Sam standing to the side, his face lit up into a proud smile. It was now time to show to my audience how spiritual love can ripple out and touch every person's heart that is open enough to allow it in.

I will never forget the first spirit to communicate that night as he was such a jovial chap. While pointing at the excessive floral arrangement on stage, the first thing he said, "Oh my God, look at this forest. It looks like the bloody three bears are going to jump out at me." Sharing that wonderful dry sense of humour, the audience burst into laughter.

As far as I was concerned, this was typical of how spirits can offer confirmation of their existence by displaying their true personality as their family would remember. People don't expect spiritual communication to be full of humour, but it most often is, and those in spirit will endeavour to demonstrate that side of their personality to establish their presence. Conversation with spirit visitors can be as amusing or even as downright dull as when they were living!

My experience with mortality has taught me some people wrongly believe that the young are in some way immune from the disabling emotions of grief. This is most definitely not so. Youth does not protect you from being totally devastated by the passing of a loved one.

This was truly demonstrated that night when the spirit of a young man around twenty years of age came forward saying he had been killed on his motorbike. I followed his directions to find his girlfriend sitting in the audience.

Once I had successfully located her, she was near enough to the stage for me to see how her young face had been traumatised by her loss. She had a harrowingly anguished look I had seen before many times, but rarely in one so youthful.

The young man in spirit identified himself as Peter, which she acknowledged was her boyfriend's name. I described his appearance, which she instantly recognised. I knew without doubt this was going to be a moving encounter.

His fresh face smiled at me. "We were engaged and going to get married at the end of the summer."

I dutifully repeated his words. The young girl became overwhelmed with emotion and tears rolled down her face. Nevertheless, she nodded.

He continued, "We were so much in love, ever since we first met at school. We were always so happy together."

As I repeated this, the young girl struggled hard to hold back her sobs. She was unable to reply, as if the act of talking might cause her to lose total control of her emotions and expose her raw grief. Instead, she just nodded furiously for a few seconds with her lips tightly squeezed together.

"He is saying he has been in the spirit world for just over two years, but for both of you, it seems like it was only yesterday he passed over."

The young girl nervously bit into a tatty piece of white tissue she was holding. With three quick nods, she gave her confirmation.

I felt a slight chill as Peter's spiritual essence changed slightly. From experience, I knew that he was ready to access the memory of his final moments in this dimension, and the unique feelings surrounding his death.

Trying to keep his emotions under control, he spoke slowly and methodically. I repeated his every word, "I was driving to work early one morning, on my motorbike ... it was so early it was still dark ... there had been a terrible storm during the night." He paused. Peter needed to recount his story accurately so there would be no doubt in his fiancée's mind that he was standing here in front of everyone, talking directly to her.

"When I drove through the industrial park where I worked, the storm had caused quite a bit of damage to some of the construction work that was going on and unbeknown to me some temporary overhead electric cable had been disturbed. Everywhere was in total darkness as all the lights were out ... then one second later ... poof ... I was dead!"

The young girl's face was now red and swollen through crying.

I knew what was coming next, and I hoped she was strong enough to hear it in front of so many people. I asked permission to repeat what was being said to me, "Can I tell you everything he is saying about his death and how specifically he died?"

Again, with no words she nodded her head vigorously. She knew what I was going to say, but she needed to hear it out loud as no one else in that room could possibly know what happened next, only her beloved deceased fiancé.

Even in these truly intimate moments that I share with people, sometimes I can feel an element of doubt from them. As much as a person wants to believe I am in spiritual communication with their loved one, there is a part of them that subconsciously installs a protective barrier which can be counterproductive in the communication process, especially in large audiences. However, on this occasion my link with the spirit world was too strong to have the communication hindered, and I could hear Peter's words crystal clear.

"Unknowingly, Peter had driven across a fallen electric wire that had been temporarily erected, and due to the speed he was driving, the wire garrotted him. It killed him instantly."

Relating this catastrophe caused a loud and unified gasp from the audience.

How could anybody not be moved by this tragic story? After feeling the emotional pain of these two childhood sweethearts, there didn't seem to be one dry eye in the house. I had to stop talking for a moment to compose myself and with the back of my hand wiped away the tears that burned at my face.

So you see, it is not easier for young people to deal with death and to come to terms with a lost loved one just because there is more life ahead of them. In my experience, even the young can be trapped in so much grief their life cannot move forward in any way, sealed into some sort of limbo where time stands completely still.

Peter had been in spirit for over two years and yet his fiancée's emotions were still so raw. Her days were spent locked in the past, not only grieving for the loss of her betrothed, but also grieving over the loss of the future she would have had with him. She needed to be freed from these burdens and be open to new relationships and new opportunities. She needed to heal and live. Peter knew this, and that is one reason why he had come today to communicate. But what he said next was as painful for him to say as it was for the young girl to hear.

"He is telling me you have to let him go. He knows how hard this will be for you, but through love, this is something you must find in your own heart to do."

Without any hesitation she cried out loudly, "No! No! I can't! I don't want to let him go. I love him far too much! Ours was a forever love."

She gasped deeply for a breath of air, and then sobbed inconsolably.

Peter continued with his spiritual message of love and in turn I had to deliver this unwelcome guidance. "Peter is telling me that the love the two of you have shared is so very special, and nobody can ever take away the wonderful memories you made together. He is saying that these are your joint experiences, and they will be part of the very essence of both of you for eternity. Having new experiences will not in any way devalue what the two of you had together. However, now you must open your heart and allow new people into your life, this is natural and you shouldn't bear any guilt for allowing this to happen. Peter is saying that soon a new admirer is going to come forward and want to be in your life."

In a flash, the young girl sat bolt upright and shook her head at the prospect of new love. This was something she did not want to hear or happen; this was a future she was not willing to accept.

"Peter is telling me he knows this is hard for you to comprehend right now, but one day you are going to be an incredible wife and a loving mother. And he truly wants this for you. He doesn't want any more tears for him. It is because he loves you so much he needs you to wake up fresh in the morning and move forward to have a wonderful life."

My role is not just to deliver a spiritual message, but to create the healing environment in which an individual stricken by grief can, through spiritual communication, find closure and move forward to lead a positive full life. This is the true essence of spiritual communication.

Are spiritual messages a form of healing? Yes, most definitely, I do believe they are.

Much later, the evening finished with enthusiastic applause. The undignified spectacle that met my audience when they arrived had now been moved on by the police.

Once again, I was disappointed that my invitations to the local press to attend and witness first-hand the love that is inspired by the interaction between two dimensions, had been ignored.

However, the next day I was invited for an interview by local journalist John Eccles. He had heard about the protesters outside the theatre and wanted to know more. Under normal circumstances I probably would have declined, but I had been interviewed by Eccles before and he had published some positive articles about my work, so a part of me felt I could trust his integrity to write a fair and honest piece.

Eccles didn't negatively respond to me in the way other journalists had in the past, with their eyes focused on scepticism and their pen eager to adjust the truth to devalue the seriousness of my work. He seemed to interview me with an intellectual understanding of the spiritual dimension and he was not swayed by misguided prejudice. He could see I was upset by the way my audience had been harangued by the protesters blocking the theatre and by how they almost lost their restraint to physically attack me when I tried to reason with them. He was sympathetic when I explained how for the life of me I couldn't understand why seemingly normal people would want to treat me in such a militant and violent manner.

Eccles believed he had the answer, and he suggested I should research a well-documented historical Christian event dating back nearly two thousand years, called the Council of Nicaea. He felt, in his opinion, this event was the birth of much prejudice against non-conformists.

At that time, I had never even heard of this, but now I was eager to find out more. After much research in the library, I discovered a very plausible explanation why people's views had become so entrenched over the years they felt justified in denouncing me. My understanding, Christianity as we have known it for the past 2000 years, was formulated by a council of bishops called together by the Roman emperor for political expediency, and in the process, interpretations and perspectives were changed to make a common religious policy. In addition, any deviation from this new religion was harshly punished, frequently by death. With such a violent enforcement of intolerance over so many hundreds of years, it's no wonder, really, that a fear of difference or deviation from the 'teachings' of Christianity still remains. If you would like to read a more detailed account of my personal interpretation, I have positioned a paragraph below for you to read.

However, on a more positive note, Jesus of Nazareth was said by his followers to be an outspoken promoter of survival after death and was always talking openly of the afterlife. Whenever the situation arose, he helped the sick with his healing hands, made a point of encouraging the most fundamental of morality – "love everyone, treat others as you would want them to treat you and you reap what you sow" – and when he did depart from his physical body, they say he specifically came back to tell his family and friends he was fit and well and having a productive life in his new spiritual surroundings.

For me, I find it difficult to understand the bigoted hostility and aversion towards me when his teachings of love and life after death are at the very heart of my own work ethic.

Council of Nicaea:
As most of us remember from our school days, Julius Caesar first invaded England in 55 BC and subsequent Roman emperors made their mark for over 400 years of occupation. It is no secret in those early days we were predominantly Druids and Celts, now often referred to as pagans.

However, the Romans had their own gods, and many of them.

The Roman Empire dominated most of the lands facing onto the Mediterranean Sea and beyond. These many countries were home to a multitude of religions. It is therefore no surprise the rulers of the empire spent a fortune policing this multicultural and multi-religious land, especially sorting out the skirmishes created by people fighting over their own particular gods.

It was the forward-thinking Emperor Constantine in the early 4th century AD who realised the empire would be much easier to manage if there was only one religion to bond everyone together – a state religion no less.

When he was younger, he had worshipped the pantheon of Roman gods as all his predecessors had done. However, in AD 312, before going into a battle, history has reported he had a vision of a Roman labarum (a military standard) with the "Chi-Rho" symbol (the first two Greek letters of the word Christ) displayed, which was used at that time to symbolize Jesus. In the vision, Constantine apparently saw the words, In hoc signo vinces – "In this sign you shall conquer".

Luckily for the Church, there was a bishop nearby to offer an interpretation to the vision. In his opinion, if Constantine fought in the name of Christ he would win the battle.

On the 18th September AD 324, Constantine, with his army's shields painted with the Chi-Rho, defeated the Emperor Licinius, who ruled the richer Eastern provinces of the empire, in what was ultimately a religious war, at the Battle of Chrysopolis. Licinius's loyalties were to the traditional Roman gods who had stood the empire in good stead for centuries.

After winning the battle, and becoming the unquestioned sole leader of the empire, Constantine had the opportunity to unify the new wave of fractious Jesus Christ cults that were spreading across his empire into one strong, identifiable body.

In AD 325 Constantine invited 1800 Christian bishops from across the empire to meet at Nicaea (present-day Iznik in Turkey), to discuss their regional religious differences and agree upon a "common religious policy".

Constantine's Council of Nicaea was not well attended and only about 300 bishops actually showed up.

For about two months the bishops argued and debated, each appealing to the Scriptures to justify their varying religious positions.

Many changes were made to ecclesiastical texts and even important religious dates were adjusted to fit into the traditional Roman festival calendar.

Naturally the bishops argued at great length debating their differences, and when they couldn't agree, Emperor Constantine had the final say... unquestionably.

Eventually, after much discussion, the new version of the Christian faith was born. However, there was one discrepancy. The translations were unclear in the debate on the difference between Jesus of Nazareth being "born" or "created" or being "begotten". Although they all agreed to recognise the God-Trinity, the debate about exactly what it meant wasn't concluded.

Nevertheless, Constantine was able to outlaw the traditional Roman pagan sacrifices and enforce his new 'Christian Religion Common Policy' on all the subjects of the empire. His brand-new State Religion.

All the valuable property and treasures of the Roman pagan temples were confiscated and used to pay for the construction of new Christian churches. This massive investment by the state into the Church's infrastructure was enthusiastically welcomed by the Church leaders, as it automatically elevated their status within the mainstream society of the empire.

As sole lawmaker, Constantine was terribly severe and enforced the new Christianity using beating and torture as the consequence of any resistance. For most people, it wasn't a hard choice, you either willingly embraced and joined the new Christian religion or risked the possibility of a painful death.

So religion became the property of the state, and the Head of State had the full backing of God – that being the one Christian God.

After fifty years of the newly formed Roman State Christianity, many of the bishops were still offering their own personal interpretation about the God-Trinity to their local congregation, which caused much friction in the ecclesiastical hierarchy. So, in order to clear up any misunderstanding, in AD 381, Theodosius, the ruling emperor, issued a decree in which all his subjects were required to subscribe to a specific interpretation of the Trinity of the Father, Son and Holy Spirit. This ultimate ruling was to define Christianity for the next two millennia; all other interpretations were now declared heretical.

To give this major ruling a more independent taste, Theodosius ordered the bishops to have a meeting to reach this same conclusion, known as the Council of Constantinople.

This tightening of Church rules was intended to bring cohesion to the people of the Roman Empire, which was coming under increasing threat from its enemies. Free thinking and education had now been successfully eradicated completely for the majority. Reading, writing and education were now only taught to the select few in the aristocracy and the Church hierarchy.

By the end of the fourth century, Christianity became the dominant religion in the Roman Empire. For the first time in a thousand years of Greco-Roman civilisation, free religious thought was explicitly suppressed, even outlawed.

The Church flourished while the Western Roman Empire went into decline, and the whole of Western Europe was plunged into the Dark Ages after Rome was sacked at the end of the 5th century.

The historic strength of the Roman army lay in its ability to fight ruthlessly under any circumstances. The old Roman gods rewarded the soldiers' ferociousness and the pursuit of dying with military honour, however the non-violent and pacifist Christian ethic ultimately drained the armies of their brutality.

However, as the empire faded, the Church was so well-established into the fabric of society, the new rulers adopted it as a perfect political tool to control the population and instill fear into their subjects.

Non-conformity or resistance resulted in torture or death – conveniently in God's name.

If fate had Licinius winning the battle back in the day, we would probably all be worshipping the traditional Roman gods throughout Europe. Now there's a thought!

19

Music to my Ears

"When words fail, music speaks."
~Hans Christian Andersen~

Watching my mother racing around Disney World with endless energy, it was hard to believe she was dying. Her only treatment at this time was my regular healing sessions. She looked and felt so well. However, I was under no illusion … this remission was not going to give me false hope of any type of happy ending.

All the Floridian theme parks were amazing! I was so happy Mum was fulfilling her wish and having the time of her life with us. These memories would be forever treasured.

It was while visiting Pleasure Island at Lake Buena Vista, a part of the Disney experience, I enjoyed a chance encounter with a most interesting and remarkable woman. Although I believe it is right that I treat everyone equally, my guilty pleasure is overly enjoying spiritual communication for people that have extraordinary lifestyles, and today I was going to be indulged.

We all sat down for a brief rest and to savour the ambience of the carnival style sideshows. Ahead of me was a queue of about thirty-five people waiting patiently to enter a very grand tent where a 'gypsy fortuneteller' advertised her psychic readings.

As I idly watched all the people queuing up, a young black woman joined the end of the line. She looked no different to many other tourists, brightly dressed in a stripy t-shirt and blue denim shorts, with long multi-coloured socks and spotlessly clean new trainers. Her large white smile and confident attitude reinforced my impression she was an American.

I turned to my family and said, "You see that young woman over there, she is the one that has the most need of a spiritual message in the long line of people. Sam is suggesting she needs to speak with me as a matter of urgency." Then, after a short pause, I added, "Come on, we are going to stand behind her."

I stood up and grabbed Richard's hand to pull him to the back of the queue. Mum said she would sit and wait with the children.

Americans are very friendly and so it didn't take long before the lady started to talk to us, and it wasn't much of a surprise when the conversation came around to psychic phenomena. That gave me the ideal opportunity to mention in passing my own spiritual sight. She embraced this revelation enthusiastically and invited me to offer what I could 'see' for her.

Even though we were surrounded by people, everyone was so wrapped up in their own conversations, it gave us the privacy we needed to converse discreetly.

With absolute frankness I explained, "I can see you constantly writing, perhaps in the capacity as a professional journalist. Your words are very powerful and influential people are directly affected by what you say and how you write. Also, I feel you have recently written a book about political life."

Her eyes shone with excitement and she replied, "Actually, I am a political journalist and I have just finished writing a book, which is soon to be published."

Now I had established a good link, the information was swamping me and I didn't want to stop. "Your book is very important. It's not a fictional story, but more about the political hierarchy in American politics and its interaction with the rest of the world. Once your book has been published, you will be travelling to South Africa as you have links with the Mandelas."

"That's very true! Actually, I am a close friend of Winnie."

"I can see you travelling to Saudi Arabia too, but this is much sooner, almost imminent."

"Yes, I am leaving for Saudi in about two weeks' time!"

And so the conversation went on; it drifted into things of a more personal nature, namely about her mother and family. The spiritual link continued to be strong and the messages profound.

It was then my link with Sam was disturbed. A spiritual entity with a female appearance joined him. They both stretched out their arms and the ends of their little fingers touched momentarily. I had never seen a greeting made in this way before and I wondered why. As they both turned to face me, I couldn't help but feel the compassion her gaze instilled within me.

Sam spoke and she remained silent. As he was speaking on her behalf, I assumed her presence to be of an angelic source. "This essence is here to warn this woman to be very careful in her travels. She faces immense danger when exposing her message. Tell her to take great care, for those near to her will try to silence her truth."

The apparition lifted her hand as if to bless us with her grace, and then vanished.

Although I was at one with Sam's presence, when other spiritual entities join him, it reminds me of the high level of his own spiritual progression.

Stressful news is never easy to impart as it is often received with resistance, even dismissal. However, there was no way I could sugarcoat what I needed to say to this lady.

Standing there amongst the Disney revellers, I whispered, "I believe you are in grave danger, it's even possible your life is at risk and you should be very wary whom you trust."

Her face paled. After taking time to consider my words she informed me the reason why she was in Florida. "As a matter of fact, fearing that some harm might come to me, I am staying in Florida incognito until my book is published. I am endeavouring to hide amongst the crowds."

So much information was flowing through me from the spirit dimension, this was becoming one of those times where I felt I knew everything about the recipient, as if their whole existence was somehow part of my very being.

On reflection, considering the need for secrecy, it seems so bizarre how forthright and honest she was being with me in a public place. At any time, she could have dismissed my words as trivia and walked away, but she didn't – she truly wanted to hear; she truly had a genuine need.

Quietly, I continued, "I sense blackmail. You are part of this blackmail in some way. However, I don't feel you are being blackmailed." I paused and looked directly into her eyes. Yes, there was a certain ruthlessness within her character, but I was confident she was not a criminal.

After careful consideration, I added, "Nor do I feel you are the blackmailer. I believe perhaps you have uncovered the blackmail … a political blackmail. As a result of your investigations, your life might well be in danger."

The lady's face softened and she smiled at me. It was hard to discern whether her reaction was of amazement that I knew these things, or relief that I had openly acknowledged the situation.

To clarify, she spoke bluntly, "During my research I discovered a blackmail amongst certain politicians that I have written about in my book. Certain people are going to be very angry with me, to say the least!" There was a light tone in her voice that was attempting to mask a serious concern for her own safety and the recognition her life was in great danger.

My role in this conversation was almost complete. "You have been questioning your own actions as to whether you have done the right thing, whether all this subterfuge is worth the outcome. I believe you have exposed the truth with good intent and your guides in the spirit world want me to offer assurance that you will not be physically harmed as a result of these actions."

On close examination, there might seem a certain ambiguity to those words, but the journalist knew exactly what I meant and was openly reassured.

The final message was delivered and my purpose here today complete. We hugged and I wished her every success. I took Richard's hand once more; it was time to rejoin the Disney fun. Moments later I looked back to wave a final goodbye, but she had gone, disappeared into the crowd.

All holidays come to an end, and before we knew it, we were returning to Wales.

Fortunately, I was coming home to a fresh beginning as our new home in Llandudno was nearing completion and it was time to organise the interior decoration and furnishing. Mum, on the other hand, had to return to Aunty Joan's house. We had already discussed that once we had made the move and settled in, Mum would come and live with us until we could get her own home habitable.

November was already upon us and it was an understatement to say that 1990 had been a rollercoaster year in terms of stress and emotion. However it now seemed that some normality was beginning to appear through the clouds of despair.

My second appearance at the Wolverhampton Civic Hall was imminent.

On the day, the massive hall was just as intimidating as it was on my first appearance six months prior. Fortunately, the quality of the spiritual communications was as prolific and profound as on that first occasion.

After a time, the interval came around and I retreated to my dressing room for a short rest.

My mouth was dry after talking so much and I was desperate for a cup of tea. You would have thought some beverages or even a kettle would have been provided in the dressing room, but there was absolutely nothing on hand to drink. So Richard, being the general gofer, had to brave the crowds, search for a refreshment stand nearby and stand in line for a tea so I could quench my thirst before I went into the second half. Not an easy task when nearly a thousand people are doing exactly the same.

He was gone for ages, but when he finally returned he had a happy look on his face and a story to tell. "There's a great buzz out there, the air is electric. Everyone is talking about how amazing you are! By the way, you'll never guess who I have just spoken to."

It was now Richard's turn to play the guessing game on me, for a change!

"An elderly chap made a bee-line towards me and asked if I was your husband. I must say at first I was a little shaken at the menacing way he stood so close to me. He took hold of my arm and held it really firm, then looked me straight in the eye. For a moment I thought he was a zealot who was going to pick an argument with me! Then in an instant his face softened and he said, 'Your wife is a living angel'. Then he went on to recap in infinite detail his healing experience with you from the last time we were here. Apparently, he was sitting in the front row and you just came right over to him and stroked your two fingers over his left eye. He told me he wanted you to know that twenty years ago he had a brain tumour removed, which left him with stabbing pain over his left eye on a daily basis. I couldn't believe how excited he was! He carried on saying, 'That girl had never met me before and she just knew it … she knew exactly where that pain was … I could tell she could feel my pain. From the moment she touched my head, the pain went away and from that day to this it has not been back. It's a miracle and she is an angel! I have come back again here tonight to specially tell you this. Please tell Helen and thank her for me. She has changed my life.' Then he let go of my arm, shook my hand and walked away into the crowd. And that was the last I saw of him."

Richard threw his arms around me and hugged me as if thanking me on the stranger's behalf. It filled my heart with happiness to know that another person had been helped by the spirit world, but now I had to focus on the job in hand and complete the second part of the evening, and the final venue of my fundraising events.

At last, the new house was fully furnished and ready for occupation.

After nearly ten months of homelessness, we could finally move out of the hotel and into our own four walls. Like so many in the area, my mother's bungalow was still under repair, so the time had arrived to invite her to move in with us for a while. I was thrilled to at last have this opportunity to spend time with Mum and live together as a normal family.

Under the circumstances, she was still keeping very well. However, as much as I knew that she would enjoy spending time with us, she would want to get back into her own bungalow when possible. Ultimately, we were very mindful she wanted to pass over in her own home.

Richard and I decided that as we were both working full-time, we needed to employ a nanny to help out with the children, be of support to my mother and generally keep the new house together.

Having proper organisation in the home enabled me to think about taking Richard to Scotland for the weekend as a surprise for his December birthday. I discussed it with Mum and she felt excited at the prospect of having the children to fuss over, especially with the nanny's help on hand.

The weather might be cold, but being locked away in a country house with a roaring fire seemed an inviting proposition. I could even do some Christmas shopping at the same time! Method in my madness, don't you think?

At first I tried to book into the well-known Caledonian Hotel in the heart of Edinburgh, but it was fully booked. So, looking through the *Johansen's Hotel Guide* I discovered the Johnstounburn Country House with its history dating back as early as the 13th century. Although it was a few miles out of the city, it looked just the ticket.

On the day we were due to leave, snow had fallen overnight, leaving a thin layer on the ground. We decided to brave the elements and continue with the plan to drive to Scotland. After all, how bad could the weather get?

Sam looked a little worried at my choice to drive and suggested we reconsider our plans, but Richard assured me that as we were sticking to main roads, everything should be fine as the major highways were always being gritted and needed to be kept open.

Living on the North Wales coast must have given us a false sense of security as the thin layer of snow looked harmless enough, but by the time we had travelled to Chester, it had started to stick on the ground. As we drove past Preston it was much heavier, and as we travelled through the upper end of the Yorkshire Dales, we were engulfed in a blizzard much thicker than either of us had ever experienced. I could sense the fear building up within me as we could hardly see a hand in front of us. No matter where you looked, it was just white. I felt this journey had become a disaster in the making.

At this stage it was pointless turning back. If we could get past the Lake District, surely the conditions would improve? However, all the weather reports we heard on the radio indicated it was going to be the worst snow conditions for years. Sam's words echoed in my mind and I knew I should have listened to him.

Richard was concentrating hard on keeping the car on the road. The journey seemed endless. Panic took over and I prayed for help.

"Oh, Sam, where are you?" I muttered under my breath. *Please help me.*

As if to answer my prayers, at that moment we saw two red lights several yards in front of us. Richard approached them as close as he dared and we were overwhelmed with relief when we realised it was a snow plough. We knew unless we kept close, we might well be left stranded and face untold disaster. After about an hour of following the plough, the blizzard eased and we could see again.

Eventually, we got to the outskirts of Edinburgh unscathed. In my mind, this was an outright miracle!

Even though the snow had stopped, the small country roads were laden with thick snow drifts. Nevertheless, with much difficulty Richard managed to slowly drive along them.

Approaching the final leg of our journey, we noticed all the villages were in total darkness. It seemed the whole area had no power. Being so dark, it was hard to discern where we were and our road map became almost useless.

Eventually, Richard's sense of direction prevailed and we found our destination. From the outside it looked dark and eerie, perhaps it was even closed under the circumstances. However, once inside we discovered the hotel had been without any power for hours. With gas lantern in hand, the cheerful porter escorted us to our candle-filled bedroom, which was made warm and cosy with a recently lit fire. Actually, apart from having no hot water, it all felt rather romantic.

We were assured that although we had arrived late, once we had refreshed, we would be able to eat in the restaurant, albeit from a limited menu. Fortunately the kitchen was gas powered!

Once at dinner, the more experienced of the two waiters introduced himself as Andrew. There were three other couples in the restaurant, and after a short while, they all retired and we were left alone.

To create a little atmosphere, Andrew came to our table and enquired about our journey. He explained that the other arriving guests had managed to check in before the main snow fall, and how the hotel manager actually didn't expect us to arrive as the roads were so treacherous.

The spirit world wasted no time in taking advantage of my being snowbound as suddenly a bright spiritual light appeared next to Andrew. The features of an elderly spirit lady soon became apparent. She stretched out her hand to rest on his arm. Although at first she was silent, I could tell by her empathy that she must have been someone very dear to Andrew as her energy gave off a deep love towards him. However, at this stage I had no idea who she was or what she wanted.

I saw Sam looking out through the restaurant window as though he was observing the snow, almost oblivious to the woman and myself. I wondered whether he had even sensed she was there with me.

Then, whether coincidently or otherwise, Andrew asked about my profession as he thought my face was familiar to him. Over the years, I had become increasingly aware many strangers I met had this same feeling of recognition. Perhaps this phenomenon was brought about by their own spiritual essence subconsciously recognising or responding to the highly progressed nature of my spiritual energy, or maybe those in spirit somehow prompt our subconscious to ask this type of question to instigate a conversation. Either way, our chat was brought around to spiritual matters, which eventually led to me offering a description of the spirit visitor standing next to him holding his arm.

This revelation made the spirit glow with a sense of happiness and within seconds of being acknowledged she started to speak to me in a thick Scottish accent, identifying herself as being a granny to Andrew, and only recently passed over into spirit.

From the window, Sam turned to look at me and smiled reassuringly. I continued to chat to Andrew about his granny and some of his other relatives in spirit. As I offered details about their lives, he became completely overwhelmed by the experience. It was then that she spoke of a kilt and a set of bagpipes, saying she wished Andrew had been given these items after his granddad had passed. Apparently, when his granddad was younger he played the bagpipes in the Argyll and Sutherland Highlanders, and his granny seemed upset because Andrew had not been given this special uniform as an heirloom to keep.

After spending a good twenty minutes reuniting Andrew with his family, I was inundated with family names that he couldn't recognise. Rather than be dismissive and suggesting I was mistaken, he showed some initiative by thinking they might be for the chef and offered to go and fetch him from the kitchen. I explained he shouldn't just spring such a revelation on the unsuspecting chap, but he reassured me that he knew his friend well enough to go and ask. Within a minute, the burly chef in all his whites was pulling a chair up beside our table eager to hear what I had to say, as he had recognised the group of names.

Trying to be an accommodating host to our new company, Richard ordered another bottle of wine to share amongst the four of us. The two members of the hotel staff sat there for about another half hour, with tear-filled eyes, engrossed in spiritual communication with their relatives.

After a long and tiring day fighting the winter elements, a good night's sleep in our cosy bedroom was most welcome.

Late the following morning we awoke to clear blue skies. The snow was still very thick and as a result of the sunshine it glistened brilliant white, nothing less than picture perfect. However, it looked like we might be snowed in for days, which wasn't an unwelcome predicament.

Fortunately, we managed to arrive at breakfast just before it had finished. Although everyone had left, Andrew was on duty and enthusiastically greeted us at the restaurant entrance to escort us to our table.

As we sat down, he told us that early that morning he had been on the phone to his mother and siblings to tell them all about his experience the night before. Also, while serving the breakfasts, he had told all the guests about his spiritual encounter. Without my knowing, this morning I had become an overnight sensation and the talk of the hotel! Actually, I was really rather moved by his open honesty with everyone that his experience had brought so much joy to his life, as quite often many who are touched in this way are tempted to say nothing in case people might view them differently.

After a perfect day, we enjoyed another romantic dinner together. Andrew was still on duty, and after showing us to our table he was again eager to express his gratitude from the night before.

He explained, "We have a very famous guest staying at the hotel with his wife. He is a well-known pop star, so I am surprised you didn't recognise him last night in the restaurant. He has already eaten this evening, but after hearing about my experience, he is really eager to meet you. He asked me to invite you on his behalf to join him and his wife for a nightcap in the lounge after you have dined."

I queried, "We didn't recognise anybody we might know. Who is he?"

"It's Johnny Marr, the guitarist from The Smiths! They really do have a massive niche following."

I glanced at Richard and by the blank look on his face I knew the name had completely gone over his head. I must say that I had vaguely heard of The Smiths, but the name Marr meant nothing to me.

Nevertheless, after dinner Andrew escorted us to meet the Marrs in the lounge.

At first we felt like gatecrashers as Johnny was in deep conversation with his wife and another gentleman. However, on noticing we were walking over, he stood up to shake our hands and formally introduced us to his wife, Angie, and the hotel manager.

I couldn't help but notice how slim and beautifully elegant his wife looked.

He apologised to the hotel manager and asked if he could be excused to carry on their conversation later as he didn't want to impose on my time. Reluctantly and with much disappointment, the manager left our company.

Within minutes the four of us were chatting like old friends.

Early on in our conversation I explained we hadn't heard of him and didn't know any of his music. But rather than being offended by my remark, he found it refreshing as our dialogue would not be centred on his musical accolades or his recent high-profile break-up with his partner, Morrissey.

Soon we learned that the Marrs had originally booked into the Caledonian Hotel in Edinburgh, but for some reason they couldn't quite put their finger on, they didn't feel comfortable there, so they checked out and by chance selected the Johnstounburn.

I explained my attempt to book the Caledonian, but couldn't as they were full and how I was drawn towards this hotel over the others.

Needless to say we all thought it a little too coincidental and wondered whether our meeting was more destiny than chance. To compound the atmosphere of coincidence, it turned out we shared the same date for our wedding anniversary. A double coincidence!

It didn't take long before the conversation focused upon my work and the Marrs seemed eager to listen and learn. Their interest was truly genuine and their questions were educated, intellectual and stimulating.

Within no time at all, Sam had brought a crowd of deceased family, friends and famous musicians to chat with Johnny, including my old spiritual acquaintance John Lennon.

We continued to talk into the early hours about all manner of spiritual phenomena. What became very evident was that Johnny was a very well read and extremely intellectual man.

Then out of the blue, in walked the hotel manager loudly playing some type of jazz on his shiny brass saxophone. With no embarrassment or care for our privacy, he made a bee-line for us and sat on the arm of the sofa opposite Johnny, as if trying to demonstrate his own musical skills.

It was evident that the Marrs were irritated by this intrusion, but too polite to complain.

Eventually, the playing stopped and with self-congratulation the manager grinned and repeatedly bowed. Politely, and with forced smiles, we applauded.

The newcomer had changed the energy within our group and the conversation became disjointed as the manager was completely focused on talking about Johnny's music. However, not wanting to seem rude, Johnny tried to include him into our group conversation about spiritual phenomena. The manager said that although he was not dismissive of such things, until he had experienced some proof of sorts, he was a little sceptical. Then he looked right at me and gave me a patronising smile.

Fortunately, I am very comfortable with who I am, and don't have the need to convert every stranger I meet in general conversation just because they require a personal revelation. I understand my role, and how my life relates to the spirit world. However, I could sense Johnny was embarrassed on my behalf and he became a tad confrontational about this man's scepticism, openly supporting the existence of the spirit world. This was unnecessary, but utterly charming. I was well-used to having to fight my own battles.

Nevertheless, I could see the spiritual manifestation of an elderly lady leaning against the bookcase on the far wall. I sensed that this was the manager's mother, as her spiritual senses were totally fixated on him.

By the time I had taken a deep breath, all manner of personal messages were being delivered to her son. The manager seemed to be amazed that his mother had so much to say and acknowledged what she said to be true.

However, over the years I have witnessed that no matter how much proof you give of a spiritual afterlife and my ability to communicate with it, people sometimes want something specific to be said they believe is the only requisite for survival evidence. In such circumstances, the recipient may well become disappointed, as I learned long ago it is not my role to wantonly convert every sceptic to believe in the afterlife in the exact way they want it to be revealed.

My role as a go-between is that of mutual deliverance – delivering a spiritual message or delivering spiritual healing energy. If your friends and family want to offer proof in a specific way, it is their responsibility to provide the information in a format you would recognise, not mine.

For instance, if a parent in spirit refers to you or themselves by their official first name and not a nickname that the family generally uses, does that make the communication weak or false? I deliver in the way it is given, not in the way you think it should or would like it to be delivered. If you issue an ultimatum or expect certain criteria, you are probably setting yourself up for let down and failure.

However, on this occasion, it worked out for the hotel manager. In a quiet but challenging voice, he announced, "Before my mother died she bought me the most beautiful fountain pen, which I know cost her a lot of money. But about a year ago, I foolishly lost it here in this lounge somewhere. I have searched everywhere, I have even had the cleaners almost pull all the furniture apart looking for it, as it really has great sentimental value. If she is really here talking with us, ask her to find it for me. Then I will know it's her for sure!"

Apparently, all the correct information I had delivered had no worth ... I had to find a long-lost pen to actually prove his mother's existence. If a fleet of cleaners couldn't find it during the past year, what chance did I have? Maybe he lost it somewhere else in the hotel or even out and about elsewhere?

Nevertheless, without any hesitation his mother pointed down the side of the armchair right beside her son. I almost chose not to offer this information as I was very dubious that it would actually be there beside us. However, what sort of medium would I be if I didn't have faith in my own communication ability?

Confidently I announced, "Your mother is saying it's down the side of that armchair next to you."

The manager laughed out loud. "That's impossible! I have had my hand down there a hundred times."

"Well, your mother suggests you have another look, just one more time!" I urged.

Still holding his saxophone in his left hand, he pushed his other down the side of the armchair. Seconds later his face lit up and he pulled out a very beautiful fountain pen. At first, he looked at it in disbelief, then realising it truly was his long-lost pen he was ecstatic. As a reward, our company was treated to a little hop-like dance around the lounge and then another unwelcome rendition on the saxophone.

Realising it was unlikely that the manager's precious pen had previously been there, Johnny and Angie reacted with a deeper level of understanding of the importance of witnessing such an apport – the rare phenomenon of transferring an object from one place to another by spiritual activity. This incident wasn't entirely about the finding of lost property, it was a truly special spiritual moment, a rare occurrence to be respected and a memory that should be cherished.

On reflection, I believe it wasn't just for the manager to have proof of his mother's continued survival, but for the Marrs to bear witness to a phenomenal spiritual consequence.

This was one of those nights that was so full of spiritual enlightenment, you just didn't want it to end. Eventually tiredness overcame us, and we all went to bed. The Marrs sadly advised us they were going home the following day, and invited us to their home to stay with them sometime in the forthcoming weeks. It turned out they only lived an hour from us, so plans were made and a friendship blossomed.

20

Let it be!

"Enjoy yourself, it's later than you think."
~Socrates~

Faced with a terminal illness, it might be said it's now time to do all the things in life you really want to do, travel to the many places you want to visit and say all the things you want to say.

How different the reality of living can be.

For some, there is just not enough time to do those things, the monetary funds to undertake the travel, nor the opportunity to say what needs to be said. Others might have every opportunity to do everything, but are physically unable as they are too ill and don't have the physical or mental energy.

My mother was relatively lucky. Although she knew she was terminally ill, for the moment at least, she had long spells of feeling comparatively well. She no longer pined to be with my father and instead had started to embrace every morsel of life. She was kinder to those she met and welcomed every new opportunity that came her way.

She had begun living at a time in her life when her body was getting ready to die.

It had now been nearly seven months since my mother's operation and the shocking diagnosis of her condition. Despite the doctors saying that she had only weeks to live, she seemed stronger than she had been for years, and after enjoying her trip to Florida, she asked me if we could go for a short weekend break to London. Mum had not been there since she was fifteen when she went on a school trip, and the nostalgia of that occasion seemed to lure her.

In a bid to lavish some luxury on Mum, I booked a January date for us all to stay at the newly refurbished Hampshire Hotel in Leicester Square. Also, we booked theatre tickets for two of the nights, and reserved a table at a very posh restaurant for dinner. These were all activities she wasn't familiar with, but nevertheless were occasions she was genuinely excited to experience.

However, her main objective was to feed the pigeons in Trafalgar Square like she had done as a schoolgirl. This was the nostalgia she craved.

On arrival at the hotel, Mum was in awe of its opulence. The interiors were lavishly decorated in heavy-wood panelling and oversized ornaments, and it had Chinese-style carpets everywhere that felt like you were walking on thick foam.

She embraced her surroundings and savoured the atmosphere.

That night we enjoyed a fabulous evening at the theatre watching the comedian Dave Allen. It lifted my heart to see my mum cry with laughter!

At midnight, we went to our rooms and during that quiet moment before sleep came over me, Sam started to discuss Mum and her welfare. He informed me he had spent some time with Mum every night since her diagnosis. I felt very touched and comforted by this knowledge. He explained of late that she would cry before sleeping. By saying nothing about this and hiding her feelings, she thought she was being brave.

Anxiously I asked, "Is she in pain?" I was terrified she had been lying and was hiding her suffering from me.

Sam thought for a second and replied, "There is no physical pain. However, her mental well-being is compromised. She wants to speak openly to you about her condition, and yet she fears what you might say."

I was well aware that many people suffering from a terminal illness, especially when enjoying long periods of good health and strong stamina, can often be in denial of their imminent fate and pretend the illness has vanished. However, I thought my mum had understood this and had moved on from denying her condition.

"What do I say?" I almost pleaded for an answer.

When working professionally with families in this same predicament, I always intuitively know what to say to bring about strong, positive change to those concerned.

However, finding the words to help my own mother, I felt hopelessly inadequate and in need of guidance.

Sam replied, "Always offer reassurance that you love her. Remind her that only she can know how she truly feels, no matter how much you try to empathise. Explain that she needs to tell you how her illness is progressing. Also, ask her to open up and tell you about what she really fears. Talk openly and honestly. Any words said with true love are never wasted."

"She must have many fears. What are they?" I asked.

Sam frustrated me with his answer. "It is up to you to ask her these things. It's not my role to tell you how she is feeling, but I know she is wanting you to talk with her."

Despite the late hour, I rang Mum's room and asked if I could have five minutes with her. She seemed in good form on the telephone and agreed to see me as she wasn't sleepy. However, when she opened her bedroom door, I intuitively knew she was hiding something from me.

We chatted as Sam had suggested.

After a while, I asked, "Are you scared of something, Mum? You know you can tell me anything."

After a little coaxing, she quietly answered, "Actually, Helen, I can't sleep at night. It's not that I don't feel tired, because I am exhausted. The problem is I am desperately afraid of closing my eyes and going to sleep in case I don't wake up again."

Then she sobbed. "I don't want to go, Helen. I want to stay here with you and the children. After your father died I begged for death so I could be with him, but now I feel nothing but guilt for asking that. I really want to live and be part of your lives. I love you all so much."

Mum shared many of her feelings with me and I listened. I was overjoyed that at last she had found the strength to want to fight for life, and for more time to be with us.

That night, by sharing our feelings, I felt we became even closer.

So often people think that because I can communicate with spirit, somehow I can also read minds. My own mother seemed to share this misconception. Like you, my dear reader, I can only know what people are thinking if they actually tell me! Just because I see spirit does not mean that my guides and angels tell me all the answers to life's mysteries. Like you, I have to develop my wisdom from life's ongoing experiences and by making many mistakes along the way.

The next morning, in the crisp winter air, we fed the pigeons in Trafalgar Square. I saw a look in Mum's face that day ... it was full of wonder and anticipation, as if she had gone back in time to when she was a schoolgirl and had the marvel of her whole life ahead.

Time went by and the first daffodils opened their unique bright yellow blooms in my garden. I knew with the change of seasons, my mother's time here was nearing completion. However, I reconciled myself to this by thinking there was most certainly a new life ahead of her, albeit in the hereafter.

The building work at Mum's home were completed sufficiently for her to move back in. She had been homeless now for over one year. I was happy she had felt at home with me, but I knew she wanted to die in her own bungalow and more importantly, in her own bed.

The dispute with the builders was still ongoing, as all they had done was wallpaper over their many structural problems. However, this was something I could tackle later, soon there would be time enough for such things. What was important right now was to make Mum as comfortable as possible in her own home.

Moving back in with all new carpets and furnishings, Mum felt at last her life was back on track. Although I visited her most days, she seemed to enjoy her new space and independence. My Aunty Joan would often pop down and stay with her so they could spend time together and even go to bingo when they wanted to.

My mother's birthday fell on the 1st May, and naturally I arranged to have a little party at my house to celebrate. At the end of the meal, I marched in with Mum's birthday cake proudly boasting fifty-three burning candles and placed it in front of her. As we all sung happy birthday, a strange occurrence happened.

There, right next to my mother, I could see a group of six spiritual entities. I could recognise my Nana Ada and my Granddad Joe, my father, my mother's guide Rosalinda, and there was another couple whom I couldn't recognise. What seemed so bizarre was that my father in spirit was holding an identical cake.

When our singing finished and Mum blew out her candles, almost simultaneously the family in spirit blew out the candles on their cake. The significance of this baffled me. Perhaps it was nothing more than demonstrating all my mother's family in spirit were celebrating her birthday too. None of them spoke to me, in fact the visitation only lasted for the short duration of the birthday verse.

Naturally I was ecstatic to see my dad and almost wept with joy as I told Mum about his visit. Then I described how I had seen her parents and another couple I couldn't recognise. After giving a description of them, she thought they might be her own grandparents.

After cutting the cake, we sat holding hands for a few minutes and had a little cry together about Dad. We both missed him so much, and on family occasions like this, grief can often show itself to remind you of its existence.

It wasn't until later when we cleared the plates away that Richard and I started to discuss the possible meaning of the visitation – in private of course.

He demonstrated a depth of understanding in his interpretation. "To me it's obvious. For so many of your family to come at once possibly signifies this will be your Mum's last birthday, as they are preparing to take her very soon. In fact, I would say from today onwards you will see a marked decline in her health. The blowing out of the candles might signify that the very life of her is being extinguished."

My eyes welled with tears. How could I not see this? Perhaps my subconscious wanted to protect me and was trying to hide this from me.

Witnessing my response, Richard became anxious. "Look, Helen, don't get upset. What do I know? Just ignore me. I am not a medium, I can't interpret these things. This birthday cake in spirit ... perhaps it's nothing more than wishing your Mum a happy birthday! Of course, it's just that."

Despite his efforts to appease me and trivialise his profound interpretation, he had triggered my spiritual instinct and I intuitively knew his initial thought was right, but I was emotionally too close to Mum to want to understand this sign. As she had been looking so well for so long, the realisation that she might not be around for her next birthday was hard for me to acknowledge.

From that day onwards, Mum's condition deteriorated and by the first week in June she was showing the first signs of the severe physical pain associated with her medical condition.

It now became apparent that if Mum was stay in her own home, she was going to need someone with her all the time. Although I visited daily, this wasn't quite the same, and when we discussed the subject, she categorically told me I was not to move in as I had the children to look after. The possibility of me staying was not a topic for discussion or compromise.

Soon after, Aunty Joan moved in with her; this was a true blessing. Although it was never said out loud, we all realised this was the beginning of the end, and Mum really needed someone on hand twenty-four hours a day. She hated hospitals and feared being in them. If it was possible to keep her at home, then that was what each of us would try and make happen for her. With Aunty Joan living in, Mum staying at home until the end was now feasible.

On the morning of 7th July, I felt Mum was in her final stages. For the last week, she had been unaware of anything as she was bedridden in a morphine-induced trance. Never had I witnessed such a fast deterioration. Only weeks before, life seemed normal and ongoing; now she just lay there, ashen grey and old, occasionally muttering random words under her breath. At times her arm or leg would erratically spasm, or maybe in her drugged mind she was trying to move her muscles to undertake a physical task she might be imagining.

Despite knowingly fighting her cancers for a year now, miraculously my mum had only suffered this degree of debility for the last month. The doctor had come earlier that morning to assess my mother's condition and to leave a new prescription for more morphine capsules for the pump that was intravenously attached to her arm.

After a while, Aunty Joan asked if Richard and I could nip out to the chemist and have the prescription filled. I didn't want to leave the room, but my aunty assured me that the few minutes it took to go on the errand would not make any difference to Mum's condition, and we would be back in a jiffy.

I lightly kissed Mum's forehead; it was noticeably cold and clammy. Leaning closer, I whispered reassurance into her ear that I would be back very soon. She looked peaceful, despite being oblivious to anything going on – the high dose of drugs had made sure of that.

We were gone about ten minutes at the most. On our return, I turned the key in the front door and I heard my aunty shout out my name to hurry me back. A chill ran through my body and I shivered. I ran into the bedroom and sat beside her, squeezing her hand to reinforce my presence. I could tell her life force was slipping away fast.

In the corner of the room I could faintly see the features of a spirit. I recognised this apparition as my mother's guide. She spread her arms wide and a wave of peace flooded right through my entire being. I blinked and she was gone. I felt relieved, almost as though Mum was to be spared this final fate. But the reality of the moment was so very different.

Aunty Joan looked straight into my eyes and said, "Judy's going! She wants to be let go. I think she needed you to leave, so she could pass. Your strong energy was holding her here, but she really needs to pass over now, Helen."

The realisation of what was happening overwhelmed me and tears streamed down my face. I knew I had to release my mother from her agony. I leaned over so our faces almost touched and whispered, "It's okay, Mum, you can go now. Let them take you over … I love you."

Despite wanting her to stay, I knew she had to go. It was her time.

With Richard by my side, I watched silently as the last shallow breath left her body. As it did, a thick white smoke started to gently flow out of her mouth. It was as if a heavy cigarette smoker had inhaled gallons of smoke and was allowing it to slowly exhale. From experience, I knew it was the ectoplasm leaving my mother's body as I had witnessed this phenomena before. I looked at Richard and Aunty Joan, and from the surprised expression on their faces, I knew they too could see this dense cloud slowly forming above my mother's head.

Richard whispered, "What's that coming out of Judy's mouth, is it cigarette smoke?"

Aunty Joan looked equally amazed, and wasn't slow in answering, "It can't be. It's been weeks since she's touched a cigarette."

Clutching at straws, trying to find a reasonable explanation, Richard replied, "Perhaps it's condensation from her breath?" He then exhaled as a controlled experiment to see if it went cloudy, but it was a sunny, warm July day, definitely not a day for seeing any type of condensation from your breath.

The room fell silent and we all watched the smoke float upwards, white and dense, stretching to about thirty inches. Then, after a short while, it dispersed and was gone. From appearance to disappearance it lasted about two minutes. However, two minutes was a very long time under those circumstances.

Richard and Aunty Joan looked at me and I knew they wanted my opinion on what was happening. I explained, "We have all just witnessed Mum's spirit leaving her physical body."

At that moment, a portal of light opened up around Mum's head allowing me to see her guide once more. Rosalinda smiled softly at me and whispered, "I will be taking your mother over."

In my mind I asked myself why my father was not showing himself. Where was he? Where were my grandparents?

As if Rosalinda understood my thoughts, she continued, "This was the way your mother wanted it to be, but rest assured your father is waiting for her." Rosalinda then faded in front of my eyes.

Once the realisation Mum had gone had sunk in, I turned to Richard, clung to him tightly and cried uncontrollably. Mum had left, never to physically share in my life ever again. Never would I feel my mother's arms around me or feel her loving tenderness in that special way only a mother can. In that moment, I thought of all the times I had taken her love for granted, believing she would never age and always be there for me … but now she was gone forever from my living world.

I was absolutely devastated.

Richard was really comforting and he held me close for as long as I needed. After a short while, I had to have some fresh air, so went outside to sit alone on the wooden bench in Mum's back garden. I sat in a daze, not really focusing on anything in particular. My mind wandered.

Out of the blue, I heard Mum's voice. "I am here! I am OK. Don't worry. I love you too, my darling girl."

For a few brief seconds, she seemed to be with me once more, albeit in voice alone.

Unexpectedly, a solitary sparrow landed right in front of me on the grass. It fearlessly hopped around within inches of my feet. I smiled, it had to be a spiritual sign as my maiden name was Sparrow! It flew up onto the wooden arm on the bench where I was sitting, and for a split second the bird looked directly at me and then took flight.

At that moment, my mother and father were suddenly standing before me, arm in arm. He was there for her as she had been for him. They were together and she looked happy. I was so pleased for her as she now had her wish to be with Dad. I longed to see my father and willed him to look at me; I so desperately wanted to connect with him, especially now. Then as one, they both turned and looked directly at me and smiled. In an instant, they were gone.

Inside I felt painfully empty. However, I rejoiced at the reunion of my parents.

Although I was devastated that I had lost my mother, I looked up to see Aunty Joan at the kitchen window peering out into the garden suffering her own grief. It struck me that she had just lost her best friend and sister. She had been so strong and caring, so thoughtful towards Mum's needs, no way in this world could I have managed without her, and neither could Mum. Aunty Joan had made my mother's wish to pass into the spirit world from her own bed in her own home come true, that was a priceless gift only a truly devoted person could give.

Thank you so very much, Aunty Joan, no words could ever express my love and gratitude.

About a week later we had the funeral. Mum was to be cremated and her ashes laid to rest with my dad at the Marble Church.

I specifically went to see Reverend Byles, the vicar in charge of St Margaret's, to personally ask him to perform the service. He had performed all the ecclesiastical duties for my family for as long as I could remember and had been very supportive of both my parents during their illnesses.

At my request, during the service Reverend Byles read 'Fruits Foreboding', the prose that had been dictated to me by George Bernard Shaw from spirit months prior. I genuinely felt the words summed up my mother's struggle in coming to terms with her illness and subsequently facing certain death.

At Mum's request, we played 'What a Wonderful World' by Louis Armstrong, as prior to her death she had learned to see the immense wealth of beauty around her in people, places and in her experiences. She wanted me to remember these words as a sort of legacy from her.

After the service, Reverend Byles came to me and remarked he was very familiar with Shaw's work, but had never read this piece before and enquired how I had come across such a profound composition. In my mind, this gave me an ideal opportunity to talk about my spirit visitors and the evening Shaw's spirit remarkably appeared to me some time previous.

However, rather than be true to my God-given natural ability, I chose to deflect from the truth. Rather than look him in the eye and tell him straight how I could see and communicate with the spirit world, I chose to mumble about how I came across Shaw's words somewhere or other – can't remember where attitude. It was as if I was ashamed to acknowledge my own spiritual abilities.

About five minutes later, Reverend Byles approached me again on the subject, and I passed it off just as quickly.

Richard was furious and pulled me to one side, he suggested this was very hypocritical of me and not true to my nature or to the divine.

Of course, he was absolutely right!

Actually, Richard went on to draw a comparison with the Bible story of the Last Supper when Jesus predicted the Apostle Peter would deny him three times before the cock crowed. Peter believed himself to be so faithful to Jesus, denying his friend could never ever happen. After the arrest of Jesus at Gethsemane, Peter did indeed deny their association and afterwards felt tremendous shame for doing so. A classic story to demonstrate duplicity.

I must say I felt truly ashamed at what I had done. Like in the story of Peter, I had denied being associated to a spiritual family to avoid any confrontation with the establishment, eluding the conflict my spiritual sight might initiate. However, this was my mother's funeral and I was suffering grief. Today I didn't have the emotional strength to defend myself in any type of religious conflict. I just wanted to honour Mum and go home to be with my family; this wasn't the time or place to subject myself to ecclesiastical debate and once again have to justify what was normal and true to me. Not here ... not now ... not today.

The next day, in restitution, I wrote a long letter to the Reverend with a full explanation of the Shaw work and how I felt I had betrayed the spirit world by not explaining its conception to him. I took this letter to the vicarage personally to discuss it with him, but he was not there, so I left it with his wife to give him.

A couple of days later, Reverend Byles rang me and we had a long chat on the subject. He was fascinated by what I had to say and suggested we meet up sometime for a more in-depth conversation. In my heart, I knew I had put the record straight on who and what I was.

Having had this experience and learned by my mistake, never again will I deny my spiritual gift to anyone under any circumstances. That said, what is vital for you to understand, having the gift of spiritual sight does not lessen the grief of losing the most precious soul of all – your Mum.

21

Hell in Paradise

"When you are going through hell ... keep going!"
~attributed to Sir Winston Churchill~

To help me overcome the loss of Mum and to bring some fresh energy into our home, Richard decided that a holiday of holidays was the order of the day. So he surprised me by planning a month away in a Caribbean paradise. What girl wouldn't enjoy that?

Nevertheless, despite my excitement, on random occasions I kept spiritually hearing the words '... daughter is going to die'. Rest assured, when you have absolute faith in your spirit messages, such a revelation makes you sit up and pay attention.

I mentioned this to Richard, but he felt I was being subconsciously influenced by my recent bereavement. Having trust in my spiritual empathy, I felt otherwise, and was in genuine fear of Fiona's safety. Discreetly, I kept an eye on her health, but she seemed absolutely fine. Nevertheless, the words in my mind came back with a vengeance and more regularly, '... daughter is going to die'.

Even though I wasn't able to spiritually tune into my mum, I had a strong feeling she was trying to get a message of warning to me. However, as Richard's explanation seemed feasible, I tried not to focus on the gravity of the message as maybe I was over-thinking the whole scenario.

To compound the situation, I was having bouts of stomach pains. In the aftermath of my mother's cancer, Richard insisted that I should visit the doctor. Meditating on my illness, I felt there was a problem somewhere in my bowel. However the doctor denied my request for tests and diagnosed that in his experience the pain was caused by emotional stress.

If that's what the doctor says is causing the problem, then stress it is! What could I possibly know?

Not wanting to interfere with the children's education, during our absence we made arrangements for them to stay with friends at their lakeside mountain cottage, near Llanrwst. The children were very excited at the prospect of their adventure, but I was most concerned about leaving them.

On the day of our departure, Richard's parents and his brother Robert drove with us to Manchester Airport for the big send off. While sitting in one of the airport restaurants, suddenly the words came into my mind again, only this time I heard '… my daughter is going to die!'

In the middle of the crowded restaurant, I burst into tears and announced I had a really bad feeling about leaving the children and wanted to go home. How could I possibly ignore this particular spiritual warning, it was far too strong?

My family were all very sympathetic and tried to placate me, and began bombarding me with all manner of clichés: It's natural, you are just worried about being apart from the kids, You are being silly, It's because you've just lost your Mum, The doctor said you're stressed.

I knew they all meant well and a very small part of me felt they might be justified. Maybe I was just overreacting! Perhaps the anxiety of both my parents recently dying, our home being flooded, living in a hotel for months, moving home, and a gruelling work schedule had taken its toll. In retrospect, any one of these situations was sufficient to be enough to trigger a severe bout of stress.

Of course, they were right. How could I not see this? I had been so foolish!

My natural instinct was to refer to Sam, but I was woefully aware his role was to enlighten me about the spiritual, not to interfere with my freedom of choice. It might well be that tragedy was inevitable, but perhaps that was necessary for my own spiritual growth. I was mindful that only by experiencing the most challenging of circumstances am I equipped to help others with similar adversity.

The information monitor displayed 'final boarding' for our flight. In a moment of weakness, I was on my way – for better or worse!

By the time we landed in Antigua, I allowed myself to believe it was stress after all! Obviously, I needed this holiday, so I made the conscious decision to enjoy every minute of it.

On arriving at the hotel, the smell of the deep-blue ocean mixed with the sun's heat seemed like a magic tonic to me. We were shown to a suite that fronted directly onto the beach; it was stunning, truly a majestic paradise setting.

We were into the fourth day when Richard and I came down with a bad tummy bug after a beachfront chicken barbecue and a few Pina Coladas. These things can happen!

After a day of sickness and diarrhoea, Richard improved, but I seemed to be deteriorating and the stomach pains didn't ease. The following day, Richard had recovered, but I was feeling progressively worse.

"All you need is bed rest," Dr Rodney Williams explained in his loud accented voice, as if the volume aggrandised his diagnosis, "and you will be fine in a few days."

Listening to his deep commanding voice, I felt more optimistic than maybe I should have been.

Suddenly, the hotel's electricity supply failed, as it often does in these parts, and the doctor produced a mini flashlight to illuminate the task of inserting a drip into my arm. Removing a picture from the wall behind the bed, he hung the plasma bag on its hook.

Lying there in the darkness, I became very frightened.

Over the next two days, despite the doctor's visits, I seemed to deteriorate and felt desperately ill. I was in agony and had the overwhelming feeling that the spirit world was becoming uncomfortably close.

I recognised a change within me and I knew I had to fight if I was to survive.

Feeling desperate, I asked Richard to ask the doctor to come immediately. With reluctance, he left my side to go to reception. As he closed the door behind him, Sam dutifully sat on the edge of the bed. His eyes were gentle and compassionate, and in my hour of need he spoke to me.

"Helen, I must leave you for a little while. It is time to make sure events happen as they should. Choices have to be made by many individuals to ease you through this suffering, and I have taken upon myself to ensure their decisions are aligned for a positive outcome."

His words worried me as I knew only too well that passing over into the spirit world was a natural phenomenon and one that is not feared by those within it. However, in my heart I knew Sam wanted me to live.

I must have dozed as it seemed like hours had passed waiting for Richard to return. His energy woke me from my slumber and he assured me he had been away for minutes.

"Apparently, our Dr Williams has several jobs. He is a part-time doctor, a part-time minister of tourism and a part-time tennis coach. The receptionist told me that he was playing tennis at the moment and wouldn't be back for a few hours. I became very frustrated, told her how ill you are and she needed to find you another doctor. She wasn't very sympathetic and told me that was not possible."

Richard was unable to see the spiritual forces at work trying to ensure my survival, so he was unaware that my life hung in the balance. Through an extraordinary set of circumstances a miracle had been aligned without either of us even knowing. Because after he'd finished talking to the receptionist, an English lady, who had overheard his conversation, introduced herself. She was the wife of a consultant gastroenterologist at London Middlesex hospital who also had his own private Harley Street practice. She suggested he could take a look at me after he'd finished his round of golf.

It seemed at last there was some hope in the air.

Later that afternoon, Dr David Silk came to see me. I felt very self-conscious as my hair was sticking to my head, my frilly nightie was stained with all sorts and the room smelt terrible.

After a thorough examination, he asked Richard to step outside into the humid evening air.

Although he spoke quietly, I could hear every word. "Helen is a very poorly girl, and I want her out of this country now and into the nearest American hospital. I am going to arrange for an air-vac to Florida, probably Miami. I suggest you pack up ready to leave."

When asked, he avoided anything specific in the way of a diagnosis and just kept stressing the urgency of hospitalisation.

About half an hour later, Dr Silk returned to tell us the air-vac was organised, but they needed an Antiguan doctor to authorise a blood test and x-ray for the paperwork. "I have arranged for you to be examined at the Holberton Hospital in St Johns," he said. "The taxis are waiting outside the hotel entrance to take us."

As soon as I stood up I felt my head spin and I knew I didn't have the strength to support myself. Sensing this, the two men supported an arm each. Richard was instructed to hold my drip as high as he could. Each footstep forward made my pain much worse and I remember thinking what I wouldn't give for a stretcher and ambulance right now.

The night air was thick with the sound of tree frogs, an atmosphere that normally I would find to be very romantic, but tonight it reminded me how far from home we were.

After a long and difficult walk, I was bundled into the back of a very old taxi. I noticed the vinyl covering on the back seats had long eroded away exposing the metal springs. Dr Silk went in another taxi to prepare the hospital for our arrival.

Our journey seemed to take ages. Each bump caused me to scream out loud in pain. It is very hard to keep upbeat when things around you seem to be going from bad to worse.

Eventually, around seven p.m., we arrived at the Holberton. By now it was very dark. As soon as our taxi pulled to a halt, Dr Silk came running over towards us waving his arms.

He looked absolutely horrified. "We can't stop here. Half the hospital roof is still missing from Hurricane Hugo. The wards are overflowing, the corridors are packed with people on dirty mattresses and I very much doubt their equipment is up to scratch. I have found out there is a small, private maternity clinic nearby where the more affluent locals go to have their babies."

After a drive through overgrown sugarcane fields, we arrived at what seemed to be a wooden shack. There was a painted wooden sign outside stating this was the Adelin Clinic.

I squeezed Richard's arm. "Please don't let them take me in there, just ask the driver to take us straight to the airport. I want to go home!"

"We won't be here long, darling," he said. "We've only come for an x-ray and a blood test."

My spiritual senses were in overdrive, and I felt otherwise. I was terrified what might await me inside that place.

On entering, it seemed that we had been transported back a hundred years. All sweaty from the humidity, we stood in the little reception area, dimly lit by a 40-watt light bulb. Everything seemed to be made out of planks of old-painted wood. Dr Silk went to organise the tests. We walked through an open archway onto the ward where we were greeted by a nurse. There were about ten beds, each decorated with mosquito netting, heavily stained with age. All the nets seemed to sway in the draught created by the solitary ceiling fan, struggling hard to rotate. Strangely, all the patients were elderly. I thought Dr Silk said this was a maternity clinic, or had I misunderstood?

I remember one old man slowly shuffled in front of us dressed in a blue hospital gown that draped open at the back, exposing folds of skin on his thin, naked body. He went into a toilet cubicle and without closing the door, we could see him urinate. A forced cough cleared his throat of stale phlegm, followed by a rasp which fired some lumpy spit into the ceramic bowl.

I didn't want to be here.

The nurse ordered, "Cumon now gurl, slip your clows off, 'n pop yurself into bed." I felt she was used to her patients unquestionably obeying her every word.

Despite feeling desperately ill, I was resolute I would not be staying. As a compromise, I lay fully clothed on top of the bed. I wasn't even prepared to slip off my shoes, as to do so seemed as if I was agreeing to stay.

Dr Silk returned and informed us the man who did the blood tests had a heart attack that day and been hospitalised in the Holberton. Furthermore, the lady who did the x-rays had gone home and didn't have a telephone, so Dr Silk had organised a taxi to go and find her to bring her back.

You might find these circumstances a little bizarre. I did! But they're absolutely true.

At that moment, a car arrived and parked at the clinic entrance. As if the driver was expected, Dr Silk made his way to greet the new arrival.

"Might I introduce Dr Bertrand O'Mard," said Dr Silk. "Although he has his own private clinic here in Antigua, he is a chief surgeon at one of the main hospitals in New York. We were lucky to find him! He only spends a short time here each month."

The doctor stepped forward towards me and exchanged pleasantries. I was very reassured by listening to his thick New York accent and his confident American swagger. I truly thanked my angels! I felt there might be a change of fortune in the air.

Another hour or so passed and still no sign of the radiographer. Dr O'Mard decided to leave, explaining he would come back once the x-ray had been taken. Until then there was nothing he could do.

Around eleven p.m., the illusive radiographer arrived, wearing a flower-patterned flannelette knee-length nightdress and a pink candlewick dressing-gown and matching fluffy slippers. To complete the outfit, her hair was crammed full of thin pink curlers. If I hadn't been in so much pain I might have even found the situation amusing! The x-ray machine was in another building to the rear. So Dr Silk and Richard once again had to almost carry me there. Outside it was very dark with only moonlight to illuminate the way. It was then I realised we were walking through a field of long grass full of goats and chickens, metal animal feeders and chicken coops. Eventually, we entered what appeared to be a large domestic garage. The room was stocked with medical supplies and in the corner was a very old-fashioned x-ray machine, which stood like it was more in storage than in practical use. With the x-rays taken, we all trundled back to the clinic while the film was developed.

Richard eased me back on top of the bed. Despite his suggestion, I still refused to remove my shoes.

After about thirty minutes, the two doctors made a theatrical entrance onto the ward side by side.

"The x-rays have shown some abnormality within the bowel. Without looking inside you, I cannot be more specific. I have made the decision that I am unwilling to authorise the air-vac as it might be fatal. With bowel situations like this, complications can set in very quickly and if left, can become fatal within a very short period of time," announced Dr O'Mard.

Dr Silk nodded in concurrence.

Nausea overwhelmed me and I could feel my heart pounding hard inside my chest.

"I don't want to stay here. Just take me to the airport and put me on a plane, any plane. I will take my chances."

Dr O'Mard was in no mood to tolerate my tantrum, and insisted he needed to have a proper look inside me. However, to do this, I had to go to his clinic where he had the right equipment.

I was convinced this was the end of the road for me, despite the surgeon's reassurance all was going to be well. Once again I had to endure another painful car journey and on reaching our destination, I was confronted by a set of very steep steps. At this moment, I'd really had enough. But somehow, I managed a slow and painful ascent up to the clinic.

Once inside, it seemed much more modern, with an American-style decor. In all fairness, the endoscopy and colonoscopy equipment looked right up to date, especially as it had the latest full-colour monitor.

Like many people, I had experienced these two procedures before under sedation with little discomfort. You can imagine my surprise when I was informed that on this occasion sedation was not going to be used. I was going to feel and see everything.

Both procedures took about twenty minutes, and they were truly a brutal act of torture.

Richard held my hand throughout. Although he tried hard to be strong for me, I could see tears rolling down his cheeks. However, the results did confirm that I had no option but to have an operation.

When we eventually returned to the Adelin Clinic it must have been well after two a.m., Dr O'Mard announced he was going home for a couple of hours sleep. He said he would be back around first light to perform the operation. Dr Silk went back to the hotel. I was now resigned to the fact there was no alternative but to stay here.

In an act of surrender, I allowed Richard to remove my shoes and loosely cover my lower legs with the top sheet while I reluctantly lay on the bed fully clothed. Richard found an old bentwood chair and sat by my side. We held hands, and together we cried. Despair overwhelmed me.

An hour passed and Richard nodded off to sleep sitting upright on the chair. At this moment, I noticed an old man walking towards me. At first, I thought it was one of the other patients wandering off to the toilet, then I realised I recognised him. My mind recollected our first visit to Antigua several years prior, when walking off the restaurant pier after our breakfast, I met an elderly man in spirit dressed in a very worn sleeveless shirt and ragged shorts, carrying a rod full of fish. There was no mistaking it – this was the same man. It was Bart the fisherman!

"Shh!" He put a gnarled finger up to his weathered lips. "I 'ave to talk t'you. You's real sick."

He stood right at the end of my bed, looking exactly the same as I remembered him. "I've been sent to help you. Your mammy, she's very worried about you. She wants you to know she loves you, an' you have to stay 'ere an' do what they say. No matter what, you'll be fine."

Bart paused and repeated himself with absolute clarity, "Your mammy says your safe. Do what the doctors say, and you'll be fine."

Then he faded away.

I wondered whether Bart knew all those years ago when we first met that I would be lying here in this clinic fighting for my life and it was his role to visit me. Is life's journey that predictable? Or was it the choices I voluntarily made that led me to this moment in my life?

Exhausted, I too fell asleep.

At first light, Dr O'Mard arrived with an Asian man who was introduced to us as Dr Sen, the anaesthetist from the Holberton Hospital. The surgeon was delighted that Dr Sen had bought some unused sterile equipment with him. Apparently, at the Holberton, surgical supplies were in such short supply, all the disposable equipment was constantly reused out of necessity. It struck me how we take so much for granted at home, and here something so simple was regarded almost as an extravagant luxury.

I suppose in certain situations, ignorance is bliss. Nevertheless, curiosity got the better of me and so I asked Dr O'Mard how this operation would differ from performing it in his own hospital.

"Well," he growled in his deep New York accent, "normally we use a laser scalpel, but here we only have the old-fashioned metal knife. Does the same job, but the scarring will be more than I would like. What concerns me most, is if you need some blood during the operation. We don't have any! Worst case scenario, if there is an emergency situation, we might find some at the Holberton, but all the blood there is unscreened so I really wouldn't want to use it."

Apparently, Dr O'Mard was blunter than expected!

"Other than that – you needn't worry about a thing." He smiled and winked at me. "Everything is going to be just fine."

The two doctors withdrew to prepare the theatre for the surgery.

Once all was ready, I hobbled through the barrier into the theatre where I was met by Dr O'Mard, all gowned up in blue. The room was tiny and dominated by a very old operating table. The equipment seemed sparse, principally an electric port lamp connected to a side table.

I lay on the operating table, and after a few reassuring words, Dr Sen instructed me to hold a thick, black-rubber mask over my nose and mouth. As the taste of anaesthetic hit the back of my throat, my body succumbed to deep sleep.

My first recollection after the operation was Richard whispering into my ear, "Don't worry, everything has been a complete success and you are going to be fine." He smiled, stroked the back of my hand and gave me a light kiss on my cheek.

A few minutes later, a nurse wheeled me off to a small private room. I thought this must be the post-natal wing as I could hear the sound of babies crying. To my surprise, despite the absence of air conditioning, I had a small ensuite bathroom with a toilet, shower and washbasin. My excitement was short-lived as Richard observed the porcelain was thick with orange sandy dust and devoid of any water! We later learned that water was only available once or twice a week and then only for an hour or so. Water rationing was enforced in order to keep the swimming pools topped up in the luxury hotels. I was horrified at the sacrifices the local community made to accommodate the tourists.

Later, when Dr O'Mard visited to discuss my post-op condition, he insisted I might need to be hospitalised for ten days, but he was willing to reevaluate this later depending on my recovery progress. I had already decided, with or without his consent, I wasn't staying here that long!

Dr O'Mard said he was returning to New York early the following morning but he would be back in ten days for my follow-up progress consultation. Pre-empting my concerns, he advised I would be left in the capable hands of the resident junior gynaecologist. Naturally, I felt abandoned and rather concerned.

That first night, Richard stayed with me until about one a.m. Once I was settled, he went back to the hotel to freshen up and have a short sleep.

After being given a sedative, I slept soundly for a short time, before waking to the screams of a painful childbirth coming from the next room.

It was then I saw Sam over in the corner, and judging by the energy that surrounded him I knew intuitively that new life was not going to be joining us this night.

After about an hour or so the screams subsided and turned to heavy sobbing. There wasn't any sound of a baby's cry. Death was in the air.

A nurse popped her head around the door to check on me.

"Sorry, dear, for the noise. But it has been a sad night."

"I know," I said. "The baby was stillborn, wasn't it?"

She looked surprised that I knew, but nodded and excused herself saying she needed to get back to the mother.

This tragic event caused me to reflect on the many mothers that had been to see me suffering grief from losing their unborn child. So often these children are loved and mourned for by their parents in exactly the same way as babies born into this world and nurtured. Lying there in the darkness, I wondered about that question grieving parents had been asking for thousands of years … so I put this question to Sam: "If a baby is stillborn for whatever reason, does that child have a soul and if so, when actually does the soul enter the body?"

Where spiritual enlightenment is concerned, Sam will always attempt an explanation to my questions. "This is a very complex happening and until your science can uncover more about the structure of the universe, much of what I say will be hard for you to understand," he explained.

In my mind, I challenged Sam to at least try and offer a reasonable insight, as this was a very important spiritual question, also one that I needed to try to understand for my own progression.

Sam knew this was crucial, not only for me, but for the countless parents who love a child that is never born alive into this world. "I will endeavour to answer as clearly as is possible so you can start to understand the basic principle. However, you have to be mindful that what I am telling you is an extreme oversimplification, which will make my explanation flawed. It is rather like someone asking you to explain the workings of a motor car to a small child in just a hundred words. What's more, even at my level of consciousness, there are constraints and limits of understanding."

I was willing to accept the explanation would be diluted and erroneous by the inaccurate vocabulary, but on the many occasions I had given counselling to grieving parents, it was fundamentally not enough for them just to accept their infant had a loving place in the spirit world – the modern mind needs more than unquestioning acceptance.

Sam explained, "Fundamentally, everything exists within the universe. Within that existence there are atoms which are the building blocks of the solid. Also, within the universe there is much that you cannot see, which is also made of its own particles. Like the universe, you are made of particles that you can see and also of particles you cannot see. To create a baby, conception needs to take pace. At the moment of conception there is a combination of egg and sperm. The egg and sperm are made of what can be seen and what cannot be seen. Within the combination of what cannot be seen in the egg and sperm, there is a further creation of something else, a consciousness. We will give that consciousness a label, and call it the soul.

"So as the combination of molecules grow to form a baby, there is an element that cannot be seen but is unique to that living life force, which is its soul. That soul is linked to every other element of consciousness and does not conform to the limitations of the physical.

"As spirit, you have always existed within the universe's energy because being spirit is part of you. This does not mean that you will automatically be born into the physical as a developed spiritual soul as you have been, it just means that your soul has existed as part of the great spirit dimension within the universal energy.

"When spirit enters the physical at conception, that soul hasn't necessarily had an 'earthly life' experience as a living being, although some have.

"The cells of male and female provide a vehicle for the soul to exist within the physical dimension. This is what earthly parents provide, a way that allows the spirit to express itself within the physical world. It is a way the two energies can merge."

As with any spiritual tutorial, one answer leads into countless more questions and my mind was buzzing. I asked, "So what if babies are terminated before they are born? Will their soul pass into the spiritual dimension?"

"Of course they will pass into spirit, because from the outset they are already part of that dimension."

I was very aware there was much physical growth from the moment of conception to full term, but I was unsure how this related to the unborn child. "So will an unviable or terminated foetus grow into a baby in the spiritual dimension?"

Sam looked a little unsure how to answer this. "The laws of physical growth have no necessity in the spiritual dimension. However, there is growth at many other levels. I believe your question is specific to the physical mortality of a very new conception. However, the answer is neither yes nor no! There are factors which I cannot verbalise at this time. But, spiritual energy which hasn't fully combined with the physical dimension may most likely return to the greater source of spiritual energy, but there are exceptions.

Nevertheless, when a foetus is fully formed into a baby, parents can become very emotionally attached. There is a bond of love and therefore an added energy within the developing spiritual soul. These babies are loved and wanted and their earthly parents grieve when they are lost. With these added energies, there is most definitely progression in the spiritual dimension."

My mind was racing; nothing was ever straightforward, especially as there was so much variation in circumstances. I asked, "What if a baby is terminated? Will the parents see that child again?"

Sam replied, "Whether a baby is lost through voluntary termination or by natural causes has no bearing on the requirement to be reunited in the spirit world, that is a matter of individual choice."

Despite the excitement of listening to Sam, I was fresh out of surgery and my body still influenced by anaesthetic, so it was not surprising that exhaustion overwhelmed me and forced me into sleep.

Sometime later, the bright morning sunshine woke me and almost immediately I felt a severe irritation down the whole of my left arm. On looking, I could see a trail of blisters along my skin.

I pulled the cord to alert a nurse to help me as the blisters were burning and I wanted to scratch them. Apparently, a pretty aggressive insect had been attacking me in the night!

At exactly eight a.m. on the dot, Richard arrived laden with three full carrier bags of all sorts – the clinic didn't provide food or refreshments for their patients, this was the responsibility of the family. Looking at the contents of his shopping, I think there was enough to feed everyone in the clinic!

As soon as he entered the room, his smiling expression turned to one of complete shock.

"What are those red marks up your arm?" he asked.

I explained what had happened.

"We have to get you out of here, Helen!"

From that moment, he only left my side for the shortest of times. Our main objective was to prove I was better off under Richard's care in a place with running water and air conditioning.

On the third day after the operation, I was relatively mobile, had all my tubes removed and managed to fully digest some food. During this time, Richard had managed to talk with the insurance company and had rented a small villa so he could nurse me back to health. Having these facilities to hand certainly gave Richard some leverage to organise my early discharge.

Thankfully, at the end of the third day I was released into Richard's care.

I was so relieved to leave the clinic.

Richard was wonderful in nursing me back to health, despite his very limited cooking skills of warming tinned soup, grilling toast, putting butter on it and boiling fresh eggs!

Ten days after the operation, Dr O'Mard returned from the States as promised. We visited him in his office for a check-up and he was pleased with my progress. During our conversation we learned that while he was on duty in New York, a young female patient died waiting for surgery in the theatre corridor with exactly the same condition as me.

So, Dr O'Mard was right – death was all too close!

I queried whether her condition was more serious than mine, but apparently it wasn't. Dr O'Mard explained that in a busy city hospital, the limited surgery capacity is constantly being overstretched by very grave emergencies taking priority over others. As a result of a more pressing emergency, this young girl died waiting. He felt that in some ways I was lucky as a less experienced doctor than Dr Silk might well have overlooked the seriousness of my condition. Also, as there were no distractions here, I had the operation exactly when I needed it by a very proficient surgeon. Other than the primitive facilities, it couldn't have gone any better!

In my mind I knew without doubt these events aligned so positively under Sam's influence.

It was only after another ten days of recuperation that Dr O'Mard eventually signed the medical papers for me to take a flight and leave the island.

Naturally, I had been worried sick about being away from the children for so long. Despite keeping in touch, we decided not to tell them about the seriousness of my operation. Their disappointment of our delay was short-lived when they realised their lakeside adventure was extended.

During my ordeal, it didn't take me long to fully understand the spirit world's warning. While I thought I was sensing the death of *my* daughter, I was sensing my own mother's feelings of imminent danger and her fears of "losing a daughter" – her daughter.

It was my mum in spirit trying to warn me.

So often with the spirit world, messages are never quite as direct as we would sometimes like. The answer is there, but it is for the medium to interpret the symbolic language as accurately as possible, and it's the accuracy of the interpretation that creates the vast difference in calibre of each spiritual medium.

On this occasion, although I correctly understood the wording of the message, because of the closeness of our relationship and the intense nature of the communication, my subconscious would not allow me to consider it was my own Mum warning me that it was *my* life that was in danger. However, with maturity, I now understand that only by experiencing life to its extreme limits can I be better equipped with the necessary compassion and empathy to more proficiently help and heal others in genuine need.

22

Hatikvah ... Lest we Forget

"At the going down of the sun and in the morning,
We shall remember them."
~Binyon~

Once back home, the routine of family life soon distanced me from my life-threatening Caribbean experience.

Christmas 1991 was almost upon us and the children were in their last two days of school before breaking up for the holidays. Not only were they excited at the prospect of Christmas, but this year I was equally as excited because Richard had arranged for us all to have Christmas and New Year at Lucknam Park Hotel on the outskirts of the city of Bath in the county of Somerset. What a thought! No cooking, no cleaning, no visitors – nothing to worry about, but enjoying the Christmas holiday.

This was my first Christmas since Mum had passed into spirit, and having experienced so much turmoil in our household over the past two years, Richard really wanted to focus on making this a perfect Christmas for all the family. I knew his intention was to distract me from my grief and the nightmare experience in Antigua. Ultimately, he wanted me to have a really special time.

Naturally, the pre-Christmas period is busy for every parent, and like so many other mothers I had my maternal duties to perform in between juggling my professional work and my home commitments. On this occasion, I had to drop off some home-baked cakes that I had been assigned to make for the children's school party. Without asking, Fiona had volunteered me for this task to her class teacher some weeks prior.

Thankfully, the school was just a stone's throw from our new home, so at least I could take them around directly after baking.

It was a small country school, set all alone along Bodafon Lane, built in a time gone by when the community only had a few children to educate. Unfortunately, it was now becoming overcrowded and was in desperate need of an extension.

The narrow lane leading up to the school was already full of the parents' parked cars. If one came in the opposite direction, I would be stuck, as even under normal circumstances there was barely room for two cars to pass each other.

As I crawled along the road looking for a space, I passed a man looking over the hedge gazing upon the open fields below. I became curious as to why he was wearing what seemed to be an old-fashioned, heavy-duty working tunic from a bygone era, as though he was in fancy dress. After parking the car, I walked back towards the school and remarkably the man was still there, seemingly totally fixated by the sea-view beyond the hedge. It was seasonally cold, but there wasn't a cloud in the bright blue sky, so on a clear day like today, the views across all the fields and onto Llandudno's crescent bay were breathtaking.

It was then I realised this was no earthly man, but a spiritual apparition.

As I approached him, he turned his stare to me, sending a chill right through my body.

To be honest, I felt completely baffled by this strange encounter, but experience had taught me to be patient at these times and keep an open heart as there was always something to learn.

A strong shimmer of energy emanated from around this man's head, and his feet glowed with a golden brightness. I felt strangely amused as he was wearing open sandals and his naked feet were exposed to the wintery weather.

He smiled at me, and I couldn't help but notice how unusually flat his face seemed, with deep dimples at the sides as though something had been removed leaving an indentation. I couldn't describe him as handsome – he wasn't – but he was extremely tall and towered above the top of the hedge.

Having my full attention, he gestured towards the ground with his finger where I saw a boulder, presumably where he wanted me to stand. I urgently needed to deliver the cakes into school, however my inquisitive mind got the better of me and I stood on the boulder so I could more easily look at what lay beyond the hedge.

I couldn't believe my eyes. In the field there were thousands of spirit children, standing silently side-by-side like soldiers on parade. They all looked directly towards me and I couldn't help but notice the desperation in their eyes, as if they had been stripped of every ounce of their identity, causing a poverty of the soul.

Some of the children even cradled babies in their arms.

Absolutely astonished, my jaw dropped open and my heart started to race. This was an awesome spectacle. I was curious why I needed to witness this sight. I remember thinking, why are they here? Why is he showing me this?

Clumsily, I stumbled down from the boulder feeling unsettled by what I had seen. At that, he faded away right in front of my eyes. I looked over the hedge again, but the children had disappeared. I was incredibly moved by what I had witnessed. What on earth was this all about, I wondered to myself?

It took me a few seconds to regain my faculties and continue up to the schoolyard. I couldn't help feeling that delivering all these cakes seemed trivial after seeing so many desperate children.

As I approached the door I saw Sam patiently waiting for me. He smiled and intuitively I knew that he was aware of the spiritual visitation I had just observed. "Something very important is about to be revealed to you. I can tell you, you have just borne witness to a rare angel indeed. You are very privileged!" he said.

"But why so many children?"

Sam replied, "These are some of the innocents of war that were separated from their families because of extermination. Those in spirit had to unite these unfortunate souls. It was important you were reminded of this."

After a short silence, he disappeared. Naturally I was extremely puzzled, but the practicalities of the day had to continue.

Over the following days, although I kept thinking of all these spirit children and the effect they had upon me, I don't remember Sam speaking to me about the relevance of the vision.

The following week we were into the Christmas holidays and preparing for our trip to Bath.

After a long journey with two excited children, we arrived at the Lucknam Park Hotel, deep in the heart of the English countryside. As we approached the long driveway, I could see that it was formerly a spectacular country house estate of historic significance. Just by being in the house's vicinity had activated my spiritual antennae, putting me on spiritual standby! I felt this historic place would be a magnet for spirit visitors wanting to reunite with their families.

On arrival, we were shown to our rooms, which were situated inside the most picturesque little courtyard villas. The children and I became very excited when we saw each room was complete with its own fully decorated real Christmas tree with the overwhelming fragrance of fresh pine.

Despite our enthusiasm, I could feel I was starting to come down with a really nasty cold. Even when the headache came and my chest began to tighten, I tried desperately hard to remain upbeat. But it must have shown in my pale face that I was falling ill, as after freshening up and settling in, Richard took the children to explore the indoor swimming pool so I could unpack our bags and then have a good rest.

When later they returned, we all got changed and went into the hotel library to relax and have a game of some sort prior to our evening meal. With cheerful optimism, we hoped we might meet some interesting people to share our Christmas spirit. We made ourselves comfy and started to laugh and chat about the day's activities. It didn't take long to notice that all eyes were upon us with a disapproving glare.

We sat and looked at each other feeling awkward. After a long silence, I noticed the only sound was the 'tick tock' of the massive antique mantel-clock sitting high and proud on the ornate marble mantelpiece. I gave Richard a wide-eyed look and without any words being spoken I knew we were both thinking the same: *What on earth have we let ourselves in for?*

I felt so sorry for the children who just looked at me in despair. Christmas was meant to be a time for kids, however it seemed all the other guests were looking down their noses at us as if we were an infringement on their peace.

Then, like a blast of fresh air, in walked a young couple holding hands with their little boy about three years old. The first thing I noticed was the cowboy boots and denim jeans the boy's dad was wearing in contrast to a room full of sombre lounge suits, crisp shirts and plain ties.

Unknown to me the children had already met in the hotel swimming pool earlier, so when they acknowledged each other, that somehow allowed us adults to strike up a conversation. That's how we met family Lewis: David, Simone and young Freddie!

Fortunately, they had come here wanting a family style Christmas too, so laughter and traditional fun soon followed and our families paid no attention to the disapproving stares of the other stuffy guests. For us, Christmas had now begun.

However, my flu-like symptoms had really taken hold and I was feeling pretty rough. Most mothers know how it is when you feel like this, you put on your best smile as if nothing is the matter, despite needing to climb under a warm duvet, have a hot toddy and go to sleep.

True to form, the group conversation eventually came around to the subject of our professions. I knew a spiritual encounter of sorts was on the agenda as it was too much of a coincidence to see Sam in the corner of the room observing David and Simone. Experience had taught me there was something important afoot!

Richard started the ritual and explained about his shops. I was second in line and explained with a respectful brevity my role in communicating with the spirit world.

Probably out of a lack of understanding, David politely interjected and expressed that he was a non-believer and that it would take something extraordinary to convince him otherwise.

I was in no mood to defend my natural spiritual abilities as this was my Christmas holiday with my family, and to top it all, my head was spinning with cold. I was happy to be in the company of sceptical folk that would have no interest in what I do and so I could relax and enjoy the festivities as a regular Mum and wife.

Nevertheless, regardless of your religious beliefs, there seems to be a universal desire to interact with our families at Christmas and New Year. If this is not possible, the majority of us make a conscious effort, at the very least, to remember them in some way. Those in spirit are no different! Therefore it was no surprise that the Lewis family, despite their scepticism, would have relatives that wanted to communicate with them and I could clearly see a mature gentleman in spirit standing beside David. It was obvious to me by his facial features that it was his father. Even though I had absolutely no desire to prove to David his father was present, I knew he very much wanted his son to know he was there with him.

It was then my attention turned to Sam. Without anything being spoken, I knew there was an importance about this communication in ways I was yet to discover. So, I took the unusual step of responding to David's comment about his scepticism and suggested I might be able to say something extraordinary, as he had suggested, to change his mind. It was apparent by his challenging smile he was highly dubious of my abilities, nonetheless he was curious and agreed.

The man in spirit now officially told me he was David's dad. I began, "I have your father here. He is telling me he passed into spirit less than two years ago, around springtime."

David's eyes lit up. In a flash he looked directly at Simone as if she had somehow inadvertently given me this information. His manner suggested he was a tad confused.

"Yes, he died in March last year," he muttered.

"He is telling me you worked together in the 'rag trade', in the clothing business."

Confusion turned to shock. David nodded his head. Although we had started the "what do you do for a living?" conversation, we hadn't actually got any further than Richard and me!

I was astonished how overwhelmingly strong this particular spirit had become in such a short time, as his presence was almost palpable. It was as if he felt he was strong enough to talk directly to his son and not through me. I rarely encounter such inclination.

"He is identifying himself as Bernard."

David gasped. I interpreted this as a yes! Within less than sixty seconds of spiritual communication, a lifetime's belief system had been totally shattered. His eyes welled up. Already it seemed David was emotionally worn out and I hadn't even started.

"Bernard is showing me a gold ring and says he always wore a small pinkie ring on his little finger."

This revelation caused David to swing backwards in his chair in shock.

There was so much more that Bernard wanted to share. "He loves Freddie so very much, and he wants you to know that he visits him every night while he is sleeping. He wishes he could give him a cuddle every night, but he can't."

David and Simone smiled lovingly, and they both turned and looked at their son in unison.

"He wants to give a present to Freddie – to do a special thing for him. He says he is going to send him a special gift … a pink balloon! Not any balloon, but most definitely a pink one. It won't happen for a little while, but when it does you will all know it is him who has sent it."

David leaned over and refreshed all our teas. Subconsciously, I think he was trying to appear relaxed and hide his obvious shock.

There was more to say. "Apparently, you are breaking into the American market on a sweeping scale. Your dad says it isn't just the raincoats, but a new venture of other clothing as well."

David looked bewildered. "Actually, Helen, our company brand enjoys national recognition and specialises in upmarket rainwear. Just before coming here to Lucknam, I finalised a deal to have new outlets all over the States! What you are saying is so right, we have just got ready to sell a range of menswear for next winter, which is totally new for us!"

Despite being in the spirit world, through spiritual communication, father and son were engrossed in business talk once again, and enjoying every minute. Over the next fifteen minutes or so they discussed in detail the new international venture as if they were in the boardroom together. The link with Bernard remained strong; he had the opportunity to be with his son, and he was determined there would be no shadow of a doubt in anybody's mind that he was having a new life in the spirit world.

Mid-sentence Bernard paused and turned to show me his wrist. I relayed this action to David. "Your father is pointing to an expensive-looking watch on his wrist, which he says has great sentimental value to him. He is telling me he left you this, but you never wear it now."

David was noticeably moved by this revelation. "When my father died he left me a rather splendid watch, which my mother had given to him on their twenty-fifth wedding anniversary. I put it somewhere safe, so safe that I have clean forgotten where it is!"

Not wanting to weaken the link, I kept focused and quickly continued, "Your father is telling me of a skin condition that he suffered when he was alive."

David resumed his nodding. No longer was he sitting across from me with challenge in his eyes, this man now totally accepted his father was here in the lounge, albeit in another dimension.

"For some reason, David, he is presenting you and Simone with the most beautiful bunch of orchids, and I must tell you they are perfect in every way. He is offering them to you as a symbolic gift."

The couple smiled at each other lovingly, it was apparent this was a special moment for them and a meaningful sign.

"He is now talking to me about Thailand, and in particular a hotel he stayed at where they used to have the most beautiful pure white orchids similar to the ones he is giving to you."

There was no stopping the flow of this spiritual outpouring.

"Apparently, he contracted hepatitis from a peanut bowl there."

"That's true!" David replied, dumbfounded at the precise detail.

We had been talking for well over an hour. Fiona and Anthony were being as good as gold, as usual, and they were being particularly helpful by playing with young Freddie.

I explained more. "He doesn't need glasses to read anymore, his eyesight is quite perfect now. Also, he is revealing to me about his love of walking, especially through the countryside … he says he'd walk for miles. He had to stop walking when he became ill as it caused him too much pain but it was a pastime he greatly missed. However, now he is walking for miles again with no pain at all … and he's happier for it!"

David and Simone were genuinely thrilled at everything they were hearing.

"Your father was very artistic by nature, and now he is settled in the spirit world he has found a new passion in painting, which he never had time to explore when he was alive."

David nodded vigorously in affirmation of this trait.

Then, out of the blue, David asked quite randomly, "Is Dad wearing a white suit like in *Randall and Hopkirk* off the television?"

"No!" I retorted rather curtly.

David blushed and suddenly looked very embarrassed. I think he thought he had insulted me in some way. Little did he know, I too loved *Randall and Hopkirk*, the TV detective partners with a difference as one of them was deceased and always dressed in white! As a child I often felt cheated when Sam never wore a bright-white suit for our tutorials together!

Bernard continued with his communication. "Your father is telling me he bought an incredible penthouse apartment in London a good while ago as an investment for your mother. However, since his passing she hasn't been able to sell it as the recession is biting too hard."

"Yes!" said David. "It has been vacant and on the market for well over eighteen months with no interest whatsoever, not so much as a sniff."

Passing on Bernard's pronouncement, I declared, "February! It will be sold by the end of February."

"But in reality, Helen, that's in just a few weeks' time!" David gasped with a bewildered look on his face. "Surely that would be impossible in such a short timescale?"

I held out the palm of my hand and blew across it. "There! Rest assured the apartment has gone, I have blown it away for you."

Spontaneously, Bernard laughed openly. "For some reason your dad is laughing out loud saying people don't get married anymore, do they? It is rather an off-the-cuff statement to make, and for some reason he is not telling me its significance."

David looked vaguely amused and explained, "Since my father's death, my mother has been living with a chap, but she has not married him!"

The link started to wane, so I knew it was time to bring this family reunion to a close. Actually, I needed the break, my head was throbbing and my red nose was becoming sore from the constant wiping.

"Before he leaves, your father really wants you to know how very proud of you he is."

It was then a woman came forward eager to communicate with David. She showed herself to me as elderly and of a maternal nature.

I announced, "Your grandmother is here wanting to speak with you."

His eyebrows lifted as if in total surprise. "Oh yes? Which one?"

I identified the characteristics that felt the strongest to me and that David might recognise. "The one with several silver tea pots who hosts the most pristine afternoon teas with beautiful dainty sandwiches and cakes. A real lady, oozing aristocratic elegance."

There was immediate recognition in David's face. "So true! She always made the most beautiful afternoon teas and I don't mean any old afternoon tea, I mean the full Monty of Victorian china cups and silver tea pots!"

The spiritual communication continued for a little while longer, but it really was time to stop. David and Simone had been reunited with their families, their outlook on life after death had been life-changing, so my job was done. And so I had to move on; I had a family that needed me now for Christmas festivities and a nasty cold to nurture!

We all stood and hugged one another with genuine affection and had without doubt all experienced the profound together.

In an attempt to take the focus away from my spiritual revelations and to bring our emotions back to a more earthly level, Richard took centre stage and openly criticised the fashion industry, especially coat manufacturers for never accommodating the smaller man, expecting all males to be around six foot. We all laughed, and David suggested he would definitely do something about it, especially for him.

We next met up with the Family Lewis after Christmas Day lunch, because Fiona and Anthony wanted to stand at the front entrance of the hotel with their new friend Freddie to wait for Father Christmas.

Imagine their faces when they saw four beautiful black horses pulling an open carriage along the long gravel driveway with Santa in his full regalia and his massive sack of presents in the rear. There were cheers from all the guests gathered at the entrance as he drew to a stop and loudly wished everyone a Merry Christmas. It was a true delight to watch him call out the children's names to give them each a present.

Suddenly, David grabbed my arm and took me to one side. "Simone and I haven't stopped talking about our experience with you yesterday," he said. "We want to say thank you so much, Helen. What we have experienced here is something big and truly amazing. I want you to know how remarkable you are and I feel without any doubt we have both had an audience with a genuine Guru."

His words moved me to tears.

The following day, the Lewis family sadly left to return home. They made me promise the next time we were in London, we would all meet up.

As I was so poorly for the remainder of the Christmas holiday, it transpired that the Lewises were the only people to be reunited with their loved ones at Lucknam. In contrast to the multitude of grumpy guests, the Lewises seemed to fully embrace the Christmas spirit … and ironically they were of Jewish decent!

On the day of our departure I decided to take a walk on my own around the extensive grounds to try to clear my head cold while

Richard and the children volunteered to pack everything into the car.

Despite it being a bitterly cold winter morning, the hotel gardens were immaculate and beautifully manicured. Beyond the hotel's boundary fence, there were miles of undulating fields of natural beauty, crisp with morning white frost. As I stood overlooking the fence admiring its magnificence, I suddenly heard someone behind me call my name.

As I turned around, I saw Sam walking towards me with another spiritual entity. His appearance took me by complete surprise as he was dressed in what seemed to be traditional Jewish clothing. I knew the items he wore had special names and specific meanings, but I had no inkling what they were.

Moments later Sam introduced me to Rouvin and explained that he was a friend of one of Simone's relatives. I was used to Sam bringing visitors to see me so I wasn't alarmed. But there was something aloof about this spirit visitor, as though there was a secret he held that he needed to talk about, but didn't as yet have the confidence to share.

Sam smiled and said, "Sometimes, Helen, there is a greater need for people to say their messages. Every so often, it is not just for a particular recipient, but for the whole of mankind. Listen to this man ... he has a story to tell."

Needless to say, I was very curious as to the purpose of this meeting.

Rouvin told me his life story. "I died in the Second World War, in Auschwitz, one of the Nazi concentration camps."

I was taken aback by this bold statement, as I had never had a spirit communicate who had died in one of those terrible places before and I was unsure why it was of relevance to me.

Obviously, I knew these abhorrent places were built for the sole purpose of systematically killing millions of people in an industrial fashion. I knew the main target had been the Jewish community, although some were from other groups, like gypsies, Jehovah's Witnesses, prisoners of war and political prisoners. The Nazi's annihilation of these people was to be the final solution in creating a master race.

However, all this happened over forty-five years ago, so why should I have someone with me from the death camps now? What was it to do with me?

Rouvin continued, "I am here because you need to see something important, and you need to remember what you are seeing. Only by you remembering will others remember too."

Confusion spread across my face as I was uncertain of what this might be.

"People often think that cruelty and suffering will stop when man recognises and takes responsibility for the violation he has undertaken – but it doesn't, it continues on and on. Why? Because man actively chooses to allow it to continue … that is why."

Rouvin was very emotional and the passion in his statement was evident in the tone of his voice.

"Look!" he exclaimed, and extended his arm to point behind me. As I turned around, I saw fields full of thousands of children, standing still and looking at me, the same spectacle I had seen previously near my home by the school. But for some strange reason their faces seemed far more gaunt and haunting.

Rouvin's tone changed and he spoke softly, "Hundreds of thousands of innocent children, the sons and daughters of our community, were herded together with their families and taken by train in cattle trucks, with no food, water or sanitation not even fresh air to survive, sometimes travelling for many days. Some died during these long journeys. We all thought this was the worst of it, but it wasn't. When we arrived at our destination almost all of these innocents were brutally murdered, the few who were chosen to survive had a torturous existence before eventually having their suffering released by death."

Looking at this sea of children's faces an utter sadness swamped every cell in my body and I ached with compassion. Strangely, I was also affected by a feeling of guilt, why, I didn't know, other than that my forefathers might have ended these horrifying activities much sooner than they did.

Rouvin continued, "My cousin, brother, mother and father and two sisters were in the same rail carriage as Simone's ancestors. When we arrived at the camp we were all told that we would only be there for a short time before being moved on. We were separated into groups – men to the right, women to the left. Then, the sick, the elderly, the children, the mothers with young children in another. A strange stench the like of which I had never smelt before hung in the air. We thought it was from factories making something for the war. Some from the crowd started to cry out, but they were quickly silenced by the SS officers who either beat them or shot them on the spot.

"If children were twins they were separated out into another special group. Parents volunteered their twins when the SS officer asked, actually some people pointed them out as though they might be saved for an easier life. No one knew why twins were so special and why the officers made such a point of wanting to know. Parents of the twins didn't know if their children were going to be murdered or saved because of the interest in them.

"After about an hour, once the segregation had finished, a group of soldiers ushered the elderly and sick into trucks, which seemed a gracious gesture to help them reach their destination with ease. The rest of us were marched off in different directions. I felt responsible for my family, so I searched around for them so I could offer reassurance, but they were gone, lost in the multitude. The soldiers kept telling us that we had to be cleansed before going into the camp and that if we didn't we would infect the others who were there. There were rumours that hot food would be waiting for us afterwards. It looked like our fate was improving after all!"

Rouvin started to cry. "I was a young man of twenty, strong and handsome, in the prime of my life, and yet all I could do was helplessly watch as the women and children were herded away like animals. I was told they were being taken to the showers. There was terror in their eyes and they were crying. Some of us younger men were singled out and told we were going to work in the camp and that we would have our showers later. It puzzled me why the women and young children were having their shower now but we didn't have to have one until later, and I tried to talk to an elder about this. Without warning I was struck hard in the stomach by a rifle butt, which made me almost vomit with fear. I was winded badly and couldn't talk. It was then I felt lucky to be alive."

I was riveted to the spot, in just those few minutes listening to Rouvin, I felt emotionally exhausted and so desperately sad for him.

He carried on. "An impeccably dressed SS officer stood in front of me and looked deep into my eyes. It was as if I was looking directly into the eyes of evil. I looked at the floor as I didn't want to aggravate him. He prodded me with a whipping crop and told me stand back. There were a few of us selected in this way and we were told we were being put to work straightaway and marched to a separate area where we were given a striped uniform and branded with a number on our arms.

"I thought that after doing this, the women and children would have showered and we would see them again. But they did not come! My heart was breaking, I wanted to find my mother and my family. I was then taken away to another area. As I walked I could see large, tall chimneys billowing out smoke in the distance and thought that they must be melting or burning something as the stench in the air grew worse. I realised I might be put to work in this factory.

"It wasn't until I was shown inside did I see what type of factory I was to work in. Never in my wildest dreams could I imagine what was happening there. The first I knew of the gas chambers was when I was told to collect the cargo from the showers. I must have been so naïve because in my mind I never thought for one moment it would be a cargo of dead people. As the doors to the showers were opened I was told to cover my mouth. There was still a lingering smell of poison, and then I saw ... I saw hundreds of naked bodies standing almost upright before me, intertwined and dead. I was aghast at this sight and the stench overwhelmed me. I wanted to run away and scream, but someone shouted that we move them quickly as more were to follow. The other inmates knew what they were doing, so without thinking I followed their lead. The bodies were pulled aside to an area where gold teeth were pulled from their mouths and the long hair of the women was shaved. I thought I had been transported directly into the darkest depths of hell.

"I wanted to scream, to kick, to fight, but such thoughts were futile as the soldiers in charge were pointing guns at us all the time. I said to the man beside me we are better dead than doing this, but he told me to shut up and do what they asked."

Rouvin stopped for a second as he wiped his tears, and Sam asked him if he wanted to stop. He shook his head. "I have to tell her, she has to know what is before her."

This statement made me wonder what he meant, and a strong shiver went through my body.

Rouvin continued, "I was told to take some of the bodies to the ovens, where a man grinned at me and told me they burned for twenty-four hours every day. As I was strong and my muscles firm, he told me to help him lift the corpses onto a metal grill he pulled out from the oven. It was scorching hot and the flesh peeled as soon as we threw them on top. As I reached for the last body that had been at the bottom of the pile, despite the shaven head and the pale, lifeless skin, I recognised a familiar face ... It was my mother!

"I screamed with terror at the enormity of what I was seeing and what I had to do. The man in charge of the oven begged me to stop yelling out or we would all be flogged.

"'It's my mother!' I cried out again and again and again. I collapsed to my knees.

"The man beside me pulled hard at my shirt and somehow I found the strength to stand.

"'Why is this man crying?' a soldier bawled and before I could answer, the man beside me at the oven shouted that I was new here and had foolishly burnt my hand. The officer laughed as if the situation was hilarious and hit me across the face with his fist shouting that I was lucky he didn't kill me. He ordered me to stay at the ovens and learn quickly. I retched as I watched my mother sliding into the scorching oven, her body blistering before being consumed by the flames. The men beside me seemed almost in a trance while they worked. These were people from our own community, and yet they fuelled the ovens with their own people, fearful to strike back at this evil.

"After a day or two, maybe more, I cannot remember – it couldn't have been too long as my body was strong with muscle and my face was still pleasing – I was stopped by a tall SS officer and he looked long and hard at me. For a moment I believed he would kill me just for his pleasure. Then he smiled at me reassuringly, and stroked my face ever so lightly with the back of his hand and then again with his fingertips. Nausea knotted my stomach at his touch as it felt lascivious and most unnatural to me. He took me away to another place to work. Why ... I do not know. I had learned very quickly that the workers of the ovens always died in the ovens."

I sensed clearly there was something personal Rouvin felt unable to share, something so intimate and so traumatic that had been inflicted upon him that he was unable or unwilling to talk about it. It occurred to me that our meeting was equally as important for Rouvin's spiritual progression as it was my own. Perhaps by recounting the trauma of others, one day he could face every aspect of his own mental and physical suffering.

Rouvin continued, "He told me that upon their arrival I had to escort people selected for their unfortunate birth defects to a medical block. I had to appear cheerful and happy to effect peace of mind within the group. Having witnessed the crematoria, I thought I had experienced the most awful of atrocities. It was only after working in the medical centre did I realise the evil these soldiers inflicted was far worse than any imagination could ever conceive.

"Here I was witness to the most intense screams of my fellow men who were being tortured in the name of medical research. Body organs were swapped, brains were examined and other useless surgical procedures performed. People were purposely blinded, crippled, paralysed or even worse by pointless medical techniques, rarely with any anaesthetics. People were filled with disease and endured exposure to conditions our bodies could never physically or mentally tolerate. These experiments always ended in death. If the experiment didn't kill the victim, once no longer needed, a fatal overdose of all sorts would be injected into them. When there was a glut of souls to eliminate in the medical block, they would be sent to the gas chambers to die with the others."

Rouvin composed himself, and Sam laid a gentle arm on his shoulder for support as they looked upon the thousands of silent children standing in the field.

Rouvin pointed to the sea of young faces. "Some of these children you see before you were taken from their mothers as they prepared to march to the gas chambers, and then subjected to all these experiments and much more. Some of these babies you see here were used as target practice by tossing them in the air so the soldiers could shoot them or they were burnt alive when hurled into the ovens or fire pits. Every single one of these children has had their innocence violated and their lives denied by this wicked Nazi regime.

"For so long I have asked why? … Why? … Why? Why does man create such atrocities? Why does man allow such things? Why does man not learn? We, especially these children, must never be forgotten. You must never forget me, for if you forget me, you forget them!"

Sam turned as if to greet another person, and without any warning a ball of bright light about the size of a tennis ball appeared by his side. Slowly it expanded, and as it did so, it became noticeably brighter.

After a few moments, I stared at three entities standing before me and recognised one as the angel whom I had recently seen in the school road overlooking the hedge, dressed in the same heavy sackcloth tunic. I describe it as a tunic, but it was merely two pieces of fabric seemingly tied together. As the garment was so ill-fitting, I could clearly see his strong, sculptured muscles protruding from underneath. Surprisingly his facial features were shockingly harsh and not stereotypically perceivable as angelic in any way.

Sam announced, "This is Angel Sandalphon. His purpose is for the protection of the earth. He is the guardian of secret thoughts and he helps people to process their emotions in healthy ways when they have passed through traumatic circumstances."

I was still very curious as to why this spiritual angel was here; why was he showing himself now? What did I need to understand and, more to the point, why was he with Sam? It was evident something profound was imminent.

A great calm overwhelmed me.

Sam came nearer and gesticulating towards the children said in a soft voice, "They are all in his care. Helen, your purpose is to see and remember them."

"See them … why?" I asked.

"To bear witness to man's evil," Sam replied.

"But the Second World War is over, the death camps are in the past, it is bygone history," I said rather naïvely.

Sam nodded and confronted me, "Hasn't history continuously demonstrated to you how it predictably repeats itself? Cultural cleansing is not in the past, it is an atrocity you will experience again in Europe. Men, women and children will be bundled together because of their ethnicity to starve in specially built camps … and in your lifetime."

I was shocked at this revelation. This was a future I was very reluctant to acknowledge.

Sam continued, "Many children are still subjected to evil atrocities in the present time. The world chooses not to control its own destructive nature by allowing such brutality to continue. These particular children are of the Jewish faith, and have suffered and died in the death camps for that one reason alone. Just look at how many you see here, and magnify that amount many times, and you may start to quantify man's inhumanity towards children that continues to this day and will continue into the future."

Within Rouvin's reminiscence there was a bigger testimony for the world to know. Hearing his voice and experiencing the visual impact of the children's faces conveyed an important message that even today, children in particular were still being wantonly tortured and killed in immeasurable numbers.

Sam spoke boldly, "Let us just consider the plight of children, the founders of the next generation and of the next generation after that. Although outlawed, slavery affects as many as thirty million people in every country across the world in one form or another, their lives undervalued and expendable. Slavery might have been abolished, but it is as active as it was in years gone by. With much sorrow, there has been a massive increase in the size and scope of how many children are affected in this way. One of the present scourges is human trafficking, especially the trading of children. Many of these are forced into prostitution in its many forms.

"We in spirit want to highlight the importance of this message. What are you doing to save the new generation of slaves? What if it were your daughters or sons who was subjected to such vile evil. Wouldn't you want to protect them?"

I now realised his message was not only to help us understand the historic suffering of his race and that of the wanton slaughter of Jews, but to help us understand the necessity for a more concerted global fight against slavery in its many forms. I was well aware of man's greed, unfortunately it seemed synonymous with our very existence. I thought of how the global drug barons controlled millions of lives through money and addiction and promoted human trafficking to supply prostitution. I thought of the global destruction of our rainforests by business moguls, extinguishing plant and animal life. Complete landscapes being destroyed through toxic waste pumped into our air, our lands and our waters. Environments changing through global warming.

When will we stop and hear the cries of the planet?

As if to counterbalance the mood, Rouvin nodded his head towards the children. Instantly, the fields of children hummed a tune, which then erupted into song ... "Hatikvah", the national anthem of Israel, meaning "The Hope".

My whole body rushed with uncontainable emotion and tears rolled down my face. The spectacle was breathtaking at every level of consciousness. As the final line was sung, Sandalphon and Rouvin joined the children and they all slowly faded out of my spiritual sight.

I turned and walked back to my own family, physically and mentally exhausted by the experience.

I found Richard and when he lovingly wrapped his arms around me, I cried uncontrollably and relayed my story of Rouvin.

In the car driving home I thought of the guests that disapproved of the children's laughter and how empty their lives must be. I suppose all they wanted from Christmas was to hear the loud 'tick tock' of the large antique mantel clock!

Days after returning from Lucknam, I prepared for the grand official opening of my new offices on Wellington Road. We decided to throw a small party on the 14th January with an open buffet, culminating with a Clairvoyance Evening to celebrate the occasion for about one hundred selected VIP guests.

I was very excited, but disappointed that my parents could not share in my pride and be present to take part in the evening.

On the night, the Clairvoyance Evening was going wonderfully well and I had been going strong for well over an hour. I had just reunited a gentleman named Cliff Poole with his recently deceased wife. She had confirmed her spiritual presence by telling her husband she was standing by him that day in the bathroom in their bungalow while he was contemplating what colour he should use to redecorate; so simple in content but yet massively compelling.

"I agree with you that it does need redecorating. You liked the pink," she told him, "and I like the pink too!"

Poole was thrilled with this life after death confirmation, "So pink it shall be!" he shouted, doubly thrilled as he had his wife's approval on the colour change.

Following this lovely reunion, a small man in spirit with neatly combed straight-brown hair, approached me. His eyes looked strangely familiar, although I couldn't place him and certainly I didn't know him.

As he came nearer, Sam stepped forward and shouted at him to stop. Something was very wrong. Sam told the visitor to go as he was not welcome here.

The spirit visitor was arrogant and called out, "I am the Fuhrer, and I shall rise again!"

There was a repulsiveness in his manner that overwhelmed me. In that split second I recognised that this was Adolf Hitler, albeit without his iconic moustache.

I suppose it was force of habit, so I repeated his proclamation to the audience.

There was an immediate outburst of surprise followed by complete silence.

Without any thought I announced, "There must be someone here that Hitler believes can in some way give him a voice to express himself."

Sam was rarely so demanding, but on this occasion he instructed me to stop.

I told everyone that I was bringing the evening to a close, and with as little fuss as possible, Richard quickly took to the stage and finalised the *Evening of Clairvoyance*.

The room was buzzing with excitement at the countless messages that had been successfully given during the evening, and everyone was curious as to the purpose of Hitler's surprise appearance.

I was shocked as I didn't expect he would be able to communicate so freely with a medium at his own convenience. I knew this was an intricate discussion I needed to have with my guide to get answers about the complexities of the darker realms and the limitations, if any, put upon the evildoers. I knew this was going to be one of Sam's future tuition sessions and that I would not get the answer I was looking for so readily.

A journalist came over to me and struck up conversation about the visitation and he felt that it was his presence that might have been the catalyst for Hitler's appearance as he was researching an article about the strong resurgence of the neo-Nazi movement over Europe and how the admiration of Hitler and his politics was escalating.

I was nauseated at this prospect and understood a little more why I was being enlightened about the suffering caused through this evil regime.

Sam whispered into my ear the unforgettable words ... Lest we forget!

23

All in a Day's Work

"Excellence beats a path to every man's door."
~Maurice Grey~

"Well? Is she any good?" the elderly man asked my new secretary, Anne Bates.

Anne had volunteered for the position of secretary after recovering from a bout of illness during a recent course of healing from me.

"Well then? Is she any good?" he repeated. "You see, I am off on a very expensive cruise next week and I am hoping to meet a lot of single ladies. My problem is, I need my tackle to work properly! What is she like for curing male impotence, as I just can't get an erection," he announced brazenly.

Poor Anne! Despite her mature years and worldly experience, she was completely stuck for words and rather flustered. Clients rarely discussed their problems with my assistants, especially ones of such an intimate nature.

The man continued pleading with Anne, "I need to make an appointment to see the healing lady ... now, for today! And I want her to put her healing hands on my 'Johnnie' to make it work. But I don't want to waste money if she can't guarantee to cure it before I go on holiday."

Fortunately for Anne, I was just finishing with my last appointment and she was able to take me to one side to ask how best to tackle this demanding pensioner.

"I really don't know what to say to him," Anne whispered in a disturbed tone.

Under the circumstances, I felt this man's query was better dealt by me personally. I walked into reception, greeted him in a professional manner and ushered him into my office so we could discuss his problem in a more dignified way.

When people express sexual intentions so publicly, I am concerned as to whether it is really others they are trying to embarrass. Irrespective of this man's intentions, there are plenty of sexual predators in this world, regardless of age. Sometimes our preconception of limitations due to age can camouflage the evil intent of a person. I wondered whether this was such an occasion, were his intentions genuine or was he invading me in a sexual way for a titillating experience. Thankfully I don't come across such situations very often, but I am always mindful for my own safety.

Looking him straight in the eye, I explained, "Impotence is caused by many medical or emotional factors. If you choose to make an appointment with me, I would spiritually assess your physical as well as your emotional condition, and then administer the healing where I feel the problem has originated. I won't under any circumstances be laying my hands on your penis."

He looked disappointed by this revelation. I couldn't make out if the disappointment was through not having me touch his penis or from not having his condition treated before going on his holiday cruise.

The way some people take a literal view of their illness or problems is very common. By that I mean, if there is a pain in the foot, the source of the problem may be elsewhere and not stemming from your foot. Quite often a physical problem is created by an emotional situation, or vice versa.

Nevertheless, it did make me chuckle the way the man thought I could heal his problem in that specific way! It made me realise that during my seminars I needed to explain more fully to people how illness manifests itself and how the healing actually works. Whatever his motive, my brand of healing wasn't the medicine he was looking for. After our little chat, he made his excuses and made a hasty exit.

Without speaking a word, Anne and I looked at each other as only two women can. I shouldn't have, but I smiled, then it was back to work for both of us.

Soon after the official opening of my new offices there was a flurry of press interest, instigated by several of the local clergy. They made false claims I was operating illegally, and incited their parishioners to lobby the local council to have me closed down. They foolishly suggested that those who came to see me risked being influenced by demonic powers. Such disparaging remarks made my new offices the centre of media attention by almost every local newspaper in the north.

I was furious!

Where were these same journalists to report on the many positive and extraordinary experiences that were being reported by my clients? Where were they when they were invited to my evenings to witness the love and joy that spiritual communication and healing brings about? Yet here they were embarking on a smear campaign, inciting the community to fear me and run me out of town. To me, it felt like a witch hunt!

Such propaganda might have worked in bygone years, as it had for nearly two millennia. However, times were changing and no longer did the church or the large national institutions have the constitutional right based on their own brand of morality to discredit my integrity because of my spiritual beliefs and my ability to communicate with the spirit world.

So you might understand why I thought the greatest tragedy in mankind's entire history may be the hijacking of morality by the religious institutions.

Foolishly, the newspapers were so eager to discredit me, they didn't research their facts before printing their lies. Actually, I was occupying my offices in a totally legitimate manner.

As usual, the criticism came from people who had never met me. You would have thought if there was any complaining to be made, it would be from my clients.

Richard was absolutely furious. Even in the few years we had been together he had witnessed so much prejudice against my work.

This time our antagonists had crossed the legal line, so Richard went to see a solicitor, and out of principle sued them all. He knew I had done nothing illegal and proved it, so all the offending publications had to settle out of court and were duty bound to print their apologies.

I didn't feel that I had won; on the contrary, my heart was breaking, as all I had ever wanted was validation and acceptance. I had spent a lifetime searching for this from my parents and now I was fighting for it once again.

In the aftermath of all this bad publicity, my offices became so popular I had to hold groups every week to satisfy people's genuine thirst for spiritual growth and understanding.

My photographer, Peter West, spoke about me to an associate of his named Ceidiog Hughes, an investigative journalist with S4C TV. Hughes requested an interview with me and some of my clients to establish what all this uproar was all about.

Having had some experience with the press already, I knew a true showcase of my work was impossible. After meeting Hughes, despite his sceptical nature, I felt he was not out to humiliate me and he offered his assurance the television feature would represent me fairly.

Actually, I am not offended by genuine doubt of my abilities, as I believe healthy scepticism can easily be dissolved when the truth is presented. I just find it quite tiresome when every time I do something that involves the media, it is never taken at face value and they are predictably confrontational at a very base level. Society would have so much to learn and benefit if only the media could move forward from this divisive stance.

As it happened, Hughes was true to his word and the feature was fairly balanced, but as expected, devoid of any showcase. While the media maintain this stance, my brand of spiritual phenomena can never be properly explored as the content is constantly being distorted and diluted through editing.

Hughes's program started with me standing in front of one of my audiences, saying: "Your loved ones come to speak to you because they love you. They know if there is something wrong in your life and if they need to speak to you about it. Or simply to let you know that they are all right! When communication is good, it's like a question and answer time.

"Tonight is for you! I stand up here and put my neck on the line every single day of the week. I have nothing to prove, I know these people are here, I know they are talking to me – you don't. You can't see what I can see. I see them as clearly as I see you."

Whenever I start one of my groups, no matter what the size, I explain the burden of proof of survival after death is on their loved ones and so is very much dependent on their ability to accurately communicate. As I have explained before, just because a loved one has passed into spirit does not guarantee their ability to engage in fluent communication between the two dimensions, so the onus is on them to develop this ability and offer me sound information.

Hughes interviewed a lovely lady called Eirlys Davies, who was in no doubt of my abilities. She told her story. "Three years ago I lost my brother in an accident. Helen told me everything that happened to him. She told me when he celebrated his birthday, that he had one son. She even talked of the time when he taught me to drive, describing the van, its colour and the number plate!" No amount of Hughes's scepticism could ever take that life-changing moment away from Eirlys.

To conclude the news feature, I reunited a lady called Ann with her grandmother. "She says you call her Mum – Mam, actually – because she looked after you so much, you were like a daughter to her, not a granddaughter. She wants to tell you that she's with you and that she loves you." Such a simple message, but one that was truly comforting and made Ann weep with joy, as their mother–daughter relationship was so special to them.

Nevertheless, I was shocked how this was edited to such an extent, all the substantial content that I had given Ann had been removed. There was so much omission, I felt the message might seem rather vague and generic to the sceptic, but perhaps that was the producer's aim – to leave the viewer with more doubt than conviction!

On occasions, even some of my clients have their own specific agendas when they come and see me.

This one particular day was progressing nicely when Anne popped her head around my office door before bringing in the next client. Despite her mature years, she had an eye for attractive men.

"I don't think I have ever seen a man dressed so smartly and looking so handsome," Anne crooned.

Minutes later she ushered in a well-dressed man in his mid-thirties. She caught my attention and playfully winked at me.

His suit was indeed immaculately tailored, his shoes expensive and his manner polite; seemingly, here was a true gentleman. After exchanging the usual pleasantries and with an air of self-confidence, he sat down in the nearest armchair.

Although it is not a conscious decision at the start of every sitting, I am always aware it's not my role to judge my client's lifestyle – it is my purpose to link the two dimensions for the act of healing and communication.

It didn't take me long to realise this man earned his money from illegal and immoral practices. Something he confirmed quite willingly as I gave him details of his life.

I talked about his younger brother being desperately ill, possibly facing death.

"I feel you are blaming yourself for your brother's condition," I said.

The man nodded and looked genuinely upset.

When you can look deep into a person's psyche, it is hard not to be disturbed by the evil you might see. Through my spiritual sight, this man's life was crystal clear to me.

"I feel you have come here today for a specific purpose." I tried to choose my words carefully so as not to judge him, but it was hard – very hard.

I looked over towards Sam for guidance, but he said nothing.

"You want to hear that you are not responsible for your brother's welfare. You want to hear that the warnings you gave him exonerate you from his condition. You want to hear he exercised his freedom of choice and he is where he is today by his own hand ... by his own choices ... by his own actions."

The man leaned forward and stared into my eyes. He looked deeply concerned. I couldn't help but wonder why such a man would even want to open the portal into the world of spirit. I had to blank my mind to such questions.

"I cannot exonerate you. Your family in spirit cannot exonerate you. Your guides cannot exonerate you. You are solely responsible for your brother's condition. The moment you allowed him to have that very first experience, a chemical imbalance occurred within him which made it inevitable he would need a second, a third … and so on. It is as if you wilfully fed him every substance he secretly stole from you."

The man looked devastated. This wasn't what he wanted to hear. The most profound sittings rarely are.

I had only been with him for fifteen minutes of his one hour consultation. I knew it was not my role to judge, but I had my own freedom of choice to uphold and I didn't want to carry on, it was my right to stop at any time. So I did!

"You have some soul searching to do before I can take this sitting any further, so I need to bring our time together to a close."

Although our parting was executed with professional dignity, the man definitely left my offices wanting, and I could tell by his demeanour he was not happy with the situation; I could tell he was used to getting what he wanted when he wanted it.

There was one occasion, however, when Sam did step in and make the decision to close down the sitting for me, probably for my own protection.

My client was ushered in as normal. He looked no different to a thousand other men that crossed my threshold. But as soon as he sat down, I knew there was something out of the ordinary about him – not in his look or appearance, but in his intent.

I sat opposite him and commenced the sitting. I always start with introducing myself, then a general introduction of what I do and what to reasonably expect. But as I talked to him, my spiritual consciousness emptied and just went blank. It was as if I had no spiritual sight whatsoever, and a dark blindness had consumed me.

My heart started to race as I was suddenly in an unfamiliar situation. I looked over to where Sam had been standing and was relieved when I realised I could still see him. Sam was calm, he didn't in any way reflect the panic that was overwhelming me. With his arms extended and his palms parallel and flat, he brought his two hands together and said, "Close the sitting … Now! And ask him leave."

On this occasion, there was no act of judgement on my part, I simply couldn't see anything to tell my client.

"I am awfully sorry," I apologised profusely. "I have to be honest, but today I can't see anything for you."

I stood up, walked over and opened my office door to signify there was no negotiation in this matter and that I wanted him to leave. By this point, probably only four minutes had lapsed from him entering the room and leaving.

From time to time, I do have to tell a client I cannot sit for them, or bring sittings to a close prematurely, but it is usually because they have important life-changing decisions to make that must not be influenced by anything I might say. But I knew this situation was very different.

As he walked past me, my spiritual sight returned, it was as if a light switch had been turned back on. The darkness cleared and I sensed a base sexual depravity with harmful intentions of the most abhorrent kind.

Anne sensed there was a problem and courteously escorted him out. For some illogical reason, I took the air freshener off the windowsill and sprayed it all around the office as if this might be able to negate any evil energy left behind.

So there is no misunderstanding, for the most part, the majority of people who come to see me are absolutely delightful. However, even the best of us have family members that without us even knowing can bring the consequence of evil into our lives. When the spirit world brings this to our attention, the repercussions can be utterly life-changing.

It is the outcome of a regular sitting with a normal middle-aged housewife that I want to share with you. There didn't seem to be anything out of the ordinary until I mentioned two boys' names and explained that they were young, alive and were close to her, although not her own.

She smiled and acknowledged they were her two lovely nephews, and she was their very proud aunt.

It was then that a feeling of utter dread filled me. For possibly the first time in my life, I didn't know how to express with honest clarity what I was being told by the spirit world. Somehow I had to find the strength to broach and resolve a secret the boys seemed to have buried away. I looked to Sam for the means to express what needed to be said to protect the boys and not compound their suffering by forcing them into further concealment.

I spoke rather gingerly, "Do you ever talk to these boys? I mean do you have a relationship whereby they trust what you say to them?"

Immediately I knew the woman's senses were alert to something foreign happening in their lives. I knew I had to be cautious. If I was imprudent in the way I worded my comments, the truth may never be exposed and young lives would continue to be traumatised.

She replied, "Well obviously I like to feel they are close to me, as I have no children of my own. I often take them out shopping for the day to give my sister a rest, but nothing more." She gave me a worried look. "Are they ill, Helen?"

Illness was not the word I was searching for. In desperation I looked to Sam for help, but he assured me I knew exactly what to do.

How could I come right out and just say what needed to be said? What if my instincts were somehow mistaken? Deep down, though, I knew they weren't.

Nevertheless, there are some things that our own sensibilities just refuse accept, so I knew I had to allow this lady to discover the truth for herself, but I had to create the setting whereby the truth would be revealed.

"I believe the next time you speak to the eldest boy, why don't you set him aside from his brother and ask him if there is anything he needs to tell you. Explain that he can feel secure and trust you in telling you anything, and if there was something that was hurting him in any way, you would protect him, no matter what it was."

"Of course, I will!" she replied. "If he's being bullied at school, then I will naturally tell his mother."

"Oh no ... I don't think it's as simple as that," I said, trying not to cause undue alarm. "I think it's his mother he is afraid of sharing his secret with. Please ... it has to be when you get an opportune moment. He must be alone and he must trust without any doubt that he can totally rely on you, and it would be for your ears only."

"This sounds serious, Helen," she said gravely.

"It is!" I replied. "But I feel I cannot say any more. You will know when he has shared his problem with you."

I could see that she was perplexed and rather upset by what I had said, but the woman promised she would let me know if anything was amiss with the children.

A week or so later she telephoned me in tears. She explained how she had done exactly as I had suggested and asked him if there was anything he needed to share with her. After some coaxing, he revealed that he had been subjected to years of abuse by his father. He blamed himself, so he kept it a secret. It was only when his young brother started being subjected to the same treatment that he knew he really needed to do something, but didn't know how or who he could turn to.

She explained since her conversation with her nephew, the police had now arrested the father and the boys were staying with her for the time being.

As we put the phone down on each other, I wondered how anyone could subject such torment and agony on any child, let alone your own children. Sometime later I learned the father had been convicted in Chester Crown Court and had been sent to jail for abusing his two sons. Once again, the interaction between the two dimensions had delivered a positive result.

The clarity of communication from the spirit world can often be beyond life-changing on so many levels, so you can understand why, by having this ability, I have a moral obligation to strive to benefit the lives of other people.

It was around this time in my own spiritual progression that two of my spirit health workers, Doctor Clark and Harry Edwards, were instrumental in the success of my spiritual healing work. Interestingly, many clients reported actually experiencing their presence during their consultations and also afterwards while participating in my absent healing program.

I received an avalanche of letters from people living all over the UK reporting their extraordinary experiences of Clark and Edwards after seeing me.

One such was from Audrey Parry-Jones, a forty seven year old theatre nurse. (No relation to me, it is a common Welsh name!) Soon after the offices opened, she heard reports about the success of my spiritual healing from her colleagues at the local hospital. Audrey was in desperate need of my healing help as she had just had drastic surgery after being diagnosed with breast cancer.

These are Audrey's own words of her healing experience with me:

I came to see Helen after a friend asked me if I had heard about this healer. I have to admit that at the beginning I was very sceptical about what was going on, and tried to come up with all kinds of alternative explanations to what it was I could feel happening to me during the healing sessions.

I could feel heat coming from Helen's hands during the healing, but thought maybe it's because she has just washed her hands in hot water. But that couldn't possibly explain it. I could also feel intense heat around my head when she held her hands over me.

I went from her after that first session and thought – No! But, a few days later I felt a lot better and so I kept coming to the Healing Centre. It does relieve the pain.

Following this, I had six terms of chemotherapy. The night before I went for my test results I was very tense, so my daughter suggested I had a nice hot bath to relax me and put Helen's picture behind the taps so I could do some absent healing.

So there I was, lying there relaxing, looking at this picture, when all of a sudden this man's face came through! Well, I was astounded, I can tell you. There I was trying to cover up my one good breast with a face flannel, because I didn't want the strange man to see me naked. I shouted for my daughter to come quick and she came running in, wondering what on earth was going on. But the face didn't disappear. It just stayed there, staring right at me.

I was shouting: 'Look. Look. Can't you see it?' But my daughter said she couldn't see anything at all.

If I had to describe it, he was like a Mills and Boon romantic type, in his middle forties. Then a second face came through. This was a man in his late fifties, with long sideburns.

Next day I went for my results and was told there was no change, which was very encouraging, but since then I have been told there is a change… for the better. I'm still doing the absent healing and the face of the first man still comes out of Helen's picture all the time.

Knowing Helen has reinforced my spiritual beliefs.

After a lifetime working in the medical profession, it was obviously very hard for Audrey to change her strong belief in the conventional, and embrace a more natural and spiritual healing program. However, she became committed to her healing sessions and to the absent healing, with strong positive results.

Another client at that time was Debbie Trotter; her experiences were so powerful she was compelled to write about them:

Before seeking Helen's help, I had been ill for about five years.

I have a condition called endometriosis, which means the lining of my womb and other internal organs bleed more than in most women. I was at a very low ebb and Robert, my husband, was the one to mention Helen and her spiritual healing to me, but he was no believer.

At my first meeting with Helen, in March 1992, I closed my eyes and tried to relax as I lay on the examination couch and she put her hands on my head. It was like a laser light, or someone with a really bright torch coming straight at me. This bright white light seemed about to hit me and just exploded in my head. I panicked a bit and nearly jumped off the couch!

I calmed down and began to feel this lovely warmth coming from Helen's hands. Then it was as if two pairs of hands were actually touching the inside of my body. I just couldn't believe it!

I was still shaking when I eventually came out from my appointment and my face was quite flushed from the warmth I had felt from the healing. Robert was sitting outside in the waiting room. When he saw me he was really concerned and jumped to his feet saying, 'My god! What has she done to you?'

I had been in there for a long time and I could hardly walk, I was so tired. Helen had also performed a psychic operation on my breast, removing a cyst that had already showed up on a hospital x-ray. For some time afterwards, there was a definite hollow where it had been. This seemed to fill itself in eventually.

On the drive home in the car I was really tired, yet so relaxed. I felt as if I had just gone ten rounds with a couple of heavyweight wrestlers. But Robert was still very sceptical and said, 'The mind is a powerful thing, you know!'

Something was going on though. My bowel and bladder problems had been causing me a lot of pain and I had been taking very high doses of Distalgesics. However, now I only need to take the odd one. Whenever I feel pain coming on, I take out my picture of Helen.

One day when I could feel the pain coming on really bad, I rang Helen up and she told me to take the photo upstairs and lie on the bed. I did what I was told and for some reason felt I had to lie on my side. It felt more comfortable. Then I could feel the invisible spirit hands resting upon me. I could feel the heat.

When I spoke to Helen later, she explained that her two spiritual supporters, Doctor Clark and Harry Edwards, were helping her heal me. Helen explained she had to lay on her side and take the pain at exactly the same time. I felt awful about that. I didn't want her to suffer the pain I had been going through. It didn't seem right.

Eighteen months before, I had an abscess on my bowel surgically removed, but it came back eight months later – even though my doctors said it was impossible. During that first appointment, Helen told me I needed a second medical opinion, as she felt something had been overlooked. She also told me there was an abnormality with my bladder. I decided to get a new opinion and the new specialist verified everything Helen had said.

Since that first healing session with Helen, my husband Robert has become a total believer. Now he always asks, 'Has Helen got any messages for me?'

The invisible spirit healing hands are another strange happening I have got used to.

I feel Helen has tuned me into something I wasn't tuned into before. The healing lights are something I see all the time when I am getting pain relief.

So, after her course of healing, Debbie maintained a much-improved level of health and wellbeing. Her commitment to the absent healing program promoted long periods of good health, and after years of suffering, she was now able to take charge of her body and make life-changing decisions.

Also at that time I decided to hold training sessions for those who showed some aptitude as a spiritual healer.

Nigel Williams and Margaret Orams-Hampton, were two such people who I met after my demonstration at the Wolverhampton Civic Hall. Subsequently, they came to see me in my offices where I discovered they were especially interested in developing their own healing abilities.

It was Margaret who astounded me the most. She had the ability to see auras and the potential to massage them to bring much benefit to the recipient. During her development classes with me, Margaret was able to hone and advance her own natural healing abilities.

This is how Margaret Orams-Hampton tells her story:

In 1989 my young handicapped sister named Elizabeth passed away. She was a real character despite her disabilities and was dearly loved by anyone who knew her.

Many people have losses I know, but for me, losing her was causing me physical pain.

Not long prior to her passing my friend Janet lost her brother when he committed suicide. Obviously her loss was great too, and to cap it all my other friend, Susan, sadly lost her husband, John. All this within six months of losing my dear Elizabeth, it was so tragic.

After meeting Helen in Wolverhampton, we all made appointments to see her at her offices in Wales.

Janet had the first sitting, followed by Susan and midway through her sitting, John brought a young lady from spirit to meet her called Elizabeth, whom he knew well. Susan confirmed this was my sister.

Elizabeth stayed to speak to me during my sitting with Helen which proved to be a very emotional experience for me. I felt as though all of my grief had somehow settled like a heavy band around my torso.

As the sitting progressed I suddenly felt as though all my grief and sadness rose up and left my body through the crown of my head and never returned.

As Helen finished up, she came outside to meet my husband Tony. I was so surprised as she began to sing Happy Birthday to him from Elizabeth, because even though no one had told her, Helen knew today was his birthday.

It was so nurturing, so comforting and knowing that Helen had lost so much in the floods yet was giving so much of herself, I made her a silk flower picture in a frame and in the centre of it was a daisy.

When I presented it to Helen she started to cry, and said. 'Do you know how important you are to me?'

She had been told by her guide Sam that when she received an everlasting daisy that her career would truly open up. What prompted me to give that daisy picture I will never know, but Helen's guide obviously did.

After my sitting I introduced Nigel Williams to Helen as we had been told by her that we had a gift of Healing. From that day, we committed ourselves to travel down to Helen's Healing Centre for team healing sessions which continued for a couple of years.

After this introduction, I attended several courses and studied to become an advanced Reiki Master. I gained my diploma in anatomy and physiology and as a Hopi Candle therapist and have never looked back.

I am so proud of Margaret's commitment to develop her natural healing abilities and reach such a high level of achievement. It is true to say many people have benefited as a result.

Her friend Nigel Williams is the most unassuming person you could ever wish to meet, and he was quite taken aback when I told him he had natural healing abilities and a modest talent for clairvoyance.

This is Nigel's own story:

At the time I met Helen, I was working as a manager in a department store. Over lunch one day my friend Margaret started chatting to me about going to see a medium called Helen Parry Jones at the Civic Hall in Wolverhampton.

Almost as soon as Helen walked out on stage we knew she was something special and that something very real was taking place. The things she was coming out with were just so accurate for the people receiving messages and I just knew this woman was in touch with the other side.

Helen made a second visit to the Civic Hall and I tried to talk to her at the end of the show by giving her a tape of when I heard her on the radio days before. As I handed her the tape, so many people were milling around her, but she took one look at me and said, 'You are Nigel, aren't you?' I was floored, how could she know my name and recognise me when we had never met before or spoken.

I later made a private appointment to see her at her offices in North Wales where Helen told me I suffered with migraines and explained that they were the caused by a buildup of pressure through blocking out the spirit world. As soon as I opened my heart and mind to spirit, the headaches would go. When I got home that night I closed my eyes and tried the absent healing Helen had asked me to try, and lo and behold they vanished.

She also talked of an old drinking buddy of mine called Billie who had died some years ago. Billie spoke of my grandfather in spirit. Then Helen said suddenly, 'Who is Floss?' Helen didn't know, but it was an auntie of mine. She continued by saying that my auntie had a cat sitting on her knee and it sounded like

'Fluffit'. Its name was actually 'Chuchit'! However, my aunty had rattling false teeth so that when she spoke the words often came out wrong and sounded a bit strange. I started to laugh because I knew exactly what Helen was talking about. She went on to say that I was going to have an association with an American and ride in a silver car with him. I had in fact been to Cyprus earlier that year and an American friend had taken me across the Turkish border… in a silver car of course!

Before the session with Helen ended, she said I had to make a really big decision, whether or not I was going to pursue Healing, as it was a huge responsibility and a step only I could decide upon. She said if I wanted to go ahead, she would help me define my abilities properly.

Shortly after I returned home I went to see another famous medium, Doris Collins, at Victoria Park Hotel, Wilton. Imagine my surprise and how flabbergasted I was when she picked me out of the audience and said you are in the process of making a really big decision about devoting your life to healing others. You may do this full- or part-time but you need to make a decision very soon.

That really made up my mind, and I enrolled for Helen to help me. She freely devoted her time through the love of her work to help me achieve my goal.

Later Helen told me two things repeatedly, 'Travel and Heal'. So ironically now I work within the travel industry where I can do both.

Meeting Helen has and always will be a life-changing experience.

Since his training with me all those years ago, Nigel's life has changed beyond belief and his confidence has grown, and his spiritual abilities have substantially progressed, bringing benefit to others.

After my appearance on television I soon became recognised in the local area. Whether I was out for a coffee or doing the shopping, it wasn't long before complete strangers would take up a conversation with me.

Actually, there are times when it is quite usual for complete strangers to engage in the most intimate and in-depth conversations, and one of these places is at the hairdresser!

It was there I first met the strikingly beautiful Ruth.

This is how Ruth Johnston tells her story:

Helen came to the hairdressing salon where I worked as a stylist. I was fascinated how she gave messages to our other clients while she was waiting. It was amazing. We go through our daily lives all wrapped up in our own thoughts and issues, not thinking or being aware of how others are feeling or what they might be going through. To see the joy, relief and comfort on the faces of these people was amazing. I was almost jealous, as nobody seemed to come through for me, but when I think about it, I had not lost anyone close to me and I did not need to hear anything; I was content.

Then I learned Helen had opened her new offices, so I went to see her for a sitting. She gave me information about my great-grandfather and he told me that I should be more knowledgeable and proud of my family history. Apparently, he was a barefoot child who worked as a bricklayer, then became one of Liverpool's master builders. His company built many famous landmarks about the city, including the Blackburn Insurance building and the Grafton Rooms. He became Alderman and was one of the founders of Everton Football Club. He was known as 'old goal drops' as he would always hand out sweets when Everton scored a goal. Subsequently I discovered I had the newspaper cutting that says all this, but I didn't realise it at the time of my sitting with Helen.

She then told me that within a year or so, she could see me standing at the alter with a fireman and I am weeping. I think… Shit! What is happening here? I am happy with my husband. Where, when and why am I going to meet this fireman? Then soon after, my friend marries a fireman, and I am their bridesmaid… and standing right beside them I wept at the altar.

The salon expanded and they opened a beauty section where Ella, a young girl of eighteen, started to work. We became great friends and during this time she lost her father. I was devastated for her, as this was my worst nightmare. One day, Helen decided to have a salon treatment, and it happened to be with Ella, my friend. Ella came out shaking, Helen had told her that her father was in the room. Helen described what they had buried him in and that he was holding a flower, also that he was mortified at the blue gown he had been laid to rest in and was laughing at himself. He was also holding the hand of a young boy, his brother, who had passed away as a child. Ella's dad told her that he loved her and that he wanted her to know that he was fine and at peace. Ella did not know about this 'Uncle' at the time, her mother explained it all to her after her experience with Helen… And it was confirmed they buried him in a blue shroud.

To be honest I could fill a library of books with people's individual stories of their experiences with me, but in the interest of brevity and in keeping with the timeline in this book, I have confined it to the selection of encounters that were given to me in those early months of my offices opening.

However, there is one more encounter I would like to share before I move on. Richard and I had a telephone call from David and Simone, the young couple who we met a couple of months earlier at Lucknam Park Hotel, inviting us out to dine with them in London. David was eager to bring us up to date with their lives after their return from Bath and in the aftermath of their spiritual encounters.

These are David's own words, recorded in an interview with a journalist gathering information about me:

There really was so much information that Helen relayed. We invited her up to stay and dine with us in London after Christmas had passed. Lucknam was such a special time and the profoundness of her gift intrigued me.

Even on our evening out she relayed more interesting facts telling me where my grandfather had hidden my grandmother's jewellery. Unfortunately he died before telling anyone!

After Lucknam and when we had returned to London, friends of ours invited us to a golf club in Wentworth, Surrey. It was a party for a child and there were around thirty or more children there all sitting in big chairs. The room was full, and I mean full, of blue and yellow balloons as it was a boy's birthday party we were celebrating.

We were talking to our friends on nearby couches when we just happened to look at Freddie. We couldn't believe our eyes, there was a pink balloon stuffed down the back of his chair. Every other balloon in the room was blue and yellow. Forty minutes later and another pink balloon appeared floating next to him and he picked it up. They were being blown up by the magician but there were only two pink balloons and Freddie had both of them! One could say it was coincidence but how in a room full of children does my son have them both? The chances of that happening are a million to one, but it was just as Helen had predicted and we knew it was a sign from Dad.

Can you imagine how I felt when on March the 1st, my estate agent rang me to say that he had shown someone around our flat prior to this date and that they wanted to make me an offer then and there! What's more the contract sailed through within just a few weeks with not so much as a single hitch. Who on earth has had that happen?

So David and Simone had the sign from Bernard that he had promised, proving he was close by and lovingly looking over them. Also, Bernard's prediction about selling his apartment in weeks had come true, despite the very short timeframe.

When I returned from London, my secretary Anne advised me she was looking for a new home in Staffordshire and so it was inevitable she would soon be leaving me. I prayed for a new person to be directed to me to assist in the offices, and my prayers were answered.

Jenny had been a secretary to a top consultant at our local hospital and was over-qualified for what I needed. However, after making a dramatic recovery after a course of treatment from me, she was delighted to volunteer her services and was happy to help me.

We had forged a relationship during Jenny's healing sessions after she was involved in a terrible car accident, which resulted in her having a serious frozen shoulder and trapped nerve. Her condition was so bad that she experienced a sort of lock jaw which made speaking impossible and gave her hours of acute pain.

Despite countless prescriptions for pain relief and regular attendance at a specialist pain clinic, nothing seemed to ease her suffering until she started to have some healing from me.

After a few sessions, Jenny announced the pain had gone and she could freely move her arm and jaw again.

As you can see, my offices became a centre of life-changing experiences for all those who visited.

For me ... that's all in a day's work!

However, personally, there was one pain that wouldn't go away. Not a day went by that I didn't think of Mum. Eventually, 1st May came around. It was my mum's first birthday after her passing. My heart ached – I missed her terribly!

It was a Friday and so I had to leave the offices a little earlier to visit the supermarket for some weekend shopping. I remember this day so vividly because as soon as I walked through the supermarket entrance – bang – it hit me! Over the store speakers they were playing 'What a Wonderful World' by Louis Armstrong, the same music that I had played at my mother's funeral.

I froze! Emotion overwhelmed me and I burst into tears on the spot. What a sight I must have looked standing there with tears rolling down my face.

But I knew it had to be a sign from her.

For me, this small sign was mammoth. Even though I see spirit every day and participate in in-depth conversations, I hadn't had any real sightings of Mum since the funeral. However small this might seem, this sign was truly wonderful for me. I felt my mother was trying to convey her love to me.

24

The Whole Shebang

"If you focus too long on an obstruction,
You can't see another direction that has opened for you."
~Helen Parry Jones~

America had excited us! We were smitten with its lifestyle and in a bid to change our own path, we explored the possibility of emigrating. However, it seemed that my profession gave the visa attorney some difficulty, as there wasn't a relevant box to tick on the forms. Richard wasn't proving much easier, as his self-employed status didn't sit well on the application either. So it wasn't going to be straightforward, but the promise of success was sufficient encouragement to keep us paying the attorney fees!

While processing our visa applications, we thought it a good idea to go on a road trip to view properties. Over the week we visited countless developments, however on one occasion Richard called in on his own to quickly pick up a property sales pack. After about five minutes he came out looking a little confused.

"Helen, I think we should have a closer look here. Last night I had this strange dream that I met a woman with a very distinct perfume. I can't remember ever smelling anything in a dream before. Well, the saleswoman in there has that very same perfume as my dream last night. I really believe it's a spiritual sign to take a closer look. Perhaps we are being guided to buy a property here."

This is how we met Betty Price, an outgoing lady in her early forties. After exchanging all the usual pleasantries, the conversation soon came around to our professions. The Americans are so much more outgoing than us Brits, so there were no quiet reservations when I spoke of my vocation. On the contrary, Betty readily admitted she was a great believer in the spirit world and was fascinated to learn more. In no time at all, she wanted me to meet her family, especially her daughter Heidi, a beautiful young lady with long blonde hair and a charismatic personality.

Knowing we wanted to move over to the States, Heidi became our self-appointed guide during the following days and went everywhere with us. She wanted us to move to Winter Park, the cultural centre of Orlando, so we could live near her.

One evening, while eating frozen yogurt in an open-air eatery, Heidi asked me about romance and the man she would one day marry.

I was in no doubt true love was imminent for her and I described in detail her future husband.

Finally, I announced, "Your guide is shouting out the name Jerry!"

Heidi was overjoyed with her messages and embraced everything I had told her. Like all young girls, she was in love with the prospect of romance, and happy to dream of the day she would meet her handsome soulmate.

Eventually, the time came when we had to return to the UK.

A few months later, I had a phone call from Heidi who wanted to share her news with us. She had been dating for a while and their relationship had become serious. His name was Lee, but despite the name difference he had the same personality and handsome characteristics I had described to her months prior.

Heidi revealed her story. "As we were so much in love and we both felt there was definitely a future together, Lee suggested I meet all his buddies, so we arranged a night out. As soon as we arrived, the guys shouted, 'Hi, Jerry!' And all night it was Jerry this and Jerry that, they never once called him by his proper name of Lee."

Naturally I was very curious.

She continued, "Apparently he was given the nickname 'Jerry' at college as they felt he was the double of Jerry Seinfeld, the comedian, and the nickname stuck."

Naturally, this was confirmation for Heidi that she had found her soulmate and she was excited at the prospect having a wonderful future and family with him as I had predicted.

Heidi wasn't the only one looking forward to having a new family, as I had just found out I was pregnant. Richard and I had made the decision a few months prior to have a baby together, but never in my wildest dreams did I expect to become pregnant so quickly.

Fiona and Anthony were delighted at the prospect of us having a new baby, and secretly we hoped sharing a sibling in the new family unit would bind all the children from both marriages together.

Meanwhile, it wasn't too long before our visa attorney wanted us to return to the States. It seemed a welcome opportunity for a little holiday to see our new friends Heidi and Betty Price again.

During our stay, an acquaintance of the Prices introduced me to some broadcasters from one of the Orlando radio stations. Once they met me and had first-hand experience of my spiritual abilities, they became enthusiastic about me working with them in the future. I became excited at exploring these new media platforms that the British broadcasters always denied me.

I must have made a positive impression, as out of the blue they rang me up with an invite to a lunch as their guests with ex-British Prime Minister Margaret Thatcher. She had left Downing Street two years prior. Whether or not you agreed with her politics, Thatcher had a very charismatic personality and she was the most amazing public speaker.

Around Winter Park, the word about my spiritual abilities was well and truly out. I could have so easily opened a clinic in the main street and filled my diary. Many people stay and work in the States on a tourist visa, but for us this was not an option as we wanted to do everything above board and legal.

Nevertheless, there was one request I could not decline. A relative of the Prices had recently given birth to a baby named Garrett. He had been born with a congenital disorder so rare, the doctors could not offer any type of diagnosis or prognosis. At first they speculated it might be his heart, but no matter what treatment they offered, it had no effect. The doctors from three different hospitals admitted they were absolutely baffled as to what it might be.

The Prices pleaded with me to help the baby in some way, otherwise it was inevitable he was going to die.

Due to the geographical distance, I was unable to visit the baby in person. However, by coordinating with Heidi, I was able to offer a spiritual assessment of his condition during an absent healing mediation. I suggested to Heidi that she would sit beside him and hold her hands over his tiny body while simultaneously I meditated on both of them. I felt my close link with Heidi would in some way amplify the spiritual channelling required for my assessment of the baby's physical condition.

After the meditation, Heidi telephoned me and I explained it was most definitely Garrett's lungs that were the problem, and if the baby had any chance of survival he needed a double lung transplant. However, despite having that information to focus upon, it took the doctors another two days of testing before they managed to medically diagnose that same problem by conventional means. The baby was flown by a special aircraft to a hospital in St Louis, Missouri, as they had the expertise required to undertake such a dangerous operation.

The parents were aware that the procedure was surgically groundbreaking, and the child's survival chance was minimal.

Obviously, I wasn't able to be present in the operating theatre. However, at the precise time of the procedure, I locked myself away in a room so I would not be disturbed, working remotely and simultaneously using my absent healing techniques. As I focussed and meditated, I could feel the baby's tiny body and struggling immune system taking a huge battering. On this occasion, the healing energy empowered me in a way that felt different, as if it was more refined or from a higher source. My hands and feet became unusually red hot and tingly – it was so intense, it was as though extremely hot water had been poured directly over them.

Although I could not see anything, I could sense an immensely strong spiritual presence standing beside me while I meditated. I realised that I probably couldn't see its form as it was so spiritually progressed and highly evolved.

Utilising the powerful force I felt emanating from this presence, I focused all of the healing energy flowing through me towards the child. Suddenly I experienced a jolt, a shock of sorts, and I felt as though the baby's tiny life had drained away. I knew he was in danger. After a short while the sensation passed and I breathed a sigh of relief as I discerned the baby had been spared death. It was then an overwhelming feeling of calm flooded through me.

After the long and deep healing meditation, I was exhausted.

The next day Heidi contacted me. The doctors confirmed the baby had stopped breathing for a time during the operation and they thought they had lost him, but miraculously he started to breathe again.

Whatever the reason, whether it was by the surgeon's hand alone or with the help of some divine intervention, even the doctors agreed it was a true miracle the baby was alive and had survived this innovative surgical procedure. He was at this time the twelfth child to successfully undergo this operation in the world.

Now he had to survive, allow his new lungs to grow and his tiny body to heal.

I agreed to continue regular absent-healing sessions on the baby to offer him a fighting chance of life.

Much later Heidi told me that in her opinion my healing had without doubt helped to save him. Since that time, I believe Garrett has become the oldest living infant lung transplant in the world. Now that's an achievement!

Maybe we had been spiritually guided through Richard's dream to meet the Prices, not as we originally thought for our benefit to find us a new home, but to ultimately introduce me into baby Garret's life to perhaps be instrumental in saving him.

Our regular visits to America resulted in our network of friends increasing. One couple that stole our hearts was Linda and Keith Garfield, with their unusually large family of animals and young son, Nicholas.

Linda desperately wanted me to meet a healer that she knew, who enjoyed great notoriety in Florida. Apparently, when Linda spoke about me to her, she became excited at the prospect of us meeting.

We met in her office and she introduced herself as Winema, meaning 'female chief'. Her bloodline was of true Native American origin and her ancestors were from the tepee camps of the Miccosukee tribes.

We chatted about similar experiences as like-minded professionals often do when they get together. During our conversation, she confided that much of her work at this time was related to the study of the aura and its relationship to our physical body. Furthermore, she was working to develop a machine to record the colours in a visual way. (I would use the word camera, but that would be misleading as from what I understood, it was a different technology altogether.)

She added, "Helen, never in my life have I seen an aura like yours, it's like a dense golden energy surrounding you. Whenever you gesticulate, it's like you are throwing out flames, or balls of fire. Unlike that of a regular aura, yours does not seem to have boundaries, it's as if you are engulfed with energy ... it's magnificent. Such a distinctive golden-bright aura like yours signifies enlightenment and divine protection ... it means you are being guided by your highest good. It is divine guidance."

I must say, I was a little surprised by her description, as strangely I don't see my own aura.

We spoke a little about her cultural traditions. She told me, "We give thanks to every living creature. If we kill to eat, then we give thanks to that animal for its life, dying to feed us. We give thanks to the planet and to the weather elements, providing us with earth, water and sunlight to sustain the crops."

Winema was very passionate about her beliefs. She announced, "We feel our planet... and it is crying. You know this, Helen, you feel the same empathy towards this planet as we do. You have that same inner character that protects and nurtures, that is why I want us to speak together."

This was proving to be a very emotional meeting. This woman reached into my heart with true love and it touched the very being of my soul.

The sun was shining, so Winema suggested we take our conversation outdoors to the coffee shop in the garden courtyard. We sat down on a wooden picnic bench. The setting was picturesque, overlooking a man-made lake with a majestic fifteen-meter fountain. The office staff used this area to have lunch or meet clients for a quiet coffee. I could understand why.

We hadn't been sitting long when suddenly the sky blackened with a flock of thousands of birds. The noise of their flapping wings combined with a piercing trill filled the air. At first it was quite frightening as it looked like we were in an old Hitchcock movie!

Then the flock landed in the garden – specifically on and under our table, nobody else's, only ours! These birds were not frightened at all and seemed oblivious to us. I wondered what on earth was happening.

Although Linda, Richard and I were astonished by this phenomenon, Winema seemed totally unfazed. "Don't move!" she said. "Just relax and observe. In our culture, we believe that a bird can be a spiritual messenger direct from the afterlife, and I am convinced they have come to acknowledge your highly evolved spiritual presence and to bring you messages from the spirit world. Soon you will be leaving the States to continue with your work, which over future years will involve you travelling across the sea many times to many countries, continually backwards and forwards."

This was something I was willing to embrace, but definitely not something I wanted to hear, as I wanted to settle down in the States to bring up my family.

She explained, "I am to warn you of climate changes over Britain and Europe resulting in horrendous storms and floods on a regular basis. Large areas of southern England are specifically going to experience the deluge and be underwater on an increasingly regular basis. In time, certain populated areas will become inhabitable due to constant flooding. You are soon to move home and when making your choice of property, always choose the higher ground.

"Use your voice to bring people's attention to mankind's abuse of the planet. Although there are many specific organisations promoting these problems, you will be able to connect with people in a very natural and fundamental way. We need to recognise as individuals that it is our place to respect and be aware of the plight of all the animals and plant life that share our planet."

It was extremely unusual for me to have any messages given to me from another spiritual person, and so I was moved by the whole experience.

Minutes had gone by and still the birds remained. This was causing quite a stir amongst the onlookers and the sound they made was overpowering, like hundreds of chattering children. Then, like a magic spell breaking, the birds took flight. Within seconds they disappeared into the sky, like an unseen force had asked them to leave.

The garden fell silent again.

The shock of this unusual exhibition faded and the coffee area returned to normal. Everyone agreed, they had never ever seen anything like it before.

Soon after this experience, we spoke to our visa attorney again. It was becoming apparent that obtaining visas in the short term was highly unlikely, as the goal posts seemed to be forever moving further away. We were becoming very frustrated at the whole bureaucratic procedure, but we had committed so much time, money and energy into this project, we didn't want to give up. It was demoralising; we wanted so much to be given the opportunity to live in America.

Perhaps, like so many potential immigrants before us, it was all just wishful thinking?

The New Year of 1993 was upon us.

My pregnancy was blooming and Richard, forever my rock, was soon to become the father of our first child.

25

Baby Cakes

Recipe for baby cakes:

1. *Take two parents who love each other.*
2. *Vow to always love your child no matter what.*
3. *Wait nine months for egg to mature.*
4. *A sprinkle of angel blessings.*

~Helen Parry Jones~

Seated in the gynaecological ward waiting for my pre-natal check-up, I chatted to a lady who had been trying for years to have a baby. Apparently, she had tried IVF several times and this was going to be her last attempt. I could see by the sadness in her eyes that she longed to be a mother. I just couldn't understand how a deserving lady like this could be denied bringing life into the world.

When you meet people who are so committed to having a child, it's hard to believe that so many are born unwanted or only know pain and suffering from parental abuse.

This was a subject I often discussed with my teachers from the spirit world, and I never got an answer that satisfied me. Even this morning on the way onto the ward, I had to walk past a group of heavily pregnant mothers huddled together smoking cigarettes. I am not being judgemental, but as any sensible person knows this can cause untold medical complications for your child. Worse still are the drug addicted mothers, whose children are born into this world with so much chemicals running through their veins that doctors have to wean the child off them once they are born.

For those of us that try our best, it's true to say that no parent is perfect – far from it. In fact parenthood is a learning challenge like everything else in life. Love covers up our mistakes, and as long as we try to provide as loving home as possible, it is all a child can reasonably expect.

I knew from experience there was not a general answer to these questions. However, these and many other parenting challenges are presented to me on a daily basis during my private consultations, and through spiritual communication I try to secure appropriate answers within the context of the individual's needs and abilities.

For some couples, though, it is the process of conceiving a healthy child that can be a major problem. For whatever reason, physical or psychological, it just won't happen!

One such couple was Claire and her husband John, a teacher and accountant respectively. They had been trying for ten years to have a child and despite all the medical treatment they had received, they could not conceive a baby.

When they first made an appointment to see me, I remember noticing how very scared they both looked as neither of them had any idea what to expect. From the outset, I detected that John was a little dismissive of the possibility of any positive changes during his healing appointment, but he was trying hard to please his wife. So despite his scepticism, one thing was certain to me, his love for his wife was not in question.

As I lay my hands on Claire, I noticed an older woman in spirit standing in the corner of the room holding an infant in her arms. It's not unusual for spirit to offer messages during my healing sessions, but they would always have a relevance to my clients healing process and welfare.

This spiritual visitor had something that was necessary for the couple to hear.

She identified herself as John's grandmother and gave her name as Winifred. She announced, "The child I am holding is their baby girl who was successfully conceived about ten years ago but was lost through miscarriage. Although the child was not full term, she has been born into the spirit world and is healthy and perfect in every way. Please tell them I have her safe with me and that I am caring for her. She grows amongst her family here and is well loved. One day she will meet with her loving parents and they will be together again. We have called her Charlotte after Claire's grandmother."

Even though I was focused on administering my healing, I simultaneously relayed this spiritual message to the couple.

You would have thought a bolt of lightning had struck them both. Claire trembled and cried. I had to stop so she could sit up on the healing couch and compose herself. As she did, John came over and put his arms around her to offer comfort.

He struggled with his words, "What you say is absolutely true. How can you possibly know this? Only our closest family knew of Claire's miscarriage. We both took it very badly."

I could hear the grief in John's voice. He was trying so hard to hide his feelings and give strength to his heartbroken wife.

John asked, "Why was our child shown to you as a baby when she would now be about ten years of age."

I explained, "The spirit world often use symbolism in their communications and this is a way of demonstrating to me it was a baby you lost as opposed to a grown child or young toddler."

After a brief respite, I carried on with Claire's healing session.

As she lay back down and relaxed, the strong healing energy flowed through my hands once more. I could feel extensive work taking place on her body, not only to physically balance its deficiencies, but to also repair the stress of bereavement the miscarriage had induced.

When a client allows their partner to be present during their consultation, I always invite them to experience first-hand the deep healing energies that can flow through me, and despite his original scepticism, John couldn't lie on the healing couch quick enough!

Two months later I received a telephone call. Claire was pregnant. Seven months later a little boy was born – they called him Charlie.

Over the years, Richard has witnessed so many childless couples come to me for successful fertility treatment, he now always jokes with young ladies we meet socially not to touch my arm unless they want a baby!

As it was, Richard and I were overjoyed at the prospect of being parents again. There was nearly fourteen years between our new baby and my oldest daughter, so in my early thirties I was now considered a mature mother by my consultant gynaecologist, which was something I had not considered. It never occurred to me that due to my age I might have problems with a pregnancy.

We decided to take no chances with the baby's welfare and booked a special private care package with the consultant. Consequently, my next appointment wasn't in the hospital but at his house. On arriving, we discovered his home was more of a country mansion, with at least an acre of manicured gardens. At the front door, we were met by his wife who escorted us to an annex area within the large entrance hall.

After a few minutes, the consultant came in to greet us and took me into his office.

He told me everything looked normal and the baby and I were absolutely fine.

However, despite the quiet and intimate surroundings, I became very distracted. Sam appeared with an unfamiliar spirit visitor who introduced himself to me.

Despite my consultant chatting on about all manner of important gynaecological jargon, the spirit visitor's presence dominated my concentration and kept insisting in a persistent but polite manner that he was a deceased friend to the consultant and it was important to speak with him. It made me inwardly chuckle as the man announced his status as deceased, as though I couldn't possibly discern he was indeed in spirit!

He went on to explain he had died in an accident involving fire, and his friend was suffering from much guilt as he felt it should have been him that died, not vice versa.

The usual dilemma overwhelmed me, how could I legitimately bring all of this to the doctor's attention! At times like this, I always look to Sam for support. We often talk through mental telepathy, and I felt him suggesting I talk about overseas holidays.

So without preamble, I announced, "I have to go to America soon, will it be safe for me to travel whilst pregnant?"

On saying those words, my spiritual eye burst open. Right before me like a translucent vision, I could see an airplane taxiing down the runway, bursting into flames and being consumed by thick, black smoke. Intuitively, I knew this was how my spirit visitor had died. But how did my doctor feature in this fireball tragedy?

Oblivious to my shocking vision, the consultant reassured me it would be safe to travel for a little while longer. Then as if he had been subconsciously prompted, my doctor announced, "Oh! I hear from the nurses up at the hospital that many of them come and see you. They say you are a very gifted lady, Helen!"

He didn't say in what – or why – but nevertheless for some strange reason, I blushed with embarrassment.

That statement created the opportunity for me to open up to him about his friend standing alongside us in spirit. Grasping the opportunity, I said, "Yes they do! Actually, I see people from the spirit world."

The consultant looked directly at me with no surprise whatsoever in his expression, in fact I believe he was demonstrating signs of genuine inquisitiveness.

I continued, "There's a man here standing beside you, he says he was a good friend of yours when he was alive. Would you mind if he speaks with you?"

The consultant looked puzzled, but nonetheless receptive. "That's very interesting ... but how so?"

Without comprehending his question, I interpreted this as consent and carried on regardless. "He is not giving me his name at the moment, but he died in a fire on an airplane."

The colour drained from the consultant's face. This was an occurrence that had not been forgotten.

I asked if I could continue and the consultant nodded, so I lunged into his friend's account of his passing. "He says you are feeling guilty. You feel it should have been you, not him. He says you mustn't feel this way, you had no way of knowing. I get the feeling you were on the same airplane as your friend. I sense a confusion in the seating arrangements and the swapping of seats." I shivered and goose pimples spread over my skin.

The consultant's professional facade faded, and in silence he closed his eyes in anguish. "I swapped seats with my friend because he wanted to smoke and I had been issued a smoker's seat in the rear section of the plane. By a twist in fate, by changing seats at that precise moment before we took off, my friend's fate was sealed."

I listened intently. The man in spirit looked on and I knew he felt relieved that this incident was being acknowledged.

The consultant opened his eyes and they were awash with tears. "The accident happened about eight years ago on the tarmac at Manchester Airport. We were both travelling with our families to Corfu, and there were not enough vacant seats to keep us all together. He came and asked me to change with him because he said he was the smoker and it wasn't fair to put me among people who did. The airplane was taxiing for take-off when a blade broke free from its cowling severing the main fuel line, but no one knew that at the time. Apparently, the pilot thought he had a flat tyre and he taxied to the runway apron, but a prevailing wind caught the fuel, which was then ignited by a spark and the plane became a fireball. It was complete chaos. I thought we were all dead. All of our group bar one survived, and he was in my allocated seat … he was my dear friend. About twenty people died at the back of the plane, mainly through the inhalation of the thick smoke." He reached for a handkerchief and wiped a tear from his eye.

As a result of this genuine heartfelt emotion, the spiritual link was strong and crystal clear and the friend in spirit continued with his communication. "He is asking you to please tell his family that he is safe and well. He says to send all his love to them. I feel that you carry much guilt and seek forgiveness … and he wants this to stop. There is nothing to forgive, his death was not your fault, and in no way whatsoever were you responsible for the accident … so stop feeling guilty."

At that moment, with the message successfully given, the spirit evaporated in front of my eyes. I could tell my consultant was deeply shaken by this encounter. I explained that my communication with his friend was over and that he had disappeared.

The consultant said just one more word, "Remarkable!"

Then as if it were back to business, the intense emotion on his face was replaced with a doctor's cheery, professional facade. With a quick recap on my medical condition, he advised I would need a scan in a few weeks' time. My appointment was over.

He ushered me back into the hall to meet Richard and said with a smile, "You have a very exceptional wife here!"

I knew he had been moved by this experience and I could tell he was trying to hide his true feelings. Nothing more was said about the encounter.

Weeks passed and it was time for my ultrasound appointment at the hospital. As I went into the room for my appointment, I noticed that a few junior doctors were also present. My consultant asked for my permission for them to remain there for training purposes while I had my scan. To be honest, I thought perhaps it was more for moral support in case any further messages came through after our last meeting!

I settled back onto the couch and he squirted cold gel on my tummy and there right on the screen was my beautiful baby. Everything looked absolutely perfect.

The consultant said, "Let's take a photo of the baby, shall we, after all he might as well get used to having his photo taken with his famous Mum." I laughed nervously as I didn't consider myself as having any fame whatsoever. However, I felt it was the consultant's way of saying something positive about my spiritual abilities.

As I was leaving, in front of everyone, he shook my hand and said he would look forward to delivering this very special baby and thanked me for my kind words at our last meeting.

"Helen, they meant more than you will ever know!"

From that day, it was like an unwritten understanding of professional integrity, we never spoke of the messages again.

Part of my private maternity package included regular check-ups at the hospital. During these visits, I was never amongst strangers, as many of the nursing staff had been to see me for a private appointment or been to one of my groups.

One of the midwives attending on me was Jo Jones. We first met while she took my blood pressure in a small room off the maternity ward. Unlike many of the other nurses, Jo hadn't actually been to see me professionally, but as she had heard so much from her associates, she was very interested in my work.

With no inhibition whatsoever she asked, "Can you tell me if you see anything for me?"

I was a little taken aback with her blunt request, but I am well used to it as I have many such requests when out socially or when interacting with others in their own professional domain. Although I am always happy to oblige, people really do not understand the true implications behind the question when I am not speaking to them in a professional environment as their chosen therapist.

If I say something profound, then they are shocked and will most probably become emotional and then respond differently towards me; if I say something trivial to avoid this, it undermines the capacity of my gift; if I say nothing, it makes me look aloof or uncaring to someone in need; if I suggest a formal appointment, then it looks like I am trying to promote my clinic. Whatever I do, it's a 'lose–lose' situation! In spite of the fact that there is now mutual consent, in such a situation delivering any type of message can compromise the professional care I need for my welfare, especially if I convey a message that the recipient is not prepared to hear. After all, people can take offence over the simplest of things.

Despite my reluctance, Jo pleaded some more.

I said, "Are you sure you want me to be truthful and tell you what I see?" I asked in the vain hope she might change her mind.

But her enthusiasm to know the unknown was far too enticing.

There was a guide by her side, so I tuned in with the knowledge this meeting was not by chance and Jo's life would be positively nurtured in some way by this experience.

I smiled, listened to her guide and allowed the information to flood through me. "I believe your marriage is very turbulent and you are even considering separating from your husband."

This statement completely took her breath away. I could see I had hit a very sensitive chord. It is at this point her professional relationship towards me could possibly change.

She nodded in confirmation saying that she had been unhappy for some time.

I continued, "You call your husband by a nickname ... Everyone seems to call him by this rather than his real name ... and although I see him working on land, I believe he had some association working with water."

Jo nodded again. "We all call my husband 'Taff' and he often works on the oil rigs."

Her eyes were wide with anticipation.

The spiritual portal widened and I could see a man in spirit walking towards me. I sensed when he was alive he was a very elderly relative of Jo's. As the spirit visitor approached me, he smiled and identified himself as her grandfather.

I continued, "I have an elderly relative of yours here, he says he is your grandfather and he has a small baby with him in spirit who had been buried alongside him, perhaps even in the same grave. Your granddad says that he is looking after him in the spirit world. He is eager to say the baby has grown into a fine young man."

Jo was amazed, and I could see tears were rolling down her face.

"I can't believe it!" she exclaimed. "That is my grandfather you are talking to Helen, and the baby is his grandson, his first grandchild born to my eldest brother. No one knows about this other than close family as we don't talk about it. The baby was born pre-term at seven months and didn't survive, so we made the burial alongside granddad as he had died just a few months before."

There was one more message that needed to be said, "Granddad is telling me your husband will start digging up the garden soon."

Jo looked puzzled at the last revelation and said there was no intention of digging up the garden, and laughed it off as some sort of spiritual error, as people often do!

After saying this, the link waned and I could sense no more.

A month or so passed and it was time for another check-up. Jo couldn't wait to take me to one side and tell me her news.

"You are not going to believe this, but last week I heard a noise outside and wondered what was going on. I looked through the window only to find that my husband had hired a small digger and was in the process of digging away mounds of earth from the bottom garden. My house is elevated and he was moving all the earth away from the bottom lawn to make the garage area bigger. To be honest, Helen, I am totally gobsmacked!"

After that experience, a longstanding friendship grew between Jo and myself.

During one of my ante-natal visits to the hospital I bumped into a young lady called Jill Josephs. I recognised her straight away as she had been to several of my clairvoyance groups at my offices. After exchanging a few pleasantries she told me that her dad was upstairs suffering in the latter stages of pancreatic cancer.

"This must be fate that we have bumped into each other like this, Helen, I have been wanting to call you for such a long time," Jill announced. "Would you please go up and have a look at him. I know there is probably nothing you can do, but he is so poorly. It's breaking our hearts just sitting with him and feeling so helpless, watching him lie there suffering. If you could even have a quick chat with him, my mum and I would be ever so grateful."

Sam stood beside her and his spiritual presence shone vibrantly. There was no doubt in my mind, fate had taken a hand and upstairs there was much work to do.

Once on the ward, Jill took me into a side room and introduced me to her Mum and Dad, named Pat and Fred.

The first thing I noticed was how abnormally large Fred's stomach seemed to be, like it had been pumped up with air, and yet you could see that his whole body was wretchedly thin. I could discern just by looking at his fragmented aura that the cancer caused his whole body to be racked in pain, despite the strong medication he was taking.

His wife spoke in little more than a whisper, "They don't give Fred any hope, they have prepared us that it's probably a few weeks at best."

She looked exhausted and devastated.

Fred's eyes met mine. I immediately sat beside him and held his wrinkled hand, an unexpected act of affection he was not expecting from a stranger. After a half hour conversation about my spiritual abilities and explaining to what extent I might be able to help him, he agreed to allow me to administer some healing to him.

The outcome of my spiritual healing comes in many different forms, especially when my patients are terminally ill. With some cancer sufferers, the healing can help in managing the condition for many years or on some occasions even offer a complete cure. However, successful healing doesn't always result in total cure.

Actually, there seems to be a time at which the body has passed the point of no return, and all that can be done is to prepare the person for their transition into the next life. This doesn't mean that healing doesn't take place – on the contrary. A miracle can happen in many ways. Just being out of pain and able to enjoy a meal and go to the toilet is amazing when you can't do these simple tasks. For some, the healing effects can empower the patient and their family to actually talk about the illness and face without denial the eventual outcome of death. Just knowing their loved ones will be there waiting can take all the fear out of dying at so many levels, so the person becomes able to pass over with complete ease and peace of mind ... this too is a healing miracle.

It could be said that the power of spiritual healing is even more profound when the circumstance is successfully easing the patient into the spiritual dimension without pain, full of dignity and with an attitude of sanguine acceptance.

Fred and his family had accepted that he was terminally ill. But despite conventional medicine saying emphatically there was nothing more they could do, I knew there was so much to be done before Fred took his first steps in the spirit world.

During my conversation with him, I could tell he really didn't have much faith in what I could do for him. It wasn't that he didn't have faith in me as I could tell even after such a short time together we had developed a rapport, it was more he didn't have faith there was anything positive that could be done for him in his most serious condition.

To break this stalemate, I suggested something to him, "What would it take to demonstrate to you that the healing can make a difference to your life."

Fred looked with dismay at me, he really didn't know what to say or what was going to happen.

"I know! This painful tummy of yours, how long has it been swollen and distended like this?"

Fred thought for a moment, "Nearly two weeks now. They say there's nothing they can do about it."

"So if I can reduce the swelling, and get your tummy feeling more normal, you would have to take it on board that the healing can do something positive, wouldn't you?"

He thought about this for a moment and then answered, "Absolutely!" And a thin smile beamed across his gaunt face.

I set to work.

By the next day, there was a marked improvement with the distension of his stomach and also in his general welfare. It was a small improvement, but a very marked one to him. So overnight Fred became committed that I should continue with the healing.

I asked, "Have you given some thought about your next goal, Fred?"

He explained he wanted so much to be at home in his own bed in the care of the two loves of his life, his wife and daughter. He also shared with me he wasn't sleeping as he was frightened of closing his eyes in case he died in the night.

"My doctors say that I cannot go home as my pain is out of control and I need constant monitoring. I know I am dying but I want to die at home, pain-free and conscious of myself so that I can pass over in a dignified way."

It seemed a reasonable request to make, but an outcome not easy to deliver. Any doctor will know that the final stages of any cancer, especially pancreatic cancer, can be very painful and cruel.

I held Fred's hand and quietly told him that I needed to administer a strong healing meditation upon him. He closed his eyes, and I focused upon the spiritual and commenced an appropriate healing ritual. It wasn't easy negotiating around the hospital bed and all the equipment, especially considering the size of my pregnant tummy.

After our session, I explained I would be in the next day to see how he was doing.

When I arrived the following day, there was a doctor in the room with Fred and his family. Jill introduced me to him. He looked inquisitively at me and announced, "Well I don't really understand what's happening here, but the swelling has gone right down in Fred's stomach and today we are easing up on his pain meds. If he continues to make such good progress, I may be able to consider allowing him to go home."

Fred was propped up in bed looking considerably more alert. I sat beside him and he automatically reached out for my hand and held it close to him like a treasured heirloom. All he talked about were his healing sessions with me and going home to be with his girls.

A few days later, Jill rang my office to say the doctors were letting Fred go home. "What has astounded them is that Dad is now on no pain medication. He is completely pain-free and his stomach is practically looking normal." Everyone was delighted.

Later that week, I went to see Fred at his lovely bungalow in Prestatyn to administer more healing. There was such a positive change in his outlook and the way he was interacting with his family. He was so happy to be at home in his own bed, looking out onto his beautiful garden. Through the spiritual healing he had mastered every single one of his goals. In his own words, "Many miracles had happened!"

There was never a promise of a cure, nor was there any promise of a longer life, so it was very much expected when the day came that Fred's body had exhausted its every resource and the spirit world were waiting to take him over.

One day, while administering the healing, it was apparent to me that Fred's illness had run its course. His whole body was utterly spent. However, there was no doubt in anybody's mind that his time here had not only been substantially extended, but his quality of life had been markedly improved.

Soon after, I made another visit and on this occasion Fred's GP was making a house-call. Curiosity got the better of him, and he asked if he could watch me administer the healing. "I would like to see what you do, Helen, because never in all my years have I seen a case like this. I believe you know that pancreatic cancer can be one of the most painful illnesses to deal with, and yet Fred is on no medication. Actually, since leaving hospital he has been calm and pain-free. It's most extraordinary."

After I finished, the doctor and I went into the kitchen with Pat and Jill for a cup of tea. Pat recognised her husband's time had run its course, and he had thoroughly wrung out every particle of quality life.

"Fred is strong in his mind but his body is frail. He could go on for days like this, Helen, and I can see he is now totally incapacitated," she said.

"If and when it might be appropriate, you know I can cut his spiritual chord and he will peacefully drift into spirit a short while later," I told her. Everyone looked at me with astonishment. I continued, "If you speak to Fred, and when he is ready to cross over, you can hold his hand and be with him when he goes."

In my previous conversations with Fred I had already discussed this spiritual procedure. He was really concerned about dying in the middle of the night all alone, and Pat finding him dead the following morning. He felt this would be particularly traumatic for her. I had explained to him that cutting the chord wasn't euthanasia, it was something that was possible only when the soul was ready to leave and clinging on to its earthly body by a mere thread of energy.

With much tenderness in her voice, Pat announced, "I am going to speak with Fred!"

About five minutes later she returned. "He says he is ready and he knows the time is right for him to go."

On the face of it, it might seem so matter of fact, as though Fred was booking himself on a train journey, but in reality all the spiritual signs were aligning to offer him a natural passing over.

For the very last time, I walked into Fred's bedroom. Pat, Jill and the doctor followed.

Fred was weak, but I could see genuine affection for me in his eyes – this from a man who found it difficult to display affection to others. "It's my time to go now, Helen," he said. This was a statement of fact, not a question.

Pat and Jill sat beside him on either side of the bed. Pat leaned in and lovingly kissed his cheek. They had spent a lifetime together, and without knowing, her energy was forcing him to live.

I asked everyone to leave the room so I could sit close and be alone with Fred. He reached for my hand. "Helen, you have become like a daughter to me, and I have told Pat that for my funeral I want you to be in the first car with Jill and her. You have done so much for us and I am eternally grateful."

I was deeply moved by this heartfelt sentiment, and I fought hard not to weep. Death stared directly at Fred, and so I placed my hand on the chakra point where his spiritual chord was already irreversibly fragmenting.

The chord was cut. I kissed Fred goodbye for the very last time.

I invited Pat, Jill and the doctor back into the room and told them it was now time for Fred to leave and that I should go to give them privacy.

Later that day I had a phone call from Pat saying Fred passed away peacefully about an hour after I had left.

Fred and his family became particularly special to me. It was an extremely hard goodbye.

The day arrived for me to give birth to our new baby.

Richard and I were in the delivery suite and he was trying to give me support in the best way any man can. He was rubbing my back, offering encouraging words and trying to stay calm.

The last thing I expected to happen right at that moment, was for the spirit world to make contact. This was one of those moments when I definitely felt I would be given a rest from my work.

I held out my hand so I could grip onto Richard. Another contraction besieged my body and I screamed out the pain through my clenched teeth. Here I was lying almost on my back in the oddly shaped birthing chair fondly known as the 'birthing bed'. It came complete with the luxury of a hospital starched linen sheet offering me the comfort of corrugated iron.

Another sharp pain cut through my abdomen.

The sweat was pouring down my face and my hair stuck to my scalp like clumped-yellow seaweed. My muscles now cramped unbearably, trying to bring a new life to this world. This was a shock to my system ... but the true shock was yet to happen.

I remember the midwife's voice distinctly as she spoke to me in a positive tone, "Not long now. It's nearly time."

As this caring lady was inches away from my lady bits, it seemed appropriate to be familiar enough to ask her name.

"I'm Judith," she responded.

I started to fidget uncontrollably, trying to find a comfortable position. Trying to behave normally, I mustered enough strength to give a forced but polite response, "Oh, that's a nice name. That was my late mother's name."

With the mini conversation over, I gave another gut-wrenching bawl. Oh, why-oh-why didn't I listen more attentively in those pre-natal classes?

Judith continually wiped and prodded around my lady bits, and in an attempt to distract me said, "Try to relax, Helen. I am sorry for your loss. My mother has passed over too!"

Relax? I thought, how could I possibly relax with my naked bottom hanging over the edge of the bed?

Then Judith asked me a seemingly simple question, as if to take my mind off the imminent contraction. "And what do you do, Helen?"

I imagine that would have worked at causing a distraction from the pain in many previous births, but my answer usually evokes all manner complications.

Judith was no different. On this occasion my answer evoked a distinct silence. She struggled to know what to say, but like it or not there was no escape for her, she was my attending midwife … and she had asked!

My legs were supported in the stirrups at a ninety-degree angle, and my body was shaking from head to toe. I gritted my teeth again waiting for the wave of pain, and tried to muster as much dignity as I could. With my eyes wide open I stared at the double doors at the far side of the room. At that moment, an elderly lady in spirit entered the room. It seemed Judith needed spiritual guidance, and apparently I was in charge of its delivery.

Without thinking I just spoke out, "I have to tell you this, Judith, a lady in spirit has just walked in, and she says she knows you."

I quickly thought through my options, especially of mutual consent. In desperation, I looked Judith in the eyes and asked her if she minded having a message from the spirit world. Without hesitation, she agreed.

"She tells me her name is Elizabeth and that she is your mother." On hearing this, my midwife slowly fell to her knees and burst into tears, using my two legs held firmly in the stirrups to support her weakened body. What a sight! Richard didn't know what to say. He was just trying to get through this ordeal the best way any man could.

Life with a spiritual communicator is never dull and it's often coloured with far too many shocking experiences, but poor Richard was not prepared for this.

Judith tried to compose herself, and while still on her knees she focused on the job in hand and started to bathe my leaks. I strained my neck to see her face and looked my shocked midwife straight in the eye. "She is talking about Michael, your son."

My hand then gripped Richard like a vice and with the other I grabbed the gas-and-air nozzle and inhaled deeply. He gently slid the plaited sweat-soaked hair out of my eyes, and reassuringly told me how beautiful I looked.

Beautiful! This was not what I wanted to hear right now! Stupid, stupid man! All I wanted was to get this baby out!

As the pain momentarily eased I began to focus on the two ladies again. On the positive side, I thought this was a different pain distraction technique not mentioned in my well-thumbed maternity book and certainly not one I had opted for and listed in my birth plan.

Between the contractions, Elizabeth discussed with Judith the problems she was experiencing with Michael and the worry of her husband's recent redundancy and assured her that there would be new beginnings for her soon. Such words of comfort not only confirmed her mother's continuing existence in spirit, but also gave reassurance that her mother was still watching over her.

It seemed an appropriate reunion of mother and daughter at a time I was to be a mother myself. The spirit world communicates for those in real need, giving support and guidance as and when it is appropriate, not on demand as some would like. I always have the right to reserve judgement and turn spirit visitors away, but on this occasion, despite the bizarre circumstances, I chose to reunite mother and daughter.

My beautiful baby son, Blake Richard, was delivered safe and sound into this world with his huge Mohican mop of jet-black hair. Judith wept tears of joy with me and vowed she would never forget this experience.

Judith's encounter became hot gossip around the hospital, and soon an orderly queue of nurses formed outside my small private room all wanting to hear from the spirit world. When my consultant made his rounds he was furious at the spectacle, and put a big sign on the door, "Helen needs her rest – leave her alone!"

Rest ... if only!

26

Heartache and Tears

*"Death leaves a heartache no one can heal,
love leaves a memory no one can steal."*
~Anonymous~

The room was quiet and still. A shimmer of sunlight shone weakly through the window in my bedroom. It was around seven p.m. in the evening and I had rested on the bed to do a short meditation while my baby was asleep.

I know all new mothers think their child is the best, but my newborn really was a perfect baby boy. He was pretty and cute, he ate, slept and gurgled all at the right moments. I put this down to my idyllic pregnancy, where I rigidly watched my diet, rested when I needed and minimised stress so I could enjoy every pregnant moment.

I often did my meditations at this time to fit in with my baby's routine and my own work pattern, but this evening my meditation had evoked a different feeling.

On this occasion, I had a vision of myself walking around a castle with its own maze and magnificent gardens, all surrounded by thick stone walls. In my vision, I felt stressed, rushed and unhappy with a deep feeling of desperation.

I was in turmoil, as although the vision of the castle seemed positive, the distressing feelings were certainly not.

Being married to Richard, I felt so blessed to have a beautiful home, a doting husband and such healthy children. I felt loved in a way I wanted to be loved. In fact, I often pinched myself to remind me that I was so content with my life and truly happy. I had no idea what my vision was trying to show me. So why was I sensing so much despair, especially in such a beautiful place?

When I mentioned my vision to Richard, he suggested that maybe we were going to sell our home and move there. I could sense his flippancy concealed a sense of vulnerability caused by an inner conflict of sorts.

Although I knew Richard was experiencing some issues with his business, he always led me to believe they were resolvable and that I had nothing to worry about. Deep down I was afraid something life-changing was about to eclipse our perfect world.

We had both been working very hard, so as a refresher before the Christmas rush, Richard decided to take me and six month old Blake to Naples Cay, Florida for a short holiday. Despite Richard's shops being summer orientated, the Christmas weeks can be the busiest of the year.

Despite the heartache of leaving the children with Richard's parents so they didn't miss any school, the holiday on our own with Blake was an absolute delight. It was absolute bliss. We could walk down from our apartment straight onto the sandy beach. We took our first swims with Blake, watching him splash around in the shallow warm sea and we continually laughed with him while sharing every new experience. I was so thankful to be alive. Life couldn't feel better!

Near the end of our stay, Richard told me we had to talk. I looked into his eyes and I had this impending feeling of doom in the pit of my stomach and knew something was about to drastically change.

He had just had a telephone conversation with his bank. His new manager had called him in for a meeting. Due to the recession, the bank was looking for a total restructure of his affairs as they felt the way the previous manager had structured all his property and trading loans had exposed them to too much risk.

So as we sat there on the beach with our new baby, Richard explained to me in no uncertain terms that when we returned home there were going to be some drastic changes forced upon his business and ultimately upon our life.

Just like that, life as we knew it was over ... my bubble had burst!

That memory is etched into my very being and to this day has always haunted me.

On returning home, Richard had the meeting with the bank. Historically, he had a good working relationship with his manager who had helped Richard's business to build over the years. However, this supportive manager had moved on and a new, younger manager had been appointed. His agenda was very different to his predecessor.

Dressed in his snazzy Next suit with his slick gelled-back hair, Richard was politely told that his borrowing ratios were not in line with the bank's current policy. He was informed that what they had accepted in the past was not something they wanted to accept now. As of now, they were changing the rules and Richard had to abide by them.

They demanded a substantial amount of money back over a very short period of time. They wanted a combination of selling property and a reduction in overdraft facilities. The bottom line was the bank wanted cash – no negotiation, no leniency and no mercy!

To us, it felt like a legalised mugging. We were now fighting for our home, for our lives and for our future.

Richard booked a meeting with a new management accountant, Nicky Tiernay, to oversee the business and to present detailed monthly management accounts to the bank, as they had insisted. With her guidance, Richard hoped to navigate through these difficult times. Although well-respected, her bedside manner was not pleasant; in fact she was ruthless. Nevertheless, she shared the common goal of saving the business.

Tiernay explained the harsh reality. "Everything that is a non-necessity for the most fundamental and basic daily life must go."

This was tough medicine, but nonetheless a remedy we were willing to endure if we could save Richard's business. I believed our love was strong enough to see us through this transition.

As if reading my thoughts, Tiernay turned to Richard, "To be honest, I doubt if your marriage will survive this transition – most wives bolt and leave the husband when the swimming pool is drained, metaphorically speaking of course, or they end up having a baby to patch up a failing relationship, and then they divorce. So be warned."

Despite my resilience, I burst into tears in front of her. *What a bitch!* I thought. However, she was speaking from a statistical truth and I had enough professional experience to know that a drastic reduction in financial circumstances can so easily lead to divorce. I have witnessed that loss comes in many forms, it often brings unwelcome change, but nonetheless it is a situation that has to be confronted.

My spiritual sight was confirmed by the accountants forecast, considerable loss lay ahead for my family. This was an outcome I wanted to deny, but denial does not negate or even diminish the outcome. There was no doubt, life as we knew it had irrevocably changed.

At face value my troubles seemed trivial compared to the suffering of many of my clients, some of whom were experiencing tragic illness and death. However, adversity at any level, no matter what form it takes, is still distressing to the recipient. Much physical illness starts with emotional discord.

When Christmas came, despite keeping a very tight purse, we put on our bravest faces for the children so that everyone would have a good time. I made sure that the fridge was full and the presents under the tree were made to look abundant.

But then another bombshell was dropped on us! Just when you think things can't get any worse, so often they really can.

On Boxing Day evening we received a telephone call from Richard's mother, telling us that his brother, Robert, had become very ill on Christmas Day. He was wracked with pain and trying to recover in bed. The local doctor had been to see him and according to Elsie he had suggested bed-rest and painkillers.

Elsie had great faith in my spiritual abilities and asked me to go down the following day to see if I could do anything.

Up until recently we were all one big happy family, and we would all go out to dinner together on a regular basis or I would cook for everyone at home. I loved these large family get-togethers, it was something I didn't experience as a child and it was an environment in which I seemed to emotionally thrive.

But something had changed.

After a failed, volatile relationship with Dina, Robert had recently got back together with her, and she had moved in with him. Since Dina had moved in, the two brothers had become estranged.

Robert was no stranger to the accuracy of my messages and listening to the advice of his guides, I pleaded with him not to return to past relationships and to pursue love and romance from new situations.

You might think that this was none of anybody's business but his own. However, Richard and I had no secrets. Very early into our relationship we exposed every aspect of our lives to each other so that at no time would the past become part of our future. I knew that before meeting me, Richard had had a liaison with Dina. It was at a time he was emotionally vulnerable after the breakdown in his marriage and Dina was vulnerable after her break-up with Robert. He realised he should have known better and this should never have happened, but it did! Life is often like that.

I advised Richard to tell his brother about it, but he insisted that if Dina loved Robert as he thought she did, she should be honest with him about her own past. He felt if they had any chance of finding happiness together, the revelation should be from her mouth not his. Robert was no innocent when it came to indiscretions within a relationship, and if after she was honest with him, he still wanted to continue with her, then we should wholeheartedly embrace her into the family.

Nevertheless, Dina continually insisted to Robert there was nothing to confess. When Richard told him otherwise, Robert believed his partner above Richard, and would hear no more about the matter.

It became an untenable impasse.

Life moved on. Robert and Richard avoided each other and all the family gatherings ceased.

When I arrived at Robert's the following morning, Elsie took me straight into the bedroom to see him. Dina looked embarrassed and scurried off somewhere out of my way without saying a word, as she knew I knew about her past with Richard.

Robert sat propped up in bed, ashen grey in colour and drained of all his energy. His eyes were black and his brow was extremely clammy. I smiled and wished him the usual festive pleasantries in an attempt to diffuse the tension radiating from him.

"Please take a look at him," Elsie begged. Then she added, "I trust you more than the doctors from our surgery."

It was obvious to me that he was gravely ill.

I told Robert in front of Elsie he should go into hospital immediately as I felt he was running a fever caused through infection and something was seriously wrong.

Elsie explained, "The doctor called this morning and Robert told him he didn't want to go into hospital as he didn't want to leave Dina alone over Christmas, so the doctor said he would have another look at him tomorrow and then reassess the situation."

The fact the doctor allowed Robert to stay at home falsely reassured Elsie that he would recover. She looked to me for this same reassurance, but I could not oblige. It was obvious she was frantic with worry and in my opinion her concerns were justified.

Robert was being stubborn and insisted he would be fine being looked after by Dina at home, but agreed that if his condition deteriorated he would consider going to hospital if the doctor thought it necessary.

I wanted to doubt my own assessment and concur with the doctor Robert was well enough to remain at home, but everything that was true to me was revealing otherwise. Against my heartfelt advice, Robert stayed at home.

Early the next morning, Elsie rang in a panic. "He's no better, Helen, in fact he's been worse in the night, I don't know what to do."

I had given my opinion yesterday and it hadn't changed. In my firmest voice I reiterated my advice, "Mum, Robert needs to be in hospital. I told you yesterday he is very poorly and needed urgent medical attention! Don't pay any notice to Dina wanting to keep him at home, you have to put your foot down as I know he won't listen to me. He needs to be in hospital right now – immediately!"

Much later that day, Elsie telephoned to say Robert had been admitted to hospital and they were keeping him in for observation. They had put him on a drip and administered some injections for the pain, and apparently he did seem much more settled.

On the one hand, I breathed a sigh of relief because at last he was being cared for in the right place, but I was gravely concerned as they needed to find the cause of the problem not just mask the symptoms, as it was obvious to me this was not a transient stomach condition.

The next day was New Year's Eve and listening to my pleas, Richard agreed to visit his brother in an attempt to reconcile before the start of the New Year.

When we arrived, Elsie and Ralph greeted us downstairs in the hospital cafeteria and explained that Dina and her family were upstairs with Robert. Richard was reluctant to go up as he felt there might be a public showdown if tempers flared, which might cause disruption on the ward.

Elsie and I went upstairs together, and I was surprised to see Robert was in a side room. He looked reasonably settled, but I could sense by the condition of his aura he was far from any type of recovery.

"He's going to be okay, isn't he?" Elsie implored in a worried tone.

I didn't answer her question, instead I responded with a request of my own, "Mum, tell me exactly what the doctors have said is happening and what they are going to do?"

Attempting to answer accurately, Elsie replied, "They say his x-rays don't show anything and he should be fine with bed rest."

Bed rest! I screamed out in my head. After the assessment I had made, I knew he needed more than that. Through my ability of spiritual sight, I believed there was a problem with the total fabric of his digestive system and we had to get to the bottom of this problem urgently.

"That's not enough!" I said out loud. "We have to get a surgeon to take him down to theatre and take a look at what's going on." Naturally, I was trying to hide my alarm, but she knew I was worried.

"What can we do, the doctors say he is now stable and nothing much can happen until the second or third of January when everybody comes back to work," Elsie replied.

"That's days away, he can't wait that long," I said with as much authority as I could muster. "I am going to speak to the staff now and then I am going to try and find his consultant."

Why was nothing more being done? I knew I had to find help for Robert.

The staff on the ward were rather complacent, so I requested a meeting with Robert's attending doctor. When I eventually spoke to him, his stance was pretty much they were short-staffed until after the holiday period and what they were doing was the appropriate treatment.

As there was no consultant to be found, there was nothing more I could constructively do at the hospital, so Richard and I drove back home.

"I want you to go to Chris Davies' House in Colwyn Bay," I told him.

"You can't just knock on a hospital surgeon's door!" Richard responded.

Richard and I had met Chris Davies professionally on many occasions as he was a general surgeon at the hospital and he happened to live near our neighbourhood. I thought it would be hard for him to say he wouldn't help if we were standing on his doorstep.

After ringing his doorbell, he answered the door to us in full black tie. Here was a man on the way out for a New Year's ball somewhere. He was dumbfounded at the sight of two former patients standing on his porch.

We must have presented our case with sufficient force as he was sympathetic to Robert's predicament and showed genuine concern. I asked him to please go to the hospital and examine Robert that night, no matter what the cost. He explained that would be impossible, but assured me that he would not leave it and would make some calls and phone us back later.

True to his word, Davies rang us back on the morning of New Year's Day. Poor man, I had probably ruined his festivities, but he was very supportive and said that he had looked into Robert's case. He couldn't become involved as he was not on call, but he had personally spoken to Mr Clark who was the general surgeon on duty, and he would call in to see Robert that morning as a matter of urgency.

In all honesty, I am surprised we achieved that level of response outside of the hospital protocol. I rang Elsie and she was amazed and grateful at the outcome. Richard suggested to his mother we go down to the hospital again, but she felt there were enough visitors and we should perhaps wait until after Mr Clark had examined Robert.

It was late afternoon and our phone rang. It was Elsie calling to say Mr Clark had been to see Robert and taken him down almost immediately for a quick exploratory examination to see what was going on. She felt it pointless us coming down until after the operation.

About an hour later the phone rang again, but it wasn't Elsie calling, it was Mr Clark.

With true compassion in his voice he said, "Helen, I need you to listen carefully … I have some bad news."

My legs turned to jelly and nausea overwhelmed me.

"I am still in the theatre performing Robert's operation, he is still under anaesthetic. I have come out to tell you he is in a bad way."

My mind started to race filling my head with all type of medical imagery.

In barely a whisper I asked, "Bad way? What does that mean?"

"He has pancreatitis, and trypsin has been released into his body. This is an enzyme and it has caused erosion to some of his other organs. His prognosis is not good and I feel if you or any of your family need to see Robert, you ought to come now. Straightaway."

My mouth dried up. "Are you saying he won't pull through this?" I managed to ask.

Why was this happening to him? Last week he was a twenty eight year old healthy young man. Of course he will pull through. It was Robert!

"It all hangs in the balance now. If he does pull through, he won't have a normal life. You just need to come down to the hospital. I will talk more later. I am so very, very sorry."

I hung up and looked at Richard. His expression was one of pure devastation. For a moment I couldn't cry, I couldn't express anything; I was in total shock.

Then a wave of emotion hit me and I started to sob in Richard's arms. We held each other tightly, and I heard him crying too. As much as I needed to cry, I felt the necessity to stop and pull myself together for my family.

Sam was, as always, close by, and I could hear him speaking to me. In no uncertain terms, I was being told that Robert was out of body and waiting to cross over to the other side.

Thankfully, we had a babysitter on standby, and also Fiona was now fourteen so she was more than able to help out with

Blake. I didn't know how Richard was going to hold up – it wasn't every day you might lose your younger brother.

We arrived at the hospital and went straight to the intensive care unit. Elsie, Ralph and Dina were there waiting in a small annex room overlooking the unit. It was also full of other relatives from other patients.

It was now a waiting game. We sat and waited.

Mr Clark came and reiterated what he had told me over the telephone. Chris Davies made a personal visit to speak to us and visit Robert. Even though I knew death seemed imminent, there was an unjustified expectancy that Robert would somehow pull through. He seemed young and strong, and had hardly started his adult life – he had everything to live for.

We sat through another agonising day. I tried desperately to administer healing to Robert but each time my hand held his, the spiritual energy returned to me, and I could see his silver chord clearly displayed becoming increasingly taut as each hour passed.

During the early morning on the third of January I could clearly see Robert standing before me with his guardian close by. His body was still alive only yards away from me lying on the hospital bed connected to all manner of machines, and yet he was standing beside me in spirit.

Robert explained his presence, "If I survive the coma, I will be forever disabled and in a wheelchair at best. I will be wracked with pain all my life. I have been given the choice, and I choose not to live like that. Please tell Mum and Dad that I love them so very much and I am sorry for leaving them."

As Robert walked back out of the room a nurse walked in, it was almost as though she walked right through him and I remember thinking, how could she not see him?

The day was spent with everyone talking of Robert, and the things we would like to do with him once he recovered. It was strange talking like this when I knew he had already chosen to take his journey to the other side, but we were all in denial.

I encouraged everyone to talk to Robert as if he was conscious and say some of the things we all needed to say to him.

Eventually the doctor was ready for his meeting with us. We gathered around him in the annex of the Intensive Care Unit. He told us Robert's organs were failing. In simple language, he explained to our small company that the enzymes in Robert's stomach, which he described like battery acid, had leaked into his whole system and were basically dissolving everything. If he was to be brought out of the coma-induced state he would be in violent pain. There was no hope and they wanted to turn off the machines that were keeping him alive.

Elsie could not accept this explanation. "You have all killed him! You have killed my baby! Why didn't you listen sooner? Why didn't you do something sooner? But no! You all left him for days and his condition worsened to this state because you all did nothing! He might have survived if you had tackled this sooner. This is one long catalogue of errors!"

Her anger was justified, and I wasn't going to stop her outburst.

In fact, no one was telling her to be quiet, because perhaps we all felt it might be true.

Once she had exhausted herself, she sobbed uncontrollably, and all we could do was comfort her.

We gathered around Robert's bed and I could see his tubes becoming increasingly congested with fluids from his lungs. Without doubt, life for his body would soon end.

Elsie sat and held her dear son's hand and started to sing in a hushed tone all the Al Jolson songs that Robert loved so much and used in his performing repertoire. Never in my life had I been so moved by somebody else's singing, made significantly more emotional as it was a mother singing to her dying child.

"I don't want him to be scared," she said, as only a mother can, "so I am singing the songs he used to sing to me. As you say, Helen, he can hear us, can't he?"

Reassuringly I nodded.

As the verses fell from her lips, she cradled her boy and stroked his head so tenderly in the same way I nursed my own new baby. There is no worse pain than a mother losing her child.

It was time ... and Ralph allowed the machine to be turned off. We all watched and waited.

With no ceremony, I saw an angel walk towards our company and stop beside Robert's bed. The anger within me grew as I felt this passing was so avoidable. I wanted the angel to go and allow Robert to live, but in my heart, I knew this was not an option. Instead, the angel knelt by Elsie's side and put his head near her knees as though he was offering some sort of comfort or even reverence. The angel stood up, arched his back and opened his arms wide, and in that moment Robert's body became still and empty of all life.

He passed silently and completely into the spirit world.

The loss was immeasurable.

We were all overwhelmed by a sense of absolute tragedy.

Following Robert's passing, Richard and I sat for days with his parents discussing all manner of things, and also how best to handle the funeral arrangements. Robert was a showman at heart, and so it seemed fitting he should have a funeral to remember, in the style of a New Orleans funeral procession.

Within a day of organising the coach and horses, the band and the singers, a researcher from HTV contacted us as they thought it newsworthy and wanted to feature Robert's funeral on the news. As Robert loved to entertain and lived for an audience, it seemed an appropriate farewell.

On the day, it was quite a spectacle to see the horses with their gleaming carriage and the procession of musicians gather outside Elsie and Ralph's bungalow. There was a slight drizzle of rain on an otherwise crisp, wintery January morning.

The procession leader held up his black parasol and the band started up; the funeral march had begun. All the neighbours lined the road to pay their respects and witness this magnificent spectacle.

By the time we arrived at the Marble Church about two miles away from the house, the rain had become much heavier. This didn't deter the hundreds of people gathered outside waiting to greet the procession. However, it wasn't until we entered the church did we realise why there was so many people outside, it was because every seat inside was taken – and this was a huge church. Never before and never since have I been to a funeral attended by so many. There were faces we recognised and faces we didn't, but it made us realise how many lives Robert had touched in his short life, to leave such a huge impression on so many was totally inspiring.

In the aftermath of Robert's death and the slow demise in Richard's business, it was sometimes difficult to find the sunshine in every day. But Richard and I loved each other dearly and in reality we needed each other more than ever now.

As Nicky Tiernay had predicted, in the wake of financial decline, I fell pregnant again. It was another huge shock as it was not something we planned, especially as our finances were critical. Like many mothers before me, I was thrown into turmoil at facing the prospect of another baby at a time when we were in financial mayhem. How on earth was I going to continue working with a toddler, a new baby and two other children to look after? I just didn't know how we would survive through this, but people do – and so would we.

Even my beautiful offices had been sold.

I relied on my meditations with Sam to keep me positive during this most challenging time.

As fate would have it, I had heard through a friend that the Warner Leisure Group had opened a hotel at Bodelwyddan Castle, and they were installing a street of shops into the historic structure. I called up there to have a look and by chance met one of the managers who had been to see me about a year before. Apparently, I had told him of a management advancement in his career, which was the position he now held, and so he was more than delighted to hear that I might consider renting a unit from the castle's new retail project to open a new healing facility. He showed me around the new hotel and its sumptuous environment. The castle's 200 acres of grounds and formal gardens even included its own maze and walled rose garden.

If I was going to relocate my offices, this was a beautiful place for the new Helen Parry Jones Healing Centre.

Within weeks, and on a shoe-string budget, I had created a two-storey establishment with three therapy rooms, a large reception lounge and an upstairs hall to seat around a hundred people theatre style so I could accommodate group classes.

In addition to my specialist services, I recruited a consortium of other holistic practitioners who could offer a full spectrum of complementary therapies.

Early one morning while walking around the magnificent gardens, Richard and I chuckled at how my prediction of walking around castle grounds had come true, but the castle surroundings I could see was not a new home for us as Richard had playfully speculated, but the rented home of my new offices.

Life was never going to be the same.

27

Foundation to Build On

"Gather all your failings
as they are necessary to build success."
~Helen Parry Jones~

In the quiet of the night when I was all alone with my thoughts, all that occupied my mind was reliving the disappearance of so much that had brought substance to my life. These losses seemed to be on a loop that just went round and round in my head. The consequence of this insomnia became long, lonely nights. My focus on all this negativity was so strong, I had no tolerance of the spirit world trying to communicate with me. Nevertheless, there were periods when depression swamped me, and I became isolated and angry that this was happening.

Despite all the loss happening in my life, travelling to the tranquility of the castle every day helped focus me on keeping myself grounded and not falling victim to the mounting stress around me – for the daytime hours at least! The days there brought me peace, and through that peace I was able to focus on the spirit world and bring comfort and healing to others. Giving joy to others gave purpose to my life when nothing else seemed to make sense.

However, at home, the darkness of depression came over me once more.

The rational part of me knew this illness had no part in my life, but the devil fed me the darkness and I willing gorged on it, and it blocked out all of the light.

Only through work at the castle did I activate my spiritual senses.

My new Healing Centre was inside the oldest part of the castle which dated back to as early as the 13th century and had been restored at various times during its history, each time making new additions onto the original.

Soon after moving into the new centre, I experienced my first ghostly apparition at that place, a genuine haunting no less!

It was always quiet during the mornings as most of the hotel guests were having breakfast. On this occasion, while having a morning mug of coffee, a ghostly spectre suddenly appeared through my office wall from the National Trust gift shop next door, walked through my reception area and just disappeared. I didn't think any more of it other than to remark to Richard that she looked as though she was from a different time period, dressed in a long frilly dress. In historic buildings, it's not uncommon for me to see such random ghostly apparitions, and Richard is totally unfazed when I tell him about them.

The next minute all hell broke loose and the shop girl on the other side of my wall came running up the path, screaming. She rushed through my office door white with fear, yelling over and over that she had seen a ghost. I sat her down in the chair and she explained what she had seen.

"I had to run to you, Helen, because I knew you'd believe me and I had to tell someone what I had just seen. I was just putting out some fresh stock, when I saw this woman on my CCTV monitor at the back of the shop. At first I was a little surprised as I couldn't remember anybody walking past me. So I went to see if she needed any help. As I approached her I noticed she was dressed in a long, old-fashioned dress, so I thought she must be in a costume for something happening at the castle. She turned around, looked straight at me then vanished through the wall to your side! It was then I freaked out and ran in here."

It wasn't long before the story had travelled on the hotel grapevine; it caused quite a stir. From then on, all the escorted garden walks included the story of our morning ghost in addition to the many other sightings people had seen over the years in different parts of the castle.

When I was much younger, I often wondered why a place can be haunted by past spirits that are not at rest. Sam explained to me that they are in a spiritual dimension of sorts, but not in a natural part of the spiritual realm – they exist apart from it. In other words, whereas spirit guides and angels and suchlike are a natural extension of the spirit world, ghosts are entities that are unnaturally confined to the physical realm for a variety of reasons, usually either through their own choice or an unwillingness to completely move on to their next level of spiritual progression. They have an existence in the state that exists between the spiritual and physical realms, effectively making them residents of neither, yet they may be subject to elements of both.

I really don't know why the ghost showed herself to us that day. However, one thing was certain, she made a lasting impression on the shop girl and me!

The hotel had a popular entertainments program and they invited a multitude of celebrity names to host special gala nights for their guests. It was prior to one of these evenings I made a special relationship with one of the celebrities.

It all started when a jovial lady named Patricia walked into my offices to enquire about a healing appointment for her husband. He had a recent golf injury which was giving him persistent pain, despite regular physiotherapy and taking various prescription drugs. She explained that he was staying at the castle for one night only and would I be kind enough to fit him in for an appointment at the end of my day.

Her request seemed straightforward and acting as temporary receptionist, Richard dutifully noted the diary accordingly. I never gave it a second thought until later when in walked Tom O'Connor, a very famous comedian of the day, asking about his four thirty appointment.

It is not unusual for me to see all manner of celebrities and people of notoriety, however I make a point of treating everyone exactly the same as there is nothing more off-putting for them than their therapist becoming star-struck or awkward. Actually, it is not hard to treat them normally as usually outside their own domain, they are as nervous and in need as everyone else.

Over the years I had found most comedians to be particularly melancholy in their private lives. However, Tom was a little different. From the moment he walked through the door everything he said was naturally funny. I don't mean he told jokes all the time, but that he had that special skill of no matter what he said, it was just funny! The comedy in his voice was accentuated even more by his thick Liverpudlian accent. In my opinion there was no nicer gentleman you could ever wish to meet.

Before I started the healing session, I advised him, as I do all my clients, to take off his watch, as the spiritual energy can be so powerful it can stop or even damage the delicate workings. However, Tom just laughed and assured me that he had won his in a golf tournament and it was worth thousands of pounds and was guaranteed to withstand all manner of stressful conditions under and above sea level, so he was sure it would cope with my healing energy!

So the watch stayed on his wrist.

As the healing session was finishing, I saw Tom's guide standing proud beside us. I am often aware of other people's guides in this way and for them to want to impart some guidance or information to their wards. Tom's guide was no different.

I announced, "I have your guide standing right beside you and there is something significant he wants to bring to your attention."

Tom looked quite excited at the prospect of having some interaction with him.

"Your guide is telling me that you drive a car with a large badge on the front, I can see it like a star, so I feel it's probably a Mercedes."

Tom seemed to take the revelation in his stride and agreed he had come down to work at the castle in his Mercedes.

His guide revealed more information, which I dutifully repeated. "I get the feeling that for some reason the badge isn't there any more, it has been lost or stolen, I can't make out which, but it is definitely not attached to the car." I paused and listened more to the guide. "Actually, about a year or two ago, you removed it yourself, Tom! That is why it is missing."

The comedian's eyes lit up with excitement. "Spot on! There was a spate of 'Merc' badges being nicked off car bonnets. I didn't want no scallywag nicking mine, so I took it off for safekeeping. But when I came to put it back on, I couldn't find the thing anywhere!"

We both laughed out loud. Even the story of why he removed his car badge sounded funny.

Tom explained, "No matter how many times I've had the car valeted, how many times I've searched under the mats or under the seats, in all the compartments, I just can't find it – it has well and truly gone!"

An extraordinary spiritual phenomenon was about to happen. "Well, Tom, I want you to go back to your car now and look in the footwell on the driver's side. The badge is there."

Tom was adamant in his reply. "No way, Helen! That's impossible. Believe me, I have had the car searched inside out for it as I'm too much of a skinflint to buy another one!"

Again we both laughed, his humour was intoxicating.

After a few minutes of some small talk, it was time for him to go, and for me to do an absent healing meditation for one of my clients before I went home.

Barely ten minutes later, Tom popped his head around the front door and grinned at Richard, like a Cheshire cat. "Where is she? Where's that lovely girl? I want to show her this thing."

Tom was holding up a three-pointed star Mercedes badge and waving it around like a recently won trophy. Richard's immediate thought was that his car had been vandalised while he was with me and that he had come in to complain.

On hearing Tom's voice, I came down the stairs to see what all the commotion was about. As soon as he saw me, he shouted out, "Just look at this, Helen!" There was a massive smile stretched right across his face. "Look what I found lying on top of the carpet under the foot pedals. There is no way whatsoever in a million years it was there when I parked the car, and I am the only one with the key."

He looked at Richard. "I think we'd better put Richard out of his misery and tell him what it's all about!"

And he relayed the story of the missing badge in its entirety. If the spirit world were out to make a grand impression, they certainly excelled themselves on this occasion.

Before he left the following morning, he popped in with Patricia not only to say goodbye and to thank the spirit world for returning his Mercedes badge, but to show me that his precious watch was not working. He even found that funny!

Finding missing objects is not a regular part of my professional agenda, but occasionally I am given spiritual insight into finding misplaced items.

One of those moments was repeated soon after Tom's discovery when Richard's mother lost her expensive diamond solitaire engagement ring. She had searched the house for three days, stripping it from top to bottom, and even had Ralph scrutinising the contents of all three dustbins.

Her engagement ring was naturally treasured not only for its monetary worth but also for its deep sentimental value, and in the aftermath of Robert's bereavement, the loss of it was causing her to cry disproportionately.

As I walked into the house I could see how desperate she had become. Within minutes of Mum telling her story, Sam stepped forward and suggested it was under her bedside lamp. This revelation really did take me by surprise, as Sam never usually involves himself with such earthly matters of inconvenience.

Quite casually, I informed her that Sam was telling me her ring was on the bedside cabinet under the base of the lamp.

Elsie was adamant, "There is absolutely no possibility whatsoever as I have turned this house upside down and searched under there three times that I can remember."

Sam smiled and suggested I look for myself. So I took her by the arm into the bedroom and lifted up the lamp. Low and behold, there it was sitting on the bedside locker, as predicted.

Elsie was shocked beyond all recognition.

It seemed once again I had been privileged to witness the unusual spiritual phenomena of a solid item being physically relocated by an apport. My first experience was finding the missing pen with Johnny Marr in Scotland, then Tom O'Connor's car badge, and now it seems with Elsie's diamond ring.

However, in my experience, the spirit world can choose to help us find what is lost in so many other different circumstances! This was demonstrated when Elsie thought after fifteen years it would be a good idea to make a pilgrimage to visit her mother's grave in the Midlands – a 200-mile round trip.

The only problem was that when we eventually arrived at the cemetery it was no longer the modest size she remembered, it had grown to such colossal proportions housing hundreds and hundreds of graves. Even after we all walked up and down the many rows of gravestones, Elsie couldn't recognise anything to establish her bearings and find her mother's stone.

In a bid to speed up the process we decided to split up. Richard and I went one way, and Ralph and Elsie went another.

After about fifteen minutes of wandering around, it became evident it might take hours to find the right gravestone.

"It's no good," Richard whispered to me. "The grave could be anywhere. Perhaps we should give up?"

At that moment, I became aware of a spiritual presence beside me. Dressed in a dark woolly overcoat with big black buttons and a colourful scarf covering her hair, it was apparent to me this was a woman who lived during the 1950s and 60s.

"I believe you are looking for me!" she declared.

Her face looked tired and weathered, typical of a life of hardship and adversity.

Within the blink of an eye she moved to a gravestone about thirty or forty yards to my right.

I took Richard by the arm and walked towards where the spirit was now standing.

Minutes later, there we were facing the old gravestone of Betsy Ashmore, surrounded by the old-fashioned mini-marble walls containing discoloured, aged marble chippings.

I excitedly called Elsie and Ralph over, and as a family we stood at the foot of the stone and reflected on years gone by. Naturally, there were some tears, especially when remembering the recent passing of Robert.

On reflection, I believe Elsie's mother showed herself to demonstrate support for her daughter at her time of uttermost loss.

Despite these events, the bringing together of families from two different dimensions is my chosen vocation and though I was still fighting my own depression, I held group meetings again in my new centre. In fact, my groups became a regular feature on the Warner's hotel program and I also gave a free demonstration to their guests once a week in the grand hotel ballroom.

I soon realised that by working from the castle, my voice was not just reaching the local community, it reached every corner of the country through the large changing population of the hotel guests. So if through my personal situation I couldn't tour the country, the spirit world had placed me where the country was actually coming to see me!

Up until now, nobody realised I was pregnant. However, my bump was at a stage I had to wear more comfortable clothes and so I had to go public about my baby. With a bigger bump came more tiredness, and this at a time I needed to be working more rather than less.

In fact, I worked right up to the day I reached full term. A week later, not only had I gone over my due date, there were still no signs of an imminent delivery.

You would have thought that now the time had come to have my baby, I would be relaxed and prepared for the occasion. On the contrary, due to my domestic and financial circumstances I was in a blind panic and my blood pressure started to elevate. Concerned for my health, my doctor made the decision to take me into hospital to deliver my baby sooner rather than later, and so an induction injection was administered.

Everything seemed to be going according to their plan, however about an hour later, I began having overly severe contractions. There was something wrong. Apparently, they discovered the baby was breech and to avoid a caesarean, the decision was made to turn the baby.

All this was happening so fast and it was all very painful.

Eventually, our little boy was born, and although he was a little blue, it didn't take long for him to pink up.

I was so much in denial during my pregnancy, I hadn't even considered a name, but when we had a family meeting later that day, we decided to call him Curtis James Robert.

"He is an old soul and his life has specific importance," Sam proudly announced.

I was curious as to the implications of this statement.

Just days after coming out of hospital, there was no alternative, I needed to go back to work.

One particular client that stands out in my mind from that time was a delightful lady called Yvonne. Although she was of Irish descent, she had lived locally in Deganwy, North Wales for many years.

On meeting her I noticed she was a little nervous, which was normal when people meet me for the first time as they really do not know what to expect, not just from me, but also from the spirit world.

Yvonne had a beautiful Irish speaking voice as the educated from the grander side of Dublin always seem to have.

She perched on the comfy sofa in my office in a very ladylike manner and after exchanging a few pleasantries, I launched into her sitting. In an instant, I had a spiritual presence standing beside me and after several profound statements Yvonne knew her mother in spirit was sharing a conversation with us.

But I could sense that hearing from her mother was not the primary purpose of her visit with me. Her grief was much more profound.

There is no wound as deep as a mother's grief at the loss of her child, and it was clear to me from the condition of her spiritual aura and the tightness around her throat chakra, that Yvonne had experienced such a loss.

As the link with Yvonne's mother waned, a brightness filled the room with a pure intensity. Through the brightness I could see a young man in his early twenties walk towards us, and as if he had physical form he casually sat on the arm of the sofa next to Yvonne.

He introduced himself to me as Paul and explained that he had died accidentally, and through me he wanted to prove to his mother he lived on in the light of the spirit world.

I knew the words would be painful, but in order for Yvonne to heal they were words that had to be said. "I have a young man here, he says his name is Paul, and by the quality of love I can feel towards you, I believe he is your son."

Yvonne was taken aback by my statement and tears filled her eyes.

The link was strengthening. "He says he didn't do it. He is telling me some people think his death was on purpose, but it wasn't. I get the impression he had a medical problem which required medication. He says that he took his tablets as usual, but he forgot he had taken them earlier in the day."

His last statement left me feeling a little confused, but I had learned many years before that to be a good medium you had to say what you spiritually hear and feel, even when at first it doesn't make sense. To try and rationalise what you are feeling and change the vocabulary to fit your own logic can often lead to massive mistakes in interpretation. So I offer my messages as I hear them, not how I feel they should be said.

Yvonne could hardly speak, she seemed still and inanimate. Eventually she stammered out in nothing more than a faint whisper that Paul was her son, and he was in spirit.

Paul looked so handsome, a lovely, quiet young man, intelligent even. I sensed he might have even be a little shy around the girls.

Yvonne nodded in confirmation as I shared these spiritual observations with her about his traits.

I continued, "He says he went out that night to be with friends, but in the morning they found him dead in his car."

Slowly, Yvonne kept nodding.

There was more to say. "He is telling me you've had a foul time since his passing. Even all your friends and family have given you a terrible time over his death."

Yvonne looked at me and I could see the utter torment in her eyes.

Keeping true to his story, I added, "He says no matter what anyone has told you, he did not commit suicide."

This was an important and profound revelation. Those five words erased years of emotional torture and within an instant her face softened and she looked younger.

Once we had finished the sitting, I was particularly drained as I often am after relaying such a traumatic death. As Yvonne was obviously shaken from the encounter, I offered her a cup of tea to help her relax. I needed a break too, so we sat and had a general chat, something I don't normally have the privilege of doing as usually I work back to back with my appointments.

During our tea break, for some reason I opened up to my client about how I was feeling. I think my post-natal hormones had flooded my system that day and I had been exposed to Yvonne's mothering instincts! It really brought home to me how important our family is to us and what a precious gift our children truly are. It reminded me how fragile life could be.

She was very sympathetic about my problems, and began to elaborate about the many aspects of her life in the wealthy Dublin suburb of Killiney, that I had identified during her sitting.

Yvonne began, "We were a very well-to-do family in the village, but when the inquest came back as suicide my friends and acquaintances completely shunned me. The response from my Church was no better, I felt they all but physically chased me out of my own home. In Ireland, a suicide judgement carries such a social stigma and I felt my whole family were put in disgrace. I couldn't even bury Paul in our family grave."

I leaned over and squeezed Yvonne's hand.

She smiled at me and continued, "I could never believe the verdict and knew my dear son would not do such a terrible thing. He knew how devout we were about our faith, he was a good lad, he had studied hard at university and had plenty of friends. In the aftermath of Paul's death, his father and I became estranged, and I had to give up our beautiful home. That's one of the reasons I moved to Wales. These days, forensic science would probably have been able to find out more, but in Ireland during the early eighties, there wasn't much available to the Garda, so as far as I was concerned the truth behind his death was never properly investigated."

We said our goodbyes and Yvonne vowed to return with her new partner for some spiritual healing, as after all these years of carrying her grief she now felt she was on the road to recovery.

Several weeks later I received a heartfelt thank-you card for the life-changing encounter she had experienced, with an open invite for coffee at her home. Also, she advised me she had written to a Mr Gay Byrne, a television presenter in Dublin, explaining about her remarkable experience and how she felt the Irish people would love me and embrace my spiritual healing abilities.

I had a little chuckle to myself at the little quote tagged to the end of her card:

May those who love us, love us.
And those who don't love us, may God turn their hearts;
and if he doesn't turn their hearts, may he turn their ankles, so
we'll know them by their limping.

By now the bank had sucked every penny out of Richard's business, leaving him in arrears with his commitments, in debt with his suppliers and with no cash to trade. Even though we had cut every aspect of our life to the bare minimum, it wasn't enough to fill the financial chasm of the banks ruthless strategy. Our life was ultimately in a downward spiral.

We had to face the realisation that, despite my busy diary, his business and life in our beautiful home would be coming to an end in the very near future.

While experiencing such level of material loss, it was very tempting to question the spirit world as to why they allowed this to happen to me as it only inhibited my propensity to help others from an attitude of security and strong mental health. However, I was well aware that to believe I would be protected in some way from any type of suffering when others were not would be rather foolish and extremely self-indulgent. Suffering and loss of any kind is not discriminatory and such life experiences have much to teach us. Only by having a multitude of experiences can I help others faced with similar adversity. Nonetheless, it was a most unwelcome realisation.

In an attempt to bring some control into our lives, we decided to surrender our home to the mortgager and move into rented accommodation at the earliest opportunity.

For my own mental welfare, I meditated most days, sometimes even several times a day. I found that this gave me solace at a time my personal life seemed in absolute tatters. Sam was telling me to follow my aspirations, but I couldn't achieve all that I wanted due to my family commitments and the financial pressures forced upon me. Life was difficult and frustrating.

This particular day I meditated specifically to seek guidance in finding a suitable home for us. In my vision I could see a house with a large garden that overlooked acres of fields in the most beautiful wide open countryside. At the garden fence stood three horses of different colours. Intuitively I knew this was going to be our new home. However, I didn't know where it was or how to find it.

We spent the next couple of weeks looking at all manner of rental property, but none seemed to have any redeemable feature that would make life there bearable. Having always owned our own homes from our early twenties, searching out budget rental property became a major culture shock for us. However, our task was made more encouraging due to my vision that we would find somewhere suitable. But this was a hard and stressful journey, especially with a newborn baby, a two-year-old and two other children.

We returned to Beresford Adams estate agents in Llandudno to see if any new rentals had become available. There we met a bubbly young lady and I got the impression she recognised me. After a brief conversation, it turned out one of her sisters had been to one of my groups at my former Rhyl offices. One thing led to another, and within minutes I was giving her a mini-sitting about her life.

As usual, Richard took all this in his stride.

When the sitting came to a close, Richard explained about my vision of the property we would be renting. After just experiencing a spiritual expose of her own life, the estate agent took Richard seriously when he requested that she shortlist our viewings to properties with uninterrupted country views with a field at the rear with three horses.

Without hesitation she walked to her filing cabinet and pulled out a folder containing some handwritten property particulars. She explained, "My manager has been out to see this place, but we haven't typed up and printed out the particulars yet. I have a feeling it resembles the property you have just been describing."

Richard immediately asked if she could arrange an official viewing for us.

The following day we met the owner at the property.

Although it was shabby in places and in need of refurbishment, it was situated amongst some of the most prestigious properties in the area. Also, when you stood in the lounge, through a massive window, there were the most breathtaking panoramic views of the undulating pastures of the Conway Valley. As we stood there admiring the view, in the field behind the hedge at the bottom of garden roamed three horses.

If we had to leave our beautiful home, there was no doubt at the budget rent we could afford, we were not going to find anything better and especially not in this location.

Unfortunately, the decision was not in our hands. The landlord's wife wanted to vet all our family, as they ideally wanted a professional couple with no children. The six of us lined up on parade in the driveway like the Von Trapp family and the landlord's wife walked along asking all manner of questions as to our lifestyle, and what was expected of us if she allowed us to rent her property. I felt so humiliated and I so much wanted to bundle her into the car and show her what a spotless executive home we had come from.

After the parade we had to wait twenty-four hours for their decision. The outcome was no prize, it was to move out of my perfect interior designed home into the makeshift and shabby. In life, there is a fine line in the material world between what you need and what you want! Richard kept reassuring me by saying that "life is the teacher ... not a punishment". I'm sure he meant well, but it didn't help!

We had a call next day to say we could become tenants, but the proviso was we couldn't bring our cat! We agreed. (But we smuggled her in anyway!)

Christmas was almost upon us and it was going to be the first one without Robert. Elsie was still experiencing much grief and she often said if it wasn't for listening about my daily encounters with the world of spirit, she didn't believe she would have pulled through as well as what she had.

It was around this time when Richard's eldest daughter, Rachel, was staying with Elsie and Ralph, and witnessed first-hand her Uncle Robert making his presence known.

Rachel loved her Uncle Robert dearly and was absolutely devastated when he died.

Richard and I volunteered to take Elsie out to the local supermarket, but Rachel wanted to stay behind at the bungalow. Before leaving, Elsie specifically told her granddaughter not to touch the new living gas fire that had just been installed in the lounge, as she didn't know how to work it and she might get burnt.

After a couple of hours of shopping, we returned, sat in the lounge and ignited the new gas fire. Out of the blue I announced that Robert had just walked in.

"Uncle Rob is here and wants to say something to you, Rachel. He is telling me that while we were out, you were messing with the fire. Don't deny it. He says he was standing right behind you and watched while you were fiddling about with the clicker thing that ignites the flames."

Rachel was a little surprised, but to be honest it might have been a reasonable guess from any adult that a new fire with gadgets was far too tempting for young fingers not to play with. The determining proof was only seconds away.

I continued, "Uncle Rob is telling me swearing at the fire was never going to help to light it. He doesn't like you swearing, so next time you try to light the fire ... don't swear!"

Rachel blushed and her eyes filled with tears. She threw her head back and exclaimed loudly, "Oh my god! That's true. Stop telling tales about me, Uncle Rob!"

There was more. "Uncle Rob is saying that you went upstairs to his bedroom, had a good rummage around and took all his photo albums out of the cupboard. He says he saw you sitting on the bed going through them and having a cry. He doesn't mind you getting them out, but next time please put them back where you found them! He says you were going through his videos too and have left them in a bit of a mess, so you better go back upstairs to tidy them properly so your nanny doesn't have to go up to do it for you."

For Elsie, such moments made life almost bearable. Her grief was still raw and her will to live very weak. However, she had a strong belief in the fact that Robert lived on in the spiritual dimension and openly shared this conviction with her granddaughter.

In my role as a therapist I have noticed that a child's grief is often overlooked and undervalued. Children need to be allowed to naturally express what they feel appropriate to their age. It is important to remember children experience grief in much the same way as adults, but tend to process the emotions differently. A way of unlocking grief is by encouraging the child to remember shared happy memories.

Children's limitations of verbal expression and their lack of life experiences often affects the way they perceive death and thus the way they respond. To avoid any imaginary scenarios a child's mind might fabricate, be honest about death and don't talk about the event or the deceased in hushed tones. Don't be tempted to delude the child by using incorrect words like 'lost' or 'sleep' when talking of those who have died.

Often children experiencing grief will ask about how the person died several times, it is the way they try to process the death, so it is important to keep your narrative true and consistent. Always give them the time and opportunity to tell you how they feel and never disregard their feelings.

For the more mature child, it is important to properly explain what happens at a funeral and offer the choice to attend, as not to do so can be interpreted as you trying to hide something from them or segregate them from the collective experience. Never underestimate the power love has in the mourning process.

My own belief is that children should be told that death is not the end, but a transition into another living experience.

Although Rachel was rather startled by the spiritual experience of Robert's visitation, she was nonetheless pleased to know her uncle was safe and well in the spirit world.

Death is most certainly not the only trigger for grief. My grief at losing my brother-in-law was further compounded by the loss of my material world as I knew it. However, without me realising, I was beginning to settle into our rental home and the routine of my offices at Bodelwyddan Castle, so I offered an earnest and thankful prayer to my guides and angels for all that was good in my life.

Maybe a chink of light was trying to prise open the veil of darkness that surrounded me.

28

Snow Far Snow Good

"A snowflake is one of God's most fragile creations,
but look what they can do when they stick together!"
~Author Unknown~

We woke up for our first Christmas morning in the rented house and I must say it was very cold – freezing cold!

However, to the joy of the children, the house, garden and all the neighbouring roads were covered in thick snow. This was going to be a white Christmas to remember. Actually, the weatherman confirmed it was the coldest and whitest for many years.

Despite the coastal salty air, this year the snow seemed to stick. Even by the time we returned to the castle to open the Healing Centre after the New Year celebrations, the hotel grounds were still snow white.

No sooner had the hotel taken down the corporate Christmas decorations, out of the blue, we had a telephone call from one of the researchers from *The Gay Byrne Late Late Show* in Dublin, Ireland. She asked if she could come over to the castle and watch me working sometime over the next week or so. Richard gave her the dates of my upcoming groups and suggested as long as she didn't expect anything special to be arranged for her, she was welcome to come to any of them.

A few days later, despite the whole area being under about six inches of fresh snow, an attractive young lady trudged into the Healing Centre wrapped up in a furry white coat and introduced herself as the researcher from Gay Byrne. She apologised for her Arctic appearance and wet boots, but her taxi couldn't manage to find traction on the icy sludge forming on the long steep driveway up to the hotel. Consequently she had to walk through the snowy mounds.

I was due to hold a healing group that day, which as it happens was looking full with about fifty people. Under the circumstances, this was a remarkable turnout, as how they all managed to attend through the atrocious weather conditions was a mystery to me.

Nevertheless, I invited the researcher to join the healing group and suggested she was treated no different to anyone else. I explained that it's only by experiencing the spiritual healing first hand would she get a true sense of my work.

The meeting was very similar to the many I had already held in my new lecture room. I spoke to the group about Spiritual Healing in general, some reasonable expectations and its effectiveness, and its place alongside other complementary therapies and conventional medicine.

During the demonstration, I relaxed the whole group into the correct receptive condition to participate in a collective healing meditation so everyone could leave with a positive experience. I explained about the channelling of spiritual energy, the existence of an aura, how it changed shape and colour depending on the state of your welfare, and also I spoke about the chakras and their positions around the body.

As usual everyone wanted to witness how I could 'see' illness and 'detect' diseased organs and identify faulty body parts. So, to demonstrate this, I walked around the group giving individual health assessments and pinpointing certain ailments past and present on random participants. In smaller groups I could offer individual attention to everyone, but in these larger situations it wasn't practical and so I would randomly select volunteers. However, on this occasion I made sure I included the researcher and without any hesitation I pinpointed the several health issues she was experiencing.

When I finished, I encouraged everyone to talk openly about their personal experiences and it was refreshing to see the researcher eagerly interacting with the other participants.

After the group had dispersed, I invited the researcher into my office to have a chat about all the other aspects of my work. She was absolutely lovely with me and offered her congratulations on how fantastic the healing group had been. She was fascinated how I went from one person to the next telling them what was wrong with them and especially how I had been so accurate in locating her own health issues.

Despite her excitement she was quite clear there was no guarantee that I would be invited on to *The Late Late Show* as apparently they researched many topics that don't make it on to the program. I had never been to Ireland, so in all honesty I didn't see any reason why they would want to invite me.

After a couple of hours of interview, it was time for her to call a taxi to take her back to Manchester airport and return to Dublin.

I really didn't have any expectation of seeing or hearing from her ever again.

Meanwhile, my workload at the castle was increasing, which was welcome on the one hand but it did cause me a little concern.

I loved being a Mum to my two new sons, but regrettably they were having to spend increasingly more time at the nursery they attended.

Richard had now reached the end of his tether. The bank was still viciously pursuing him on a daily basis and in desperation, and to save his own sanity, he had no alternative but to go to the courts and declare himself bankrupt.

If I didn't know any better, I might have thought the bank deliberately forced Richard into a position of default so they could seize back all his properties at rock-bottom prices. I thought to myself, a bank couldn't be that immoral, could they?

The bankruptcy was life-changing far beyond our expectations. During our nine years together we had experienced many losses. We experienced all manner of loss during our divorces, we lost everything in the North Wales Flood and we had both lost close family through tragic health problems.

And now this. Emotionally, the cost of this bankruptcy was exorbitant.

We both felt that we had reached rock bottom. Our only hope was that from now on our situation could only improve.

Richard had always been my knight in shining armour, but now his horse was lame and his armour in rusty tatters. But I loved him completely, more than words could express, and I had true faith that as fate had brought us together, our union had a greater purpose yet to be fulfilled. Nevertheless, to be very honest, this optimism was extremely hard to muster.

A few days later, the phone rang, it was the researcher calling from Dublin. I had been selected to feature on the *Gay Byrne Late Late Show* during March. In a couple of weeks' time they would fly Richard and me over to Ireland, arrange a chauffeur to collect us from the airport and accommodate us in a luxury hotel.

Yes, I told them with enthusiasm, of course I would love to come!

So as one door closed in our life, perhaps another one was about to open.

The day of our leaving for Dublin came around quickly and naturally I was very nervous to be invited on to a national television chat show. True to the researcher's word, we were met by an elderly gentleman called Miles, Gay Byrne's personal chauffeur, who drove us to our hotel in Byrne's Mercedes.

On the forty-five-minute journey to our hotel, Miles entertained us by recounting anecdotes of the many celebrities he liked and many of those that had upset him during his great number of years in Byrne's employ.

Being outspoken, he was not shy about telling me how fascinated he was with my work. He suggested that when it was time to take us back to the airport, he would like to pick us up earlier and give us a guided tour of Dublin so he could continue chatting with me about my healing abilities.

Miles dropped us off at the hotel, explained our researcher would be in touch and said he would be back tomorrow evening to take us to the RTE Donnybrook studio.

The following morning we explored the famous Grafton Street in the city centre with its many shops and diverse street entertainers. After a really exciting day, Miles picked us up at the appointed time and chatted incessantly during the short journey. As he opened the car door at the special guest entrance, a lone photographer took pictures of me. How bizarre, I thought, nobody in Ireland would have heard of me so why would he want any pictures?

There was someone waiting to greet us and I was shown to my dressing room. Inside there was a large bouquet of flowers waiting for me and even before I read the card, I had an inkling Richard must have organised these. I knew how proud of me he was.

The researcher came in to have a quick chat about the scheduled format of the evening's events. Apparently, I was appearing tonight with the ever-popular British comedian Lenny Henry and Hollywood actor Hugh Laurie who was promoting his latest film.

There had been some major contention on the running order of the guests. My researcher had arranged for me to go on after Lenny Henry, and his people wanted him to go after me. I couldn't understand the point of the discord, I was just glad to be here and to showcase my spiritual abilities.

I was allocated a personal runner, a person who moves you to where you need to be when you need to be there, and fetches you what you might fancy to keep you happy. Already I was feeling very seduced by this celebrity treatment.

It was time. The runner ushered me to the make-up department.

As I walked in there was quite a buzz and I became the focus of everyone's attention. The girls had already been warned about my spiritual abilities and they were absolutely thrilled to meet me. With considerable ceremony, they sat me down and kept asking all sorts of questions about how I could see spirit, what I could see for them ... about everything really! The room was loud with laughter and electric with excitement.

In walked Lenny Henry, and gosh was he tall.

I thought, we are on live television together tonight – this is going to be absolutely great. Lenny Henry had been a regular face on British TV for many years and I must admit I was a bit of a fan. It was apparent he could sense the electricity in the room, and I had visions of him joining us with some playful banter and perhaps giving me some professional advice on being interviewed

– after all, he had been doing this type of thing for a very long time and it would be second nature to him.

One of the make-up girls stood up and invited Lenny Henry to sit next to me to have his pancake put on and ultimately to encourage some dialogue between us. After all we were going to be expected to interact in an entertaining manner in about two hours' time. His runner would have told him all about me as I had been told about him!

He glanced at me in a very indifferent way, "I'd prefer not to sit there, thank you." He walked to the opposite end of the room with not so much as a hello or how are you – not even any eye contact!

Was this the way celebrities felt they could treat people? Perhaps this is the way they treated people who they felt shouldn't benefit from such media platforms. Or is this the way they treated each other?

As he was a longstanding professional entertainer, I'd had the fanciful notion of him wanting to put the new girl at ease and point her in the right direction.

How wrong I was!

Nevertheless, I refused to be fazed by his unfriendliness as I thought maybe he was tired or this was the way he prepared himself for a performance. So, we carried on with our little party while he sat on his own looking dreary.

The time just flew by, and before I knew it the researcher had come to collect me. Taking a firm grip of my arm she escorted me to the apron of the stage.

The butterflies started in the pit of my stomach. What had I let myself in for? I had totally underestimated the importance of what I was doing here.

I was now on a two-minute countdown.

The researcher gave me my final confab before I had to face Gay Byrne in front of the live cameras. It suddenly dawned on me, this was prime-time television, watched nationally by nearly every household in Ireland; actually this show was widely regarded as an Irish institution. It finally registered that from tonight, the majority of Irish families would know my name, who I am and what I do!

This was a daunting thought. Adrenaline was flooding my body. My heart felt as if it was going to explode out of my chest.

"Sixty seconds, Helen," the researcher announced. "Just so you know, there are people placed in the audience that Gay Byrne will call upon to express strong opinions opposed to you. Then at some time after that, he will take you down to the audience so you can demonstrate what you do and to prove your abilities."

What's happening here? I felt absolutely ambushed!

I thought I was coming on the show to talk about my spiritual abilities and share some of my many extraordinary experiences. I thought I would be treated like all the other guests that come on these types of chat shows, to share their funny and interesting life experiences and anecdotes; heaven knows I have had enough of them! I didn't realise I had travelled all this way to be confronted by complete strangers and have to defend myself – yet again.

I started to doubt myself. Had my naïvety allowed me to believe I could be accepted for who I was? Was I going to be manipulated into being humiliated in front of a nation? With so much loss in my life, was I now going to be stripped of my dignity and reduced to a laughing stock? I didn't believe my emotions could withstand more misfortune and setback.

Despite the strong lights on the live studio stage I could clearly see Sam.

His thoughts became as one with mine. "Don't fear, chile. Your message is strong and true. If your words and your healing can touch just one heart, then it has been worthwhile, as through that one heart, others will benefit from the good that your work can achieve.

My visits are purposely to help and guide you. Through your own instruction, I am here to administer your spiritual will. As my role dictates, I will remain close to you to enable spiritual protection of any dark deeds that may try to encounter you. Remember, through your presence your energies are connected to everyone and every living thing you come into contact with. Rest assured you are strong, your natural abilities are omnipresent and your light will be recognised and seen for its purity."

Although Sam was trying to be encouraging, I was terrified by what he said, and I had to access every part of my very being to conquer that fear and honour my abilities.

I was comforted, though, by knowing that no matter how this night went, Richard would be waiting for me in the studio's Green Room with pride in his eyes and love in his heart.

"Ten seconds, Helen …"

I heard Gay Byrne announce my name … there was no turning back.

"Five seconds …"

From here on in, whatever happened on that stage tonight, success or failure, I knew my life would never be the same ever again.

"Go …"

In that moment, I heard Sam's voice in my mind, "Helen, it is only by *you* losing everything that *you* are completely free to embark on the new."

I took a deep breath and focused on Sam to help steady my nerves. With much sincerity and true faith in my heart, I walked out to embrace my own destiny.

The End … just for now

Epilogue

The show went extremely well despite the attempts to discredit me by carefully selected members of the audience. However, under Sam's guidance, with love and positivity I successfully opposed them, and eventually finished to a rapturous applause.

However, what did concern me was that Lenny Henry poked fun at me on live television and while doing so his chair mysteriously collapsed bringing all manner of stage scenery on top of him. Thankfully he wasn't hurt and he did make a classic comedy moment out of the calamity, albeit at my expense.

Was this a random accident? Or might it have been in some way orchestrated by the spirit world for trying to trivialise me? That's a mystery that I will most definitely reveal to you the next time we meet!

Afterwards, I joined Richard in the Green Room and nearly burst into tears believing this incident had spoiled my contribution to the show. Richard thought otherwise, and said my appearance would be forever remembered and kept current in people's minds because of it. How right he was, as it is shown time and time again on all the out-take programs regularly shown on television and more recently featured on YouTube.

At the time, I totally underestimated the importance of *The Gay Byrne Late Late Show*. When I returned to my Healing Centre at Bodelwyddan Castle, without expectation of any feedback, I was overwhelmed to find my answering machine was completely full with enquiries that had been made within the first twenty minutes of the broadcast.

Also, it seemed the response at the television studio was unprecedented and RTE had to dedicate a telephone line specifically to deal with enquiries about me, which they kept in operation for a considerable period afterwards – well over a year I was led to believe.

Due to the phenomenal response to my appearance on *The Late Late Show*, the researcher approached me about returning later in the year, which she told me was most unusual and almost never done. I vowed to myself to be better prepared for the next time!

Incidentally, during my second appearance, the show's ratings peaked, beating those of that night's *Coronation Street*, one of the UK's most popular soaps. I was so pleased as another one of Sam's predications had come true. I have learned never to doubt him!

Being introduced to Ireland was one of those life-changing moments for which I am eternally grateful. As a result of the show, the Irish people took me to their hearts and I soon became known as "Helen the Healer". Needless to say, this was the start of a new direction in my life, which fortunately has continued to this day. The love and loyalty given to me by the Irish people has been remarkable and as a result I have spent a substantial part of my life travelling from my home in Wales across the Irish Sea to almost every corner of the Emerald Isle with extraordinary consequences.

Thanks to that one appearance, I subsequently had many more interviews on Irish television and radio. Later on, I even had my own radio show for a while, where people would telephone in for guidance, a sort of spiritual agony aunt. Unfortunately, even in these progressive times, due to the lack of acceptance of spiritual enlightenment outside the context of organised religion or the feel-good factor of *mindfulness*, this is something I doubt would ever be allowed by mainstream British broadcasters.

I had to finish this book somewhere, and being introduced to the Irish nation seemed a good place to have a pause ... and for you to contemplate.

Without question, my spiritual abilities have brought therapeutic comfort, both mentally and physically, to people and animals in the most unusual of circumstances and in some of the strangest of places. My healing hands have not only taken me to places all over the United Kingdom and Ireland, but also the world.

In my next book, I will continue with this exciting new era of my life, and I can't wait to tell you about these spiritual experiences in the very near future.

For example, I will share with you an extraordinary spiritual visitation I had whilst at the famous shrine in Knock, Ireland, which has mysteriously left me with a permanent scar in the form of what can only be described as a St Brigid's cross. Also the time when I had an unscheduled meeting with an agent from MI5, the United Kingdom's domestic counter-intelligence and security agency, which shocked him to the core. How a Catholic bishop followed me at speed in his car and flagged me down as he wanted me to give healing to a very sick nun. How, when I was with a British television film crew at the Waterford Glass factory in Ireland, the change in energy caused by my entrance into the massive showroom triggered every light in the building to fuse and drained the camera batteries of power. How, when a medical doctor brought his patient to see me, he proclaimed in a television interview that the information I gave about her condition was as if I had all his patient's medical notes in front of me, despite the fact we had never met. There are so many fascinating experiences for me to share!

Such daily encounters prove without any doubt how the spiritual dimension constantly interacts with us, with or without our realisation; with or without our belief; despite our religious preferences; despite scientific proof; despite our cultural prejudices; and that ultimately our life energy lives beyond this earthly existence.

Despite this ability to interact with another dimension, my own life is not protected from the hardship and adversity experienced by each and every one of us. The mental and physical challenges I have had to overcome in my life have frequently taken me to the brink of despair. However, it is only by using my own experiences and that of the greater consciousness beyond our earthly boundaries, I can help others overcome their own adversities.

I truly hope the spiritual lessons I have learned and shared with you in *Beyond Boundaries* not only proves our continued existence beyond death, but will bring untold peace and inspiration into your own live.

"The best view comes from the hardest climb."
Author unknown

Absent Healing

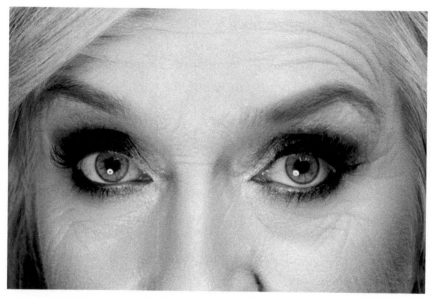

How to achieve the best results from your Absent Healing.

- Carry out in any appropriate place where you feel warm, comfortable, secure and relaxed.
- Allow yourself 5–10 minutes. Play relaxing music if inclined.
- Have my photograph positioned nearby. My presence will act as a focal point.
- As you settle down, become aware of how steady your breathing becomes.

- Slowly take three deep breaths: in through your nose - and out through your mouth.
- Continue steady breathing and focus deep into my eyes, allow your mind to empty and your whole body to feel heavy and relaxed, from the tips of your toes to the end of your fingers.
- Continue to focus on my eyes, or maybe allow your eyes to comfortably close.
- In your mind, respectfully ask the universe for the Healing to be given.
- Allow the Healing to flood your body for the time you have allotted.
- As the session is nearing completion, slowly become aware of your muscles and gently move them.
- If your eyes are closed, open them and focus on your surroundings.
- Never consciously wonder what changes have happened, rest assured positive changes happen.
- Be thankful and continue with your day with a renewed sense of improvement.

For a more personal Absent Healing, visit my website www. helenparryjones.com

Available through the website, free colour photograph of my eyes. (Postage extra.)

About the Author

Helen Parry Jones has been able to connect with the spirit world since her earliest childhood recollections. Since then, her abilities have developed far beyond recognised Spiritual Communication and Spiritual Healing, to a much higher level of consciousness.

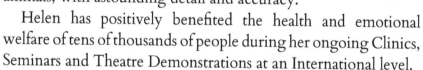

Through her advanced ability, Helen Parry Jones is able to locate illness and discover malfunctions within the human body and that of animals, with astounding detail and accuracy.

Helen has positively benefited the health and emotional welfare of tens of thousands of people during her ongoing Clinics, Seminars and Theatre Demonstrations at an International level.

Furthermore, honesty, trust and integrity is synonymous with the name Helen Parry Jones, which has held fast during a successful thirty year career as a professional therapist.

Her career has been consistently well documented in the press, on radio and during television interviews in the UK and Ireland.

Helen has complemented her career with her own weekly radio phone-in show in Ireland, to deliver her unique brand of emotional and physical healing to a wider audience.

Over the years, she has accomplished substantial recognition and is highly respected as at the top of her profession. People find her remarkable, her audience become spellbound as she speaks and people really love her.

For many years Helen has had an online presence through her website www.helenparryjones.com and more recently she is endeavouring to use various social media. Helen Parry Jones is soon to launch her own web-casting and You-Tube channel.

Bibliography

Andersen, H. C. (n.d.). *Hans Christian Andersen quotes.* [online] Available at: https://www.goodreads.com/quotes/90636-where-words-fail-music-speaks [Accessed 11 Dec. 2017].

Anonymous and author unknown quotes are available at: https://quotefancy.com/quote/22090/Anonymous-Death-leaves-a-heartache-no-one-can-heal-love-leaves-a-memory-no-one-can-steal [Accessed 11 Dec. 2017]. http://izquotes.com/quote/288495 [Accessed 11 Dec. 2017]. http://www.thequotablecoach.com/the-best-view/ [Accessed 11 Dec. 2017].

Aristotle (n.d.). *Aristotle quotes.* [online] Available at: https://www.brainyquote.com/citation/quotes/aristotle_119068 [Accessed 11 Dec. 2017].

Binyon, R. L. (1914). *For the Fallen.* [online] The Great War 1914 – 1918. Available at: http://www.greatwar.co.uk/poems/laurence-binyon-for-the-fallen.htm [Accessed 11 Dec. 2017].

Francis of Assisi, Saint (n.d.). *Francis of Assisi quotes.* [online] Available at: https://www.brainyquote.com/citation/quotes/francis_of_assisi_121023 [Accessed 11 Dec. 2017].

Kennedy, J. F. (n.d.). *John F. Kennedy Quotes.* [online] BrainyQuote.com. Available at: https://www.brainyquote.com/quotes/john_f_kennedy_100269 [Accessed 8 Dec. 2017].

Seattle, C. (n.d.). *Chief Seattle Quotes.* [online] BrainyQuote.com. Available at: https://www.brainyquote.com/quotes/chief_seattle_564107 [Accessed 8 Dec. 2017].

Seneca, L. A. (n.d.). *Seneca Quotes.* [online] BrainyQuote.com. Available at: https://www.brainyquote.com/quotes/seneca_405078 [Accessed 8 Dec. 2017].

Schopenhauer, A. (n.d.). *Arthur Schopenhauer Quotes.* [online] BrainyQuote.com. Available at: https://www.brainyquote.com/quotes/arthur_schopenhauer_103608 [Accessed 8 Dec. 2017].

Socrates (n.d.). *Philosophy Paradise: Famous Socrates Quotes.* [online] Available at: http://www.philosophyparadise.com/quotes/socrates.html [Accessed 11 Dec. 2017].

Unknown (commonly attributed to Prime Minister Winston Churchill), (n.d.). *Quote Investigator: Exploring the Origins of Quotations.* [online] Available at: https://quoteinvestigator.com/2014/09/14/keep-going/ [Accessed 11 Dec. 2017].